Discovering Aquinas

Discovering Aquinas

An Introduction to His Life, Work, and Influence

Aidan Nichols OP

WILLIAM B. EERDMANS PUBLISHING COMPANY
GRAND RAPIDS, MICHIGAN / CAMBRIDGE, U.K.

First published 2002 in the U.K. by
Darton, Longman and Todd Ltd

This edition published 2003 in the U.S.A. by
Wm. B. Eerdmans Publishing Co.
255 Jefferson Ave. S.E., Grand Rapids, Michigan 49503 /
P.O. Box 163, Cambridge CB3 9PU U.K.
www.eerdmans.com

Printed in the United States of America

07 06 05 04 03   7 6 5 4 3 2

ISBN 0-8028-0514-0

The author and publishers are grateful to the Saint Austin Press for permission to
reprint the chapter 'Thomas in his Time' from *Beyond the Blue Glass: Catholic
Essays on Faith and Culture* (London, 2001), vol. 1.

Designed by Sandie Boccacci

Contents

Preface   vii

Part One: *The Man*
1. Thomas in his Time   3

Part Two: *The Doctrine*
2. Revelation   21
3. God and Creation   37
4. The Trinity   60
5. The Trinity in Man   74
6. Angelology   82
7. Grace and the Virtues   91
8. Christ, Church, Sacraments   110

Part Three: *The Aftermath*
9. Thomas in History   129

Part Four: *The Tools*
10. Thomas and the Practice of Philosophy   147
11. Thomas and the Idea of Theology   167

Conclusion   181
Bibliography   185
Notes   195
Index of Names   212

Preface

In John Gray's novel *Park,* set centuries hence, Dlar shows his visitors an item of furniture of outstanding beauty:

> See the best of all, as to the embellishments; and with that he displayed the painted inside of the boards, in glowing *opus lense*, golden without the use of gold. Scenes from the *Summa*, said the giver, in reverent and delicate banter. Such indeed were the subjects; for there may be lovely and exquisite emblems of what is abstract.[1]

'Natural forms', writes Thomas in the *De veritate* (the 'disputed questions about truth'), 'are as it were images of immaterial realities'.[2] Brought into play re-wrought as symbols, they can stand for deep or complex concepts.

A theological thinker for whom that is a congenial reflection is useful to those of us who need the help of the poet's sensibility if we are to be awoken from the prose of our metaphysical slumbers. Certainly, there is a difference of intellectual temper between those who approach the topic of theology with a robust assurance of the power of philosophical argument and those others, more affected by images than by ideas, who look to history and experience for the presentation of religious theory. (Immanuel Kant would call the contrast one of *Verstand* with *Vernunft*, but centuries earlier Thomas had spoken of *intellectus* and *ratio*.) It is easy for the supporters of either to make a caricature of the other. And yet they are, or can be, complementary. It is in the spirit of Thomas – who approved of distinctions but disliked the 'either/or' – to follow up *both* approaches. Though at one point criticising Plato for 'proposing everything in figures and by the art of symbols', a selection of images is vital to Thomas – who was both a conceptual thinker and a poet – in the setting forth of sacred truth.[3]

I like to think of this as Thomistic interpretation 'in the English manner'. I have suggested elsewhere that the particular contribution of the English Dominicans of a pre-Conciliar generation to the Thomist patrimony lay in the furnishing of a powerfully incarnational idiom for its articulation.[4] In this they belonged to a wider common tradition. Religious metaphysics, whether Catholic or Anglican, in modern England – in Hopkins and Chesterton, Lewis and Sayers, Farrer and Mascall – delights to put ideas and images together in words, not to keep them apart. There is, I hope, a touch of this in what follows.

It is far from irrelevant to the historical St Thomas: the one who actually lived. His prose may not seem especially imagistic. It is far more so than some Thomistic manuals would suggest. In the course of giving a brief answer to a couple of objections to some thesis, Thomas is perfectly capable of switching from the most austere metaphysical analysis to some extravagant metaphor taken from a Greek Father or a Carolingian monk. But more to the point is the whole texture of his thought. In his commentary on *The Divine Names*, a treatise of fundamental theology by the sixth-century Syrian monk who used the pseudonym of 'Denys the Areopagite', Thomas remarks:

> We do not know God by seeing his essence, but we know him from the order of the whole universe. For the very 'university' of creatures is proposed to us by God so that through it we may know God insofar as the ordered universe has certain imperfect images and assimilations of divine [things], which are compared to them as exemplary principles to images.[5]

This Christian-Platonist comment yields up a presupposition of Thomas's entire vision and warrants that kind of imaginative commentary on the severer conceptual reaches of his thought in which such English commentators on the angelic doctor as Thomas Gilby both delighted and excelled.[6]

A later generation of English Dominican writers were more restrained. Influenced by the predominantly logical and language-analysis concerns of contemporary Anglo-American philosophy,

Gilby's younger collaborators in the Cambridge bilingual *Summa theologiae* like Herbert McCabe, who died in 2001, or friars, like Brian Davies, of a later generation still, discussed (and discuss) Thomas in a way well suited to the Anglophone philosophical climate of our time.[7] In this modest introduction to the life and work of Aquinas, the present author, though conscious of debts to his brethren of the English Province (in particular, those of the pre-Conciliar period), owes more to the French-language reception of Thomas in the twentieth century: notably, to the metaphysically and dogmatically meaty studies of Thomas's thought produced by the Dominicans in France.[8] Some acquaintance with the flourishing garden of American Thomistic scholarship is also exhibited in these pages.

At certain points, where it seemed illuminating, or, from the standpoint of the good of the Catholic intellectual tradition, pastorally pressing, I have also tried to bring Thomas's thought into critical correlation with theological predecessors and successors – some of a very different ilk, in our own day. The 'line' taken is that Thomas constitutes the classic theological moment of Latin Christendom. This is not only because he had a pre-eminent gift of synthesising the materials of Scripture and patristic Tradition, revelation's witnesses. It is also because he honed a metaphysic that was up to the job of being that revelation's philosophical Instrument – in the traditional language, its serviceable 'handmaid'. It is hardly surprising, then, that any major derogation from Thomas's achievement (to be carefully distinguished from enrichment of it by the provision of complementary insights) will tend to create difficulties for the articulation of Catholic faith.

I began this Preface with a citation from John Gray that considers how Thomas's work might be reflected in the visual arts. Christian iconographers have from time to time fashioned 'lovely and exquisite emblems' for the picturing of Thomas himself, in an effort to make manifest what his *oeuvre* signifies for the Catholic interpretation of the Gospel. Shortly after the middle of the fourteenth century, Tommaso da Modena painted the chapter room of the priory of St Nicholas at Treviso with a number of frescoes of Dominican saints and scholars. Thomas is shown standing before a desk at a lecturer's chair. In his right hand he holds the book of

Scripture while his left hand rests on a tiny church onto, and into, which rays of light are streaming from a sun gleaming on his breast. Here is Aquinas diffusing light for the Church – the Church on which, however, he in turn depends.[9] The burning sun emblemises (John Gray's word!) Thomas's teaching that theology, unlike other sciences, being as it is a knowledge of the divine mysteries seen from the viewpoint of divine Wisdom herself – 'a certain impression of the divine knowledge'[10] – requires an ascetic and spiritual effort of purification, at once affective and intellectual. Hence the need in the theologian's life for charity, the supreme evangelical virtue, and the Gifts of the Holy Spirit, those ways in which human powers become more finely attuned to divine leading.[11]

In his reading of the Gospel of St John, Thomas himself has this to say:

> Just as a lamp is not able to illuminate unless a fire is enkindled, so also a spiritual lamp does not illuminate unless he first burn and be inflamed with the fire of charity. Hence ardour precedes illumination, for a knowledge of truth is bestowed by the ardour of charity.[12]

In retrospect, we can read that as a self-portrait. It is because of the wonderfully integrated character of his wisdom – integrated not only as supernatural with natural but also as *thinking with love* – that the Church in our day should not leave him as a fresco on a wall, but find inspiration from his teaching and example. Some words of his commentary on Second Corinthians may whet the appetite:

> Between ordinary science-knowledge and faith-knowledge there is this difference. The first shines only on the mind, showing that God is the cause of everything, that he is one and wise and so forth, whereas the second enlightens the mind and warms the heart, telling us that God is also saviour, redeemer, lover, made flesh for us. Hence the savour of this knowledge, and the fragrance spread far and wide. 'Behold the scent of my son is as of a field which the Lord hath blessed.'[13]

BLACKFRIARS, CAMBRIDGE
All Saints of the Order of Preachers, 2001

Part One: *The Man*

1.
Thomas in his Time

Background and vocation

Saint Thomas was born in 1225 into a pro-imperial Italian aristocratic family, the de Aquinos, who had land and a castle at Roccasecca, half-way between Rome and Naples, just to the east of that great thoroughfare, the Via Latina. His parents – Lombard on his father's side, Neapolitan on his mother's – sent him to the boarding school run by the monks of Monte Cassino and arranged for him to become an oblate there, planning so to make use of their local influence as to have him, in due course, elected to the abbatial dignity. For Cassino was, to the feudal nobility of the region, a great prize. When he was 15, however, and could have made solemn profession (the oblateship was understood in this period in a way which makes it comparable to simple profession in the modern Latin Church), the abbot of Monte Cassino advised his parents to send him, rather, to the emperor Frederick II's *studium generale* at Naples – probably because skirmishes between emperor and pope were making Cassino too hot for comfort.[1] He would have lived, no doubt, in the Neapolitan study house owned by the Cassinese monks, the dedication of which – a significant pointer to the half-Greek character of southern Italy in the Middle Ages – was to St Demetrios of Thessalonica.[2]

Naples was a cosmopolitan place, as were generally southern Italy and Sicily under the influence of a ruler who sat lightly to his own religion (and anyone else's). There Thomas was introduced by one Michael the Irishman to the latest ideas in the shape of the natural philosophy of Aristotle.

Arab astronomy and Greek medicine would also have been

capital in this University milieu. Catching a whiff of pagan naturalism at Naples was important: in Paris at the same period the study of Aristotle was officially forbidden.

At the age of 19 Thomas joined the newly instituted Order of Friars Preachers – a priory had been founded at Naples in 1231 by Jordan of Saxony, St Dominic's successor. He did so in the teeth of opposition from his family, who resorted to such low tricks as abduction and (attempted) seduction: abducting Thomas while he was on his way, in the entourage of the Master of the Order, John the Teuton, to the 1244 General Chapter in Bologna, and attempting to seduce him by introducing a prostitute from the camp following of their military retinue into his room at Roccasecca, during his 'house arrest'. The claim that the reason for their opposition was social embarrassment, much as if a son of the Duke of Buccleuch had absconded from Eton to become a hippy in Islington, though widely made by socially radical Thomists in the 1960s, looks less plausible when we learn that the friar who gave him the habit, his namesake Thomas de Lentini, shortly after became bishop of Bethlehem, papal legate and patriarch of Jerusalem. Benedictine influence would in any case linger in the form of Thomas's habitual citation of Gregory the Great (nearly 2,500 times), and especially of the latter's *Dialogues*, on the life and miracles of St Benedict, which Thomas drew on heavily in his theological defence of the religious life. Thomas's last known writing is a letter of 1274 to abbot Bernard Ayglier of Monte Cassino where, as his most recent biographer, Père Jean-Pierre Torrell, writes, he 'refound spontaneously his language as a young monk and presented himself as "a son always ready for prompt obedience" '.[3]

In all probability, St Thomas passed over to the Dominicans chiefly because he saw there greater opportunities for the study and communication of the fruits of contemplation to others, a task for which he had already developed the aptitude at Cassino – though we cannot rule out, as a possible secondary factor in his renunciation of life in that well-endowed monastery, a desire for evangelical simplicity. Père Marie-Dominique Chenu called his departure from Cassino 'the exact replica of the gesture of Francis of Assisi',[4] inasmuch as St Francis repudiated his father's wealth, St Thomas the great riches of his abbey. In his treatise in support of the friars,

Thomas will call religious poverty an outstanding lesson of the Cross of Christ.[5]

Whatever the blend of factors in his motivation, it was typical of Thomas that he used his enforced leisure at Roccasecca to read the Bible right through and to begin his study of contemporary theology. Blind to blandishments, then, Thomas persisted, powerfully aided, no doubt, by the excommunication and deposition of Frederick in 1245. Henceforth Aquino hostility to a papally mandated Order lost its *raison d'être*. Making doubly sure of their candidate, however, the Order despatched him for the completion of his noviciate, and subsequent study, to Paris, the pre-eminent University city of the age.[6] We have from this student period, in Thomas's handwriting, the commentary of St Albert the Great on Denys the Areopagite's *On the Celestial Hierarchy*, produced in the characteristic *peciae* or separate fascicules which were the hallmark of Parisian manuscript production. Given the unspeakable awfulness of St Thomas's handwriting, if as some scholars suggest, Albert was deliberately employing him for this purpose as a secretary, the great German philosopher-theologian must have been singularly impractical – or kind-hearted. From Paris, the young Thomas set out to accompany his master when in 1248 Albertus Magnus returned to Germany with the mission of founding a new general study house of the Order at Cologne. It was at Cologne that Thomas would have heard Albert lecture on *The Divine Names* of Denys, the paramount source for the Christian-Platonist element in Albertine thought, as later in his own, and also on the *Ethics* of Aristotle, all ten books of which had just been translated for the first time by bishop Robert Grosseteste of Lincoln.

Early teaching

Almost certainly it was at Cologne that Thomas was ordained priest. And above all it was at Cologne that he began, modestly enough, his professional teaching career as a 'biblical bachelor', with literal commentaries on Jeremiah and the Book of Lamentations, as well as on Isaiah, though the *Super Isaiam* also included spiritual exegesis in the form of marginal notes.

In 1252, the Dominican Master-General, John of Wildeshausen, anxious to strengthen the role of the friars at Paris, was prevailed upon to return Thomas, whose outstanding gifts had already been noted, to the Ile-de-France. Accordingly, at an age below the normal, and after relatively abbreviated preparation, he graduated that year as a bachelor in theology, a sort of junior lecturer whose task it was to comment on the *Liber Sententiarum* of Peter Lombard, a systematically thematic presentation of texts from the Fathers on the articles of the Creed – *sententiae patrum,* 'the views of the Fathers' – and the theological manual in most widespread use ever since the Fourth Lateran Council had strongly recommended it in 1215. Thomas's commentary on the *Sentences,* the *Scriptum super Sententiis,* is far from being merely footnotes to Lombard, however, for Aquinas introduces a new principle of organisation – of theological intelligibility – all his own. He considers all things inasmuch as they come forth from God, the Alpha or absolute Beginning, in dependence on the procession from the Father of the Word, and inasmuch too as they return to God, the Omega or absolute End, by the grace which depends on the procession from Father and Son of the Holy Spirit.[7] Thomas provides us here with a first sketch of the plan of his future *Summa theologiae,* the 'Summa of Theology', with which his name will always be connected. Indeed, it now seems that even ten years later Thomas was still working on improvements of this 5,000-page work, something known from the discovery of an alternative, more incisively argued version, at Lincoln College, Oxford, in the 1970s. Meanwhile he also found time to help out his brethren, who were floundering, evidently, in the swamps of metaphysics, by writing two small treatises, 'On Being and Essence' and 'On the Principles of Nature', where we have a first glimpse of his debt to the Arab philosophers, and to their Jewish contemporary, Maimonides. Here we see in action that 'intellectual charity' which formed so distinctive an aspect of his sanctity.[8]

The mature teacher

By the time Thomas had finished even the first version of his commentary on Lombard, he was no longer a simple bachelor. In

1256, at the exceptionally early age of 31, Thomas became one of the twelve masters of the Sorbonne – a sort of medieval equivalent to the holder of a chair in a modern Faculty of Divinity. His role was to raise, discuss and resolve theological problems on the basis of, above all, his biblical knowledge: hence the title *magister in sacra pagina*, 'master of the sacred page'. He was fortunate in this, since his appointment coincided with the climax of a campaign against the friars mounted by the secular masters, in the course of which the French king, Louis IX, had to send archers to protect the Dominicans against the secular clergy and populace. Thomas was assisted by the bull of Pope Alexander IV, *Quasi lignum vitae*, which bade the chancellor of the University quell the uproar of the secular masters against the friars and give them their rights.

In thirteenth-century terms, his task was a threefold one: *legere, disputare, predicare* – to comment on Scripture, to dispute, to preach. We see him at work in this period in these three distinct ways when, firstly (*legere*), we read his commentary on Matthew, the full text of which was discovered only this century in a library in Basle (Switzerland); when, secondly (*disputare*), we study his 'disputed questions' *de Veritate*, 'on truth'; or, thirdly (*predicare*), we dip into his University sermons – preserved, alas, so differently from Newman's, only in note form. (The Sunday and feast day sermons, passed down in the *opera omnia* of Thomas in times past, are now recognised as spurious.[9]) And of course, on top of all this, Thomas had to do his bit in setting out a theological case for the presence of the friars among the professors. Here his thesis was that no work of spiritual mercy – and preaching and teaching were for him certainly that – is unfitted to be the distinctive purpose of a religious order.

Parisian chairs changed hands rapidly, and, strange as it may seem, at some point in 1259 Thomas found himself at rather a loose end. The next year or so of his life is shrouded in obscurity; it is probable that he returned to Italy, where the historian soon finds him. From a whole variety of indices, ingeniously assembled by scholars (they range from the character of the parchment and ink Thomas used, to developments in both his documentation and his doctrine as well as back references in other treatises), we can infer that it was in this shadowy period that Thomas started composing the *Summa contra Gentiles*, the first of his two masterpieces. The claim was made in the sixteenth century that Thomas wrote this work as a 'missionary handbook' for Catholic representatives in the world of Islam, but attention to its contents suggests a wider aim, negatively convicting of error those who brought arguments against the faith from a great diversity of standpoints, from out-and-out pagans to Christian heretics and, more positively, showing the beautiful intelligibility of the suprarational wisdom of divine revelation, where the truths of philosophy fructify in their definitive, God-provided context. Since Thomas died before he could finish the successor to the *Summa contra Gentiles*, the *Summa theologiae*, it is to these earlier syntheses of theology that we must look for his account of eschatology, the last or ultimate things.

In the autumn of 1261 St Thomas was named conventual lector of the priory of Orvieto, a little Umbrian city with an outsize cathedral, perched on an isolated and almost perpendicular outcrop of rock, originally an Etruscan fortress and later a refuge in times of distress for the medieval popes. One supposes that Thomas's duties were not especially exigent, and it is from the Orvieto period that we have the widest variety of his writings – most commonly produced in response to requests from correspondents near and far, whether eminent or virtual nobodies. Thus Thomas's analysis of the views of the Greek Fathers on the issues increasingly separating the Greek and Latin churches was made at the request of the pope (it was unfortunate that so few of the excerpts in the anthology that Thomas was sent were authentic) while the treatise *On the Reasons for the Faith* was put together for an anonymous 'cantor of Antioch' – a minor cleric in the crusader state in Syria. Other short books were despatched to an Umbrian archdeacon and a Sicilian archbishop.[10] Here too, in all likelihood, Thomas wrote the most Christian-Platonist of all his works, the commentary on the *Divine Names*, from the pen of that mysterious Greek-speaking Syrian Christian of the sixth century who went by the name of Dionysius the Areopagite, a companion of Paul in the Acts of the Apostles; the *Commentary on the Book of Job* (generally regarded as the best crafted and most penetrating of his biblical works); the *Catena Aurea* or 'Golden Chain', an exposition of the four Gospels from texts taken from the Fathers (which the still Anglican Newman valued so much that he had a team of Tractarian scholars translate it); and, not least, St Thomas's only known poetry, the liturgical office for the newly introduced feast day of Corpus Christi (promulgated as an intrinsic part of the Roman liturgy by Urban IV in 1264). Thomas's expansion of his knowledge of the Fathers and Councils of the Church in his Orvieto period doubtless owes much to the fact that the archives of the papal curia were currently based in what was now his home town.

'Now' – but not for much longer. In September 1265, the Roman Province of the Order to which Thomas belonged asked him to go south to Rome itself, and set up a house of studies in the City – almost certainly at Santa Sabina, the residence of the Master. The late Father Leonard Boyle, Prefect of the Vatican Library, believed this was a unique experiment, what he termed a *studium personale*, essentially a one-man study centre where Thomas was free to develop courses as he thought fit.[11] The fact that it did not survive his departure from Rome is therefore entirely unsurprising. The title of Boyle's study, which argues this case, 'The Setting of the *Summa theologiae* of Saint Thomas', makes plain the claim to glory of Thomas's stay at Rome: it was then that the most important of all his works was conceived. Just when and where the different parts of the *Summa* were actually published is a matter of scholarly debate, but perhaps the dominant view would ascribe the *Prima Pars* to Rome, the *Secunda Pars* to Paris (on Thomas's return there in 1268 or 1269), and the *Tertia Pars* to Naples, when in his ending of his great task he returned to the place where his University studies had begun.

The Great *Summa*

The *Summa theologiae* opens by asking what theology is, and its answer is that theology is orderly reflection on the content of revelation, biblically attested as this is, and summed up in the articles of the Creed. This orderly reflection is carried out in the light of God's own knowledge of himself and his saving plan – which light, as communicated to ourselves, we call 'faith'. It is, then, in the broadest possible terms, an integration of faith and reason, and while Thomas allows that charity may give the unlettered person a kind of intuition or instinctive judgement in matters of faith, normally it requires study and hard work. The rest of the *Summa* falls into three parts which follow broadly what has been termed an *exitus-reditus* – literally, 'coming out, going back' – scheme. The fount or source of creatures is God whose existence is, for Thomas, known by reason but the mystery of whose being, in its concrete character, requires revelation for its description. After describing this fontal being, which is totally complete self-communicating goodness expressing itself through the interplay of three subsistent relationships (Father to Son, Son to Father, Father and Son to Holy Spirit), Thomas considers the issue from God of the created world: first, that of pure minds, the angels; then, that of the natural order as a whole; and finally the place of man, who is embodied mind or (in Thomist anthropology) intellectualised body. Creatures come forth from God, structured in the way that natural philosophy indicates but dependent on God for their existence and, in the case of rational creatures, ordered to him by their tendency to seek a goal beyond themselves.

Thus the first 'part' of the *Summa*, the *Prima Pars*. The second part begins by an account of human happiness which is, for St Thomas, the purpose of morality, just as it was for Aristotle. Thanks to the doctrines of creation and redemption, however, the content of such happiness must be re-described so as to include – indeed, centre on – the vision of God. This is our aim and destiny, 'return' to God in beatification. Thomas then uses a combination of Aristotelian ethics and the ascetic and moral writings of such Church Fathers as John Cassian and Gregory the Great to give an account of the basic emotional drives of human nature and how these, like mind and will, are distorted by sin. So ends the first half of the second part of the *Summa*, entitled less cumbersomely in Latin the *Prima Secundae*.

Next comes the first explicit treatment of the difference Christ makes: the gift of a new interior principle of acting, Christ's Holy Spirit. Thomas explicitly puts the question, What is the Gospel in itself? Is it, for instance, morals, or cultus, or teaching to be believed? He answers that primarily it is none of these things but the power of a new love which unites us with God and with each other. The teaching element, the written Gospels, dispose us to receive this Holy Spirit; the sacraments actually mediate this life to us, and it proceeds spontaneously to express itself in Christian living. The Spirit of Christ supernaturalises our natural drives not just through modulating the moral virtues but also and more specifically in two particular ways – the 'theological virtues', new God-directed dispositions, and the 'Gifts of the Holy Spirit'. First, then, that Spirit elicits faith, hope and charity, which make us tend to the God of the saving revelation as he is in himself, giving us real contact with him. And secondly, he bestows on us those gifts or endowments proper to the messianic child in the Book of Isaiah, applied by Church tradition at large to the messianic people of the New Covenant and associated by the Latin Church with, especially, Confirmation. For Thomas the Gifts essentially concern making the Christian life easy: they enable us to love God and our neighbour in thought, word and deed with happy facility.

The remainder of the *Secunda Secundae* is what we might call a phenomenology – a reflective description – of the Christian life, a life informed by charity and articulating itself in both practical goodness and contemplation. This enables Thomas to sum up in the final question of this 'second half of the second part' his earlier broadsides against those secular clergy of the time who had attacked the friars as interlopers. The best way to be a Christian is to unite contemplation and practical goodness; the highest form of practical goodness is to pass on understanding of the Christian faith, since this alone is helpful not only for time but also for eternity; so the best way to follow the Gospel is *contemplata aliis tradere*, to 'give to others the fruits of contemplation' – in other words, to become a Dominican!

The third and concluding part of the *Summa* shows what actually made (and makes) possible this return of rational creatures to God. Having spoken of our origin and our goal, Thomas must now make clear the path that connects them, and this he identifies as Christ, the *iter ad Deum*, or pathway to God. The incarnation, life, death and resurrection of the Word bring together the origin and the goal, and we encounter them in their salvifically connecting capacity in the sacraments which, for Aquinas, are efficacious symbols – signs that actually bring about what it is that they signify. As he will write on the *iter ad Deum* in the *Compendium theologiae*:

> The totality of the divine work finds its completion in that man, the last created creature, returns to his source by a kind of circle, when by the work of the Incarnation he finds himself united to the very source of [all] things.[12]

Compare the beautiful verbal icon of the structure of the *Summa* composed by the Cambridge theologian Nicholas Lash, who writes:

> We might almost say that, for Aquinas, the 'soundness' of his 'educational method' depended upon the extent to which the movement of his exposition reflected the rhythm of God's own act and movement: that self-movement 'outwards' from divine simplicity to the utterance of the Word and breathing of the Gift which God is, to the 'overflowing' of God's goodness in the work of his creation ('Prima pars'); the 'return' to God along that one way of the world's healing which is Christ ('Tertia pars'); and, because there lies across this movement the shadow of the mystery of sin, we find, between his treatment of the whence and whither, the 'outgoing' and 'return' of creaturely existence, the drama of conversion, of sin and virtue, of rejection or acceptance of God's grace ('Secunda pars'). And this by way of explanation of how in a summary of *Christian* theology, Christ can make a central appearance only towards the end.[13]

Rome to Paris

Convenient as it may be at this juncture to offer an overview of the shape of the *Summa theologiae*, I am running ahead of the story. Something more needs saying about the other works of Thomas's Roman period, and indeed about his second, very fruitful, engagement as professor in Paris – not least because for contemporaries, whatever may be the case for us today, the *Summa theologiae* did not prove (to judge by the diffusion of manuscripts) the sort of *succès de réclame* that might have been expected. Or, to put the matter more fairly, it would be known in the Middle Ages more by vulgarisers and abbreviators than for itself. From the Roman period we have, for instance, the *De Potentia*, 'On the Power [of God]', a series of disputed questions crucial to Thomas's meta-physics of the creation – for him at once totally dependent on God and yet (or rather, *and therefore*) totally free to be itself; the little jewel called the 'Compendium of Theology', where we find a very simple and moving précis by Thomas of what it is we believe in and hope for; more answers to questioners; and the first of his commentaries on the texts of Aristotle, a treatment of the *De anima* – perhaps suggested by the fact that much of his recent work, like the *Prima Pars* of the *Summa*, had obliged him to consider more closely the nature of the human creature, as a unity of body and soul.

Why Thomas was made, or chose, to return to Paris, we can only conjecture. The scholars suggest that the reason lay in the deteriorating intellectual situation (for an orthodox Christian, for a Dominican, for a sympathiser of Thomas's kind of thought) in that academic capital of thirteenth-century Latin Christendom. What was at stake was threefold. Firstly, there was well-founded anxiety over doctrinal orthodoxy, for a school of Latin – and thus, in prin-ciple, Christian – supporters of the Muslim philosopher Averroes had arisen, who maintained (through, it would seem, a tendentious misreading of their master's teaching) that human beings share one universal mind, and thus can expect no personal immortality. Secondly, there was the question of the retention of influence by the Order, for the crying havoc of the secular masters had started up again. And thirdly, under threat were also the rights of citizenship within the Church of what would later be called 'Thomism' – for conservative theologians hostile to the use of that rather too earth-bound philosopher Aristotle were bent once more on a formal con-demnation of the use of his writings in Catholic thought. All of which helps explain why the personal presence of Thomas was deemed desirable if not indispensable – as also the fact that so much of this second professoriate at Paris was taken up with expounding and, where necessary, salvaging from 'Averroist' interpretation the works of Aristotle. It was as though Thomas foresaw, and attempted vainly to forestall, the bitter disputes precipitated at Paris by his death.

For although the Platonism of Saint Thomas is quite as important as his Aristotelianism, it was the Aristotelianism which was controversial. Aristotle had asked, fundamentally, two questions. What is reality like, and what are the rules of argument which get us from one conclusion about it to another? The first kind of question is answered in his *Physics*, *Metaphysics* and *Ethics*; the second in his logical writings, the *Organon*, a name we can paraphrase as 'the philosopher's tools of trade'. The latter had been percolating through, in dribs and drabs, for some time, but a logical rule is empty unless you have some content for it to deal with, and it was the philosophical and ethical writings that caused the stir. In them, the different kinds of things in the world around us, including man, are analysed in terms of general principles of being and action which all beings in different ways exemplify; happiness is said to be the goal of specifically human life; it is reached by the exercise of virtues which are ways of being at harmony with myself and my human environment. There is little in Aristotle about the divine, for the philosopher lacked the concepts both of creation and of the personal nature of God, even if he saw a place for an unmoved Mover to keep the whole cosmic process of coming-to-be and passing-out-of-being in operation.

Thomas's achievement was to integrate such naturalism into the traditional Christian vision of life which the earlier monastic theologians entertained. In the early Middle Ages theology had been by and large the spiritual theology practised in the monasteries. While issues of logic were beginning to exercise monastic minds (one thinks of St Anselm), and such ruminations on the fundamental grammar of theological discourse were even more at home in cathedral schools, the aim was predominantly (not least in Anselm) the expression of the prayerful orientation of man to God. Preferred theological themes were closely relevant to spiritual living: religious self-knowledge, one's status as creature and sinner; the grace of Christ and how it heals from sin and raises up to share the life of God; the goal of earthly pilgrimage in the beatific vision, sitting down with the Trinity at the banquet of heaven in the celestial city. Monastic theology, so well described in Dom Jean Leclerq's *The Love of Learning and the Desire for God*, included, as that title tells us, ardour for erudition.[14] The same monastic milieux transmitted, after all, much of the pagan classical inheritance as well as the Church Fathers. It was Thomas's conviction, evidently, that this programme could be taken much further. The naturalism of the pagans at their best – the thinking, both theoretical and practical, of the 'good pagans' – could be textured into the fabric of Christian theology, without losing – and here is the point that Thomas's more rationalist disciples in later centuries were in danger of forgetting – the spiritual and eschatological (in a word, the *heavenly*) orientation of theology itself.

It is from his second Parisian period that we have, at least very probably, Thomas's treatise *On the Eternity of the World*, which accepted, against the English Franciscan John Peckham, the philosophical case that in principle the world might always have existed, while maintaining against neo-paganising naturalists that we know from revelation that in fact this is not the case. Around the same time, Thomas produced his book *On the Singleness of the Substantial Form*, where he argued (not especially originally, for a generation earlier, among the first of the high medieval Scholastics, this view had been fairly general) that the same soul, the form of the body, carries out at different levels all the functions, from mere physiological growth to the highest reaches of contemplation, of which the human person is capable. One of the fears here was that, to deny, as Thomas did, a distinct *bodily* form might mean in Christology that we cannot say of the body which hung upon the Cross that it rose self-identically on Easter Day (since, evidently, its intellectual form, the rational soul, had been separated from it in the meanwhile). For Thomas, however, the identity of the body of the Passion and that of the Resurrection is guaranteed by the fact that the divine Word is its enduring subject. The *De unitate intellectus*, against the 'monopsychism' of the Latin Averroists, already mentioned, belongs here too.

Thomas now took further two of the three classic genres of his first Parisian period which correspond so neatly to the three chief duties of a theological master in his time. He brought out his great commentary on John (he may well have seen this as the rightful successor to his work on Matthew: the first Gospel of the Canon could stand for the second and third, since all three Synoptic evangelists were primarily theologians of the Saviour's humanity, the fourth evangelist of his divinity). And he resolved a great range of 'disputed questions', many belonging to the 'question-box' or 'ask what you will' variety known as *quodlibets* which most of the masters assiduously avoided, since in such perilous games of intellectual self-exposure reputations could all too easily be lost.

If we do not have examples of his preaching to be assigned with security to these years, then the lacuna is filled by a medley of minor compositions whose subject matter ranges from the angels, and the metaphysics of the Platonists, through scientific cosmology and topics that raise the issue of Providence like astrology and making choice by lot, to questions of social ethics such as how to treat the Jews. And above all, this is the great period of Thomas's work on clarifying and interpreting the corpus of Aristotle. His expositions of two of Aristotle's logical writings, the *Peri Hermeneias* and the *Posteriora Analytica*, are, naturally enough, among the most technical of his works, yet the way his wider philosophy enhances the coherence of Aristotle's text has been admired.

The *Sententia libri Ethicorum*, Thomas's re-writing of Aristotle's *Nicomachean Ethics*, is, however, more ambitious than that: the Gospel re-makes morals; it leaves logic largely as it was. The commentaries on the *Physics* and *Metaphysics* of Aristotle testify to Thomas's perennial interest in the structure of nature and its relation to its Prime Mover – but also to his determination to 'read' the Greek philosopher via his own creationist metaphysic of being, which was far from Aristotle's mind. However, he never completed studies of some other minor treatises of Aristotle on the physical world, nor for that matter his commentary on the latter's *Politics*. In all these enterprises, we should note how Thomas is not primarily concerned with the historical reconstruction of texts from the fourth century before Christ: to think so would be on our part both an anachronism and a serious under-estimate of the *apostolic* aim of all Thomas's writing. Rather, his intention in seeking the original author's mind was to seek the truth, a truth clearer in the light of revelation than to Aristotle himself.

Last years

When Thomas came to the end of his second period of Parisian teaching in 1272, less than four years of life were left to him, and the sheer expenditure of energy on so massive a literary output (contemporaries commented on the frenetic way he worked, wrote or dictated, in sharp contrast to the later idealisation of the serene, eternity-absorbed master, or even the early memories of a bovine and therefore presumably placid 'dumb ox') must have taken its toll – even if he did use secretaries, amounting perhaps in his later years to what Torrell calls 'a veritable workshop of literary production'.[15] But there was no rest for the wicked, or in this case, the righteous, as indeed the more sharp-witted contributors to the Wisdom Books of the Old Testament had long ago noted. Assigned to Naples, he was given once again the task of creating a study house of the Order, this time no personal affair, however, but a *studium generale* in a city which would remain, until the late eighteenth century, among Europe's greatest capitals. As befitted one whose earthly span, though he knew it not, was closing, the subject matter he now taught was, in its period, non-controversial and apt for contemplation. the Psalter, the Pauline letters and the mysteries of the life of Christ, which were to form the lion's share of the last part of the *Summa theologiae*. It is thought-provoking that Thomas's presentation of the life of the Saviour, while from one viewpoint absolutely straightforward – a re-statement of the narrative structure of the Gospels themselves – is, to judge by the way he entitles its chief parts, a sort of *reprise* of the *Summa* so far: he begins with the *egressus*, or coming forth of Christ from God into this world; moves onto the *progressus*, or development of his public ministry, before attending to his *exitus*, or redemptive leave-taking of the world to return to God, and subsequent *exaltatio* or raising to God's right hand as the mediator of human glorification.

That *Tertia Pars* was, as already mentioned, never completed. Thomas fell into a trance while celebrating Mass in the chapel dedicated to Saint Nicholas in the priory at Naples, some time around St Nicholas's day (6 December) 1273 – later remarking that, in comparison with what he then saw, all his writings were as straw. He never set pen to parchment again. Thomas died on a journey between Naples and Rome, on the Appian Way, while obeying the injunction of the pope, Gregory X, to take part in the Second Council of Lyons, one of the abortive reunion councils between West and East, which was to open on 1 May 1274. The probable cause of death was a blood-clot, caused by hitting his head against a low-lying branch while on donkey-back. The monks of the nearby Cistercian abbey of Fossanova nursed him in his last days, and hours, and were rewarded for their pains by an improvised commentary on the Canticle of Canticles, the great love song of Yahweh and Israel, Christ and the Church. Thomas died among the sons of Benedict just as he had lived with them as a child; and this was fitting because his theology, no matter how speculative its flights, had never had an ultimate goal different from that of Benedict or Bernard in the heavenly city of God.

Part Two: *The Doctrine*

2.
Revelation

The nature of revelation

To address what St Thomas has to say about 'revelation' is to raise a number of interrelated questions. The more important trio are these. First, how did Thomas view the supernatural knowledge of God and his plan for the world, the heart of the biblical covenant, especially in its New Testament and therefore Christian form? Secondly, by what means did he regard that revelation as undergoing transmission to successive generations and so to ourselves? Thirdly, how did he see the act of faith, which in all theologies, in one way or another, is the subjective correlate of revelation, the way revelation is appropriated by the individual heart and mind?

Let us turn without further ado to our first question, how would Aquinas have understood the supernatural or strictly revelational and salvific knowledge of God and his plan that is typical of the biblical faith? The first thing we must register – and, *prima facie*, a somewhat shocking thing it is for those of us brought up on some variant of a theology of salvation history (whether drawn from 'biblical theology', or the documents of the Second Vatican Council, or the mainline Catholic theologians of the mid to late twentieth century such as Daniélou, Balthasar, Congar) – is that revelation for Thomas does not consist principally in public events. It is not to be found, for instance, in the Exodus and Sinai events of the Old Testament or even in the Incarnation, Life, Death and Resurrection of Christ in the New. And this is because, for Aquinas, revelation – with one caveat to be entered – is essentially an interior event, and more justly still, it is an intellectual event. It consists in cognitive acts, acts of intellectual appropriation, in which the mind judges relevant materials (and *those* may be events like the ones just mentioned) by a light superior to the ordinary lights that the mind normally works by in this world. God gives the recipient of revelation what Thomas calls a *lumen propheticum*, a 'prophetic light', which enables him or her to judge of their experience in a way that echoes the divine judgement of the realities concerned.[1]

In ordinary common-or-garden knowing of the world, two things – so Thomas thought – are required: a capacity to register in a receptive way what is other than the mind (what Thomas, following Aristotle, called the 'patient intellect'), and the power to penetrate what is thus registered and draw out its intelligibility – in plain English, make sense of it (for which we need that other kind of mental activity which Aristotle and Thomas call the 'agent intellect'). And all this is with a view to showing something for what it is, by the natural light of human understanding. What we find in strictly supernatural knowledge – revelational knowledge, salvific-ally relevant knowledge – has to be grasped by analogy with this twofold process. What the mind receives may be impressions from the naturally or historically formed world around it – the life of the cosmos, say, so important to the Wisdom writers of the Old Testa-ment, or the miracles or the Passion of Christ in the New. Or again, what the mind registers may be materials directly infused by God – images or ideas which God, who is immediately present to the soul as to every other reality, can place there by his action. But in either case what the mind is patient of cannot be called 'revelation' unless it has actively grasped its content by an act of judgement made through a light higher than that of natural understanding because sharing in the light of the divine mind, the mind of Truth itself.

This analogy with our variegated natural experience of the world and of ourselves within the world enables Thomas to do two things simultaneously. First, he can admit, in line with the biblical witness to revelation, the extraordinary variety of materials that divine Providence has utilised for communicating supernatural knowledge. Perhaps his fullest statement of the diversity of the media of the Judaeo-Christian revelation comes in his commentary on the Letter to the Hebrews, where the biblical writer opens, 'In many and various ways God spoke of old to our fathers by the prophets' (Heb. 1:1), on which the English Dominican interpreter of Thomas, Victor White, commented:

> St Thomas stresses the extraordinary richness and variety to be found in the methods which God has devised to make his saving ways known to men – even in the Old Testament alone. The extraordinary variety, in the first place, of all sorts and conditions of men whom he has chosen to be the recipients of his revelation. Then, the extraordinary variety of historical conditions in which revelations have been made . . . and the manifold adaptations to the particular needs of those conditions.

And this is not all. For there is:

> Thirdly, the immense variety of the kinds of things that have been the subject of those revelations – divine and transcendental things, temporal things belonging to past, present and future; promises and threats; absolute things, contingent things and conditional things. Fourthly, the immense richness and variety of symbolism which revelation has employed for its medium, ranging from the crudest of inanimate stocks and stones . . . to the most sublime and dazzling visions.

Nor is the list ended here. We must add:

> Fifthly, the diversity of clarity of apprehension of what is revealed, ranging from the darkest night both of sense and of understanding through every degree of twilight to relatively clear daylight vision. Next, the unlimited variety of modes of expression and literary form which will be given to communicate the revelations . . . Finally, the limitless variety of men to whom the revelations are to be communicated, and their corresponding adaptation to the needs of each . . .[2]

Variety, then – to sum up the message of Thomas's Hebrews commentary – in immediate recipients, historical conditions, subjects treated, symbols used as media, clarity of apprehension, expressive forms in which the immediate recipient will go on to articulate the revelation received, and revelation's ultimate destinees – namely, all human beings.

I said there were two things that Thomas's comparison of revelation understanding with natural understanding enables. And after this exhibition of the *diversity* intrinsic to the revelatory process, modelling revelation on the analogy of the Aristotelian account of ordinary knowing also enables Thomas to bring out the basic *unity* of revelation as a happening in the human world. This unity lies in the fact that all instances of revelation share a single common feature. In every case, be it apparently prosaic, as with Solomon observing the herbs growing in the garden wall, or utterly exotic, as with the apocalyptic visions of St John, a judgement is pronounced by the receiver of revelation, thanks to that supplementary strengthening, or further illumination, of the mind which the *lumen propheticum* provides. And just as the *lumen naturale* of the agent intellect is given by God as Creator to enable us to find our way in intelligent fashion in the ordinary world, so the *lumen propheticum* is given by God as Redeemer, to enable human beings (a few of them directly, all of them indirectly) to locate and interpret aright the ultimate goal of human life, a goal entirely supernatural because consisting in the open vision of the Trinity, and hence transcending finite, created nature altogether.

Thomas has already told his readers, or students, in the opening question of the *Summa theologiae*, that divine revelation is necessary to us because the purpose and meaning of human existence is ultimately to be found only in the God who is invisible and incomprehensible, and yet that purpose has somehow to be made known to humankind if human objectives and activities are to be aligned with their final end. For only in that goal does *salus*, 'salvation' – health and well-being for spirit and body alike – ultimately consist. What is necessary, then, is some way of abolishing the distance that separates human cognitive capacity from awareness of the divine offer of salvation, and this can only be done by God himself. He does this by bestowing the 'prophetic light' on chosen individuals – chosen so that they may witness to divine revelation on behalf of all.

The supernatural prophet is thus enabled to see something from the standpoint of eternity, to see something present whose significance lies in the last analysis in the eternal. As a reflection of the divine knowledge, prophetic knowledge can make use of anything in creation since anything, as known by God, can serve to mediate an understanding of human salvation. The prophet's judgement may fall on a paranormal occurrence like the content of an ecstatic vision, or on something absolutely commonplace and everyday. That is why Thomas, unlike modern exegetes or indeed the rabbis, who divided up the Hebrew Bible into particular kinds of books, regards the entire scriptural revelation as prophetic, not just the scrolls of the classical prophets, from Isaiah to Malachi, the only prophets in the pre-medieval and post-medieval senses of that word. He states in his commentary on the Letter to the Romans, for example, that the Books of Kings are prophetic books inasmuch as they describe not only the deeds and sayings of prophets but also the historic events on which the prophets' judgements were made.[3] And in the *Summa theologiae* he devotes the longest article in that guide-to-theology-at-large to the prophetic character of the ritual prescriptions of the Pentateuch, since these provided the sacred writers with symbols of the salvation which was to come.[4] So whatever the raw material of prophetic knowledge – whatever its material character – formally speaking, when considered as a distinctive kind of understanding, it is all the same.

The role of the Incarnation

Here, however, I must introduce a caveat, which concerns the difference made to the structure of prophetic understanding (the structure of revelation, then) by the Incarnation. For Aquinas, the enlargement of the judgement of a prophet – that is, an immediate recipient of revelation – comes about in the Old Testament through angelic mediation. Though Thomas was extremely interested in the angels, and has the most sophisticated angelology of any medieval author (hence, no doubt, the ignorant anti-Scholastic jibes about the numbers of angels on pinheads), this view of revelation in Israel is not what it may appear: a blatant case of reading into the biblical text metaphysical theories drawn from elsewhere. The idea that the Old Law was mediated by angels is clearly found in both the speech of Stephen in the Acts of the Apostles and in the Pauline Letters, notably Galatians, and it is crucial to the argument of the Letter to the Hebrews.[5] What Thomas does is to broaden this claim to the extent of a categorical denial that the Old Testament was ever the effect of unmediated divine agency. When in Exodus 33 we hear that the Lord spoke to Moses face to face, as a friend speaks to his friends (verse 11), we can read those words only because, so Thomas somewhat sweepingly declares, *secundum opinionem populi loquitur Scriptura*, 'Scripture speaks according to the opinion of the people' – describing the causality of things as it was generally viewed. The real causality was certainly angelic. As Aquinas explains, the function of angels is communication (the very word 'angel' tells us so). Now the angels themselves enjoy the Beatific Vision. So these immaterial substances are able to communicate not that Vision itself, which is infinite, but some of its finite effects, some knowledge of God's eternal designs for his world. This they do by working in and and through matter, obeying its laws while exploiting its resources. By what Aquinas calls a 'commotion of the bodily spirits and humours' – in more modern language, by modifying the processes of human physiology – the angels are able to stimulate mental images, or indeed stimulate the external sense-organs to produce aural or visual images, images which then form the raw material of revelation. At the same time, the angelic powers also clarify and strengthen the human intellect by means of the *lumen propheticum*, augmenting the light in which relations between images and ideas are seen. Thus, as Thomas puts it in the *De veritate*:

> The human mind is raised to understand in a certain way conformably to the manner of immaterial substances, so that with utmost certitude it sees not only principles but also conclusions by simple intuition.[6]

Such angelic mediation ceases, however, with the transition from the Old Testament to the New – on that 'turn of the ages' between the pre-Incarnational and Incarnational epochs. Thanks to the hypostatic union, the human mind of the Word incarnate is immediately open to influxes from the divine mind, for it is the human mind of one who is personally God. The revelation from which the Christian religion takes its rise is, in the first place, a vision in the inspired human intellect of Jesus, in the human soul of Christ.

His knowledge of the divine Trinity and its saving plan was incomparably greater than that of the Old Testament prophets – including in that phrase, as Aquinas does, all the writers of the books of the Old Testament and those who by their experience contributed to them. This uniqueness of revelatory fullness in Christ is what makes Thomas call Jesus in his human nature *primus et principalis doctor*, 'the first and principal teacher'.[7] And the Christ who, as God, is truth itself and, as man, possessed all supernatural knowledge relevant to salvation in the highest degree, proceeded to teach the apostles by *both deeds and sayings* (here the dimension of public event at last makes its full-dress appearance),[8] and they pass on his teaching *verbo et scripto*, 'by word of mouth and by writing'.

The faith of the apostles

It follows that the apostles enjoy a crucial status in Thomas's account of revelation. What knowledge did the apostles have of the truths of faith? Since the development of nineteenth-century historical scholarship the tendency has been to reply, A very confused and imperfect knowledge. We find that reply already given by a Catholic theologian (though not an especially orthodox one), Anton Günther, in the 1840s. Thomas's reply, by contrast, is that the apostles enjoyed a particularly clear and comprehensive grasp of all that the revelation of the new covenant contains. In his commentary on First Corinthians, Thomas echoes Paul in holding that the apostles enjoy the first rank among the ministers of the Church.[9] In his commentary on the Letter to the Romans he explains why it was that they received at Pentecost greater graces than all subsequent Christians. It was so they might become the universal and definitive doctors of the Church. When Paul writes in Romans 8, 'we who have received the firstfruits of the Spirit', the 'we' here, according to Aquinas (following in this Origen and Ambrose), refers to the apostles. It is for Thomas a soteriological principle that God gives someone grace in proportion to the mission for which he or she has been chosen. So, to cite his Romans commentary:

There was bestowed on the man Christ the most excellent grace there can be, because he was chosen in order that in him human nature might be assumed into the unity of the divine person [of the Word]. After him, it is blessed Mary who possessed grace in the greatest plenitude, having been chosen to be the Mother of Christ. Among the others, the apostles received by sharing it the highest dignity. Receiving from Christ himself immediately [receiving, Thomas means, the deliverances of Christ's uniquely inspired prophetic mind], it was indeed incumbent on them to communicate to others what regards salvation, to the degree that they are, in a certain manner, the foundations of the Church.[10]

It is the unique proximity of the apostles to the fullness of time (cf. Galatians 4) when, with the climax of salvation history at the Incarnation, the first and principal teacher, the God-man, was manifesting clearly the substance of divine revelation in its maximal form, exteriorising his understanding in words and deeds, that gave the apostles a perfect knowledge of the mysteries of faith in which they were confirmed or stabilised by the outpouring of the Spirit at Pentecost. And so, in a characteristic comparison, just as a human being finds herself in her most perfect condition in youth, so the people of God of Old and New Testaments was in its most perfect condition for grasping revelation when it had left behind the childhood of Israel and was full of abundant life, fully developed yet still showing no sign of the ageing process. Directly taught by their master, Christ, from the outside, and taught from the inside by the Spirit of Pentecost, the promised Paraclete, the apostles stand head and shoulders above all other teachers of the faith. However, Thomas adds a caveat. The Gifts of the Spirit that the apostles received by way of wisdom and knowledge were sufficient for the teaching of the faith for all future generations. But the apostles, the men of Galilee, were not called upon to propose the faith by means of reasoned analysis, systematisation or precise enunciation. So after the apostles there was still in the Church work for theologians to do. That is the consequence of what a French Dominican interpreter of Thomas called the 'lack of correspondence between the magnificent infused faith of the apostles and their uncultivated human intellectuality'.[11] Here is the lacuna which the charisms of teaching in the later Church are to supply.

Bible and Tradition

But how are later theologians, or any later members of the Church for that matter, to encounter the message of the apostles? Thomas's principal answer is, through the Holy Scriptures and, in a derivative manner, through the Apostles' Creed. As he writes:

> The truth of the faith is contained in the Holy Scripture diffusely and in different ways, some of which envelop it in obscurity. That is so much so that to extract from Sacred Scripture the truth of the faith much study and application are required, to which most people, absorbed as they are by other concerns, are in no position to give themselves or to attend. That is why it was necessary to draw from the Scriptures and to formulate as a summary something absolutely clear which could be proposed to the faith of all. Nonetheless, it is not a question of things added to the Holy Scriptures but of things drawn out of them.[12]

The Bible is clearly quite central to Thomas's picture of Christian theology considered as investigation of what divine revelation contains.

In fact, so much is this the case that Catholic spokesmen have sometimes been embarrassed by the succour Aquinas seems to give to what, in the wake of the Council of Trent, might be considered typically Protestant notions of the sufficiency and perspicuity or self-evidence of the biblical record. Thomas rarely refers to sacred Tradition, for a reason I shall give shortly. For the moment, however, let us notice the few occasions when he mentions it. In Second Thessalonians Paul writes to the Church at Thessalonica in terms frequently cited by Catholic apologists on this subject:

> So then, brethren, stand firm and hold onto the traditions you were taught by me, either by word of mouth or by letter (2:15).

In his commentary on the epistle, Thomas can hardly avoid all reference to this text. What he says, however, needs some unpacking. It is clear from Paul's words, writes Aquinas, that much of what the apostles taught was not set down in the apostolic writings. The apostles, he explains, citing Denys the Areopagite, whom he believed to be a younger contemporary of Paul, thought it 'better to hide much'.[13] Deliberate concealment of the mysteries of faith by, of set purpose, not describing them in writing was, doubtless, more important to the sixth-century Christian Platonist than it had been to the apostle of the gentiles. Denys's project had been aimed at showing how the teachings and sacraments of the Christian religion were that divine truth and saving reality of which the message and ceremonies of the pagan mystery-religions were but a caricature. At the same time, Denys was appealing to a memory of what, historically, had once been the Church's practice. His account of unwritten and indeed unpublicised tradition could find some justification in the 'discipline of the secret' by which the sacraments and, above all, the Eucharist, were guarded from profane and potentially hostile eyes, at any rate at times and places, in the pre-Nicene Church. Interestingly enough, Thomas refers to sacred Tradition by name chiefly in allusions to the sacraments, as when, for instance, he writes that the form of the sacrament of Confirmation is known to us through the *traditio apostolica*. This would be a good example of what he had in mind in his Thessalonians commentary, for his conclusion in the passage I have been discussing was that the unwritten provisions of the apostolic teaching must be 'observed', *servanda*, in the later Church – with the distinct implication that they are more matters of practice, like the Liturgy, than they are of credal confession, like the articles of faith. (In fairness I must add, though, that in his commentary on the Book of Job he speaks of the identity of Satan as a fallen angelic intelligence – a truth of faith, evidently, as something that we know by means of *traditio ecclesiastica,* 'the Church's tradition'.)[14]

The chief reason why Thomas does not, by and large, speak of Tradition as a fount of revealed understanding distinct from the Scriptures is that he thinks of Scripture as *itself transmitted by Tradition. Traditio sacrae Scripturae*, the 'traditioning' or handing on of Scripture within the Church as a whole, is the norm of Christian faith. And so, for instance, he emphasises – and there could be little less Protestant than this! – that the Fathers of the Church must never be separated from or counterposed against the biblical authors. For the Fathers are the authentic transmitters of Scripture – and here he will be thinking of not just the textual tradition but also the salvific meaning of the biblical writings. Even though the authority of the Fathers in theology is only 'probable', unlike that of the apostles, which is 'certain', the witness of the Fathers remains a reliable witness of what the Church believes. Thus a Dutch Dominican student of Thomas's theology of revelation-in-transmission has effectively equated Thomas's formula *fides totius Ecclesiae*, 'the faith of the whole Church', with the post-Tridentine formulation *unanimis consensus Patrum*, 'the unanimous consent of the Fathers'.[15] Also worth noting here is his conviction that the general Councils of the Church are authoritative interpreters of Scripture. Illumined by the Holy Spirit, the Fathers – in the sense, this time, of the bishops assembled in Council – explained infallibly the meaning of the sacred text. Moreover, so as to set aside errors in the interpretation of the faith established by biblical revelation, there can be (and is) in the Church appeal to the pope, who in Thomas's ecclesiology represents both the unity of the Church and Christ himself in his pastoral care for the congregation of the faithful. Hence, as Aquinas puts it:

> We must stand by the decision of the pope rather than the opinion of other men, even though they may be learned in the Scriptures. For the pope has the right and duty to determine concerning the faith, a determination he indicates by his judgment.[16]

This passage alone serves to show that Thomas's statements about the *sufficientia* and *perspicuitas* of Scripture are not to be taken in a sixteenth-century sense.

Thomas's near-identification of *sacra Scriptura* with *sacra doctrina*, 'the holy teaching' – namely, revelation-in-transmission as expounded by the Church's theologians – is not, therefore, so unilateral as it may at first appear. What might strike us as more odd, indeed, is Thomas's willingness to describe Scripture as itself *scientia*, 'science'. Three considerations explain his so doing. First, for

Thomas, science is always a knowledge of something through its causes, whereby we get to the bottom of something by uncovering its foundational principle. But the knowledge found in Scripture derives from God's own knowledge of himself and his eternal design for the world, and nothing can be more cognitively fundamental than that. Secondly, like more mundane sciences, Holy Scripture, Thomas points out, itself uses reasoning, as when, for example, in his First Letter to Corinth, Paul argues from the Resurrection of Christ to the resurrection of all mankind. And then thirdly, Scripture offers to thought the unity which is typical of scientific under-standing, for all the matters dealt with by Scripture are covered by the gift of prophetic inspiration only insofar as they are *revelabilia*, 'revealable', objects of revelation. And to have in this way one single, formal perspective on all the topics that this body of literature (the Bible) treats of is precisely what enables a kind of knowing to be unitary and in that sense scientific.

Principles of biblical exegesis

Here we have, then, even when all necessary caveats are entered, a very high doctrine of the primacy of Scripture and of Scripture as the soul of theology. And if we go on to ask after not, as just discussed, the authority of Scripture (*vis-à-vis* revelation on the one hand, and theology on the other) but, rather, Thomas's principles for interpreting Scripture, we shall not be surprised to find that he lays the greatest possible weight on the meaning under-stood by the biblical authors. This follows *logically* from his understanding of revelation as prophetic knowledge. If revelation chiefly happens not as events in the public world but as interior occurrences in the minds of prophets and doctors (Christ and his apostles), then the ability of the biblical literature to capture and express the intentions of those minds is what makes it the vehicle of revelation in the later Church. So crucial is this to Thomas that it created something of a difficulty in dealing with the spiritual sense of Scripture on which the Fathers of the Church so often rely. Thomas's general position is that the spiritual sense of Scripture consists in that meaning which *God* attaches to the *res* ('realities';

these could be events or people) to which the literal sense of the human authors of the text refers. That God does so attach further meaning to events and persons – happenings and personalities in the Old Testament as prefigurative of the New, happenings and personalities of the New Testament as prefigurative of eternity and the life to be lived now by humans in order to get there – is plain from the Church's teaching and practice. It is plain most obviously from the Liturgy where, for example, we celebrate the return of Israel from Babylon as a type of the Resurrection and of holy baptism, and the Ascension of Jesus as a type of our own entry into future glory. So strong was Thomas's adherence to the primacy of the literal sense that he insisted on verifying claims for such spiritual interpretation of biblical passages by reference to other texts of Scripture where, at any rate, some of the same claims could be validated in terms of the literal sense. Only after he discovered, probably in his Orvieto period, that the Fifth Ecumenical Council had condemned as heretical the denial by Theodore of Mopsuestia that certain texts of the Hebrew Bible were Christologically prophetic did Thomas, consistent with his understanding of the role of Councils, change his tune. Beginning with the final version of his commentary on the Gospel according to Matthew, he begins to argue that the spiritual sense can sometimes be included within the literal sense. So when, for instance, in his commentary on John he discusses the evangelist's locating of the Baptist's debate with the Pharisees at Bethany, Thomas gives two reasons why St John might have mentioned this detail of place.[17] First, the topographical datum would interest any contemporary eyewitnesses who might get hold of the Fourth Gospel. Secondly, because Bethany means 'house of obedience', the evangelist was indicating that any of his readers who did not yet believe must come to Christian baptism through the 'obedience of faith'. Students with tidy minds sometimes ascribe to Thomas, therefore, a position in these matters that they dub 'virtual pluralism'. Thomas's 'hermeneutic' is one where a text can have a superordinate literal sense whose content is the same as the spiritual senses in other hermeneutic schemes but without detriment to a subordinate literal sense of a less exalted kind, construed by simple reference to the primary signification of the words used.[18]

The act of faith

But of course the interrelation of Scripture and Tradition and the principles of understanding Scripture within its own traditioning are only of personal importance to us if we have that subjective correlate of divine revelation which is faith. We have seen how Thomas understands the prophetic light of revelation by analogy with the natural light operative in ordinary human knowing. By 'light' here we can understand whatever causes something to become manifest in some order of knowledge. In Thomas's writings, the word 'light' represents, to put it grandiloquently, the causal principle in cognitive manifestation. And now we must add that there is not only, for him, the *lumen naturale* and the *lumen propheticum*. There is also the *lumen fidei*, the 'light of faith'. And this for Thomas is a light issuing from God as Redeemer, just as is the *lumen propheticum* – not, however, to give us direct knowledge of revelation, as with that more intense if also (in many cases) more transient light, but to allow us to adhere to the First Truth, God himself, by assenting to what, through veridical witnesses (that is, through testimonies he has guaranteed as true), God invites us to believe about himself and his everlasting purpose for us.

In his analysis of the act of faith, Thomas distinguishes between *credere Deo*, believing by or through God; *credere Deum*, believing God; and *credere in Deum*, believing in God. All these elements are present in faith's act and therefore in the 'virtue' or stable disposition which is the principle of all Christian believing in the life of the faithful.

First of all, *credere Deo*. Believing is 'by' or 'through' God in that only God can activate interiorly the instinct we have for our last end, and thus, by means of the will, move the intellect to give its assent to the truths he teaches – truths which reach us from him through the Church's presentation of the canonical Scriptures which are themselves the expression of the preaching of those apostles who, as doctors of the faith, participated in the knowledge of the unique Witness to divine truth, the God-man. Thomas offers a psychology of the act of faith – a psychology of a metaphysical sort – under this heading of *credere Deo*. Although the truth of divine revelation to which the will bids the intellect adhere is not, as it was for its immediate recipients, something evident, nonetheless this revelation is worthy of our assent. That we can grasp from the way the will is attracted to the share in our final good which revelation promises. A secondary but important factor for Thomas is the manner in which God confirms the credibility of his revelation by furnishing its transmission with conditions that only he could originate – in the fulfilment of prophecy, the occurrence of miracles, the manifestation of outstanding sanctity on the part of revelation's representatives. These signs demonstrate that it really is God who has spoken by means of revelation's recipients, and thus intervened in human history, centrally in Jesus Christ.

Still, such 'signs of credibility' do not bring it about that we actually believe in the First Truth for its own sake, taking it as the very measure of our own minds and doing so with absolute certitude. Here is where the necessity of a new light – a new formal principle of knowing – becomes plain, and Thomas discusses it under the heading of *credere Deum*, 'believing God'. *Secondly*, then, to know God by means of his own word is actually to share in his divine knowledge. Faith is such a sharing, albeit an imperfect one, but not so imperfect that it does not orient the human mind towards the future vision of God in its wondrous fullness.

And this brings us to the third dimension of faith, faith as *credere in Deum*, 'believing in [literally, 'unto'] God'. By its own dynamism faith tends towards the supernatural blessedness of seeing the Holy Trinity. But this vision is a gift of God to which we must respond by a perfect will. As the Swiss Dominican Benoît Duroux has explained:

> This formal quality of the mind [the *lumen fidei* making *credere Deum* possible] which consists in having as the medium of knowledge the First Truth itself, is incapable of finally beatifying man unless charity renders this adherence operative and deserving of the gift of the beatific Light.

And Duroux goes on:

> That is why faith, which informs man obscurely but with certitude about the everlastingly True, and by this very fact

determines in principle man's speculative intellect, also represents God to him as the Goal to be rejoined by love and thus can extend itself into the order of action.[19]

With *credere in Deum*, this active movement of the mind in love towards the God who is its ultimate goal, St Thomas reaches the end of a theology of faith. For the noblest aspect of faith is its character as the *inchoatio gloriae*, the beginning of glory. As the monastic theologians of the early Middle Ages saw especially clearly, faith has an eschatological quality. The life that flows from faith is anticipation of life with the Trinity in heaven. There the *lumen fidei* – made possible, historically speaking, by the *lumen propheticum*, itself a supernaturalised version of the *lumen naturale*–will reach its full term in the *lumen gloriae*, the light of glory.

3.
God and Creation

One way of connecting our last topic – revelation – to the theme of 'God and creation' is via Thomas's account of the ways of knowing God as found in the opening of the fourth book of his *Summa contra Gentiles*.

Three ways of knowing God

In that text, Thomas writes that there are three kinds of knowledge of God enjoyed by man.[1] First, there is the sort given by the light of natural reason, whereby man 'ascends' or rises up through creatures to the knowledge of God. The second is when the divine truth which surpasses human understanding 'descends' or comes down to us by the mode of revelation – not, however, Thomas adds, 'in order to be seen but in order to be believed as by a word passed on [from one to another]'. And then thirdly, he says – and here he comes to questions of the highest form of mystical experience as well as to the beatific vision in heaven – knowledge of God also comes about when the human mind is so raised up as 'perfectly to intuit those things that are revealed'.

If we leave aside the latter – the issue of the knowledge of God enjoyed by the saints after death (and for Thomas experiences of mystical rapture on earth, such as the one reported by St Paul, consist in a momentary sharing in the vision of God proper to the blessed)[2] – we have here two forms of cognitive approach to God, one ascending and the other descending, one working through the *lumen naturale*, the other, in dependence on the *lumen propheticum* of prophets and apostles, working through the *lumen fidei*, the light of faith. Revelation is received through faith, but that is not to say there is no valid rational approach to the mystery of God.

This distinction between the natural and the revealed knowledge of God is an elementary one, but Thomas makes it more sophisticated in a way that takes us to the heart of the matter in hand: God and creation. For Thomas, metaphysical knowledge reaches out to God thanks to analogical reasoning based on what is common to both created being and uncreated Being, doing so in virtue of the real yet limited community which joins finite being with infinite. By contrast, the knowledge of faith attains God as he is in his own inmost mystery, for in that knowledge given through revelation God utters himself as he really is. True, the images, concepts and analogies used by faith are taken, like those at work in the philosophical knowledge of God, from the natural world. But when used in faith they have been divinely selected as media for God's self-revelation. That is attested by their presence in the Scriptures. And the judgement that the believer, as distinct from the philosopher, makes on such media is carried out not by any natural light, but in the light of faith which is a share in God's own knowledge of himself.

Laying aside, then, mystical graces of rapture, few and far between as these are, we have in this life two fundamental modes of knowing God. To introduce two key terms which were vital for the later Greek Fathers and in modern Western dogmatics for Hans Urs von Balthasar, we know God both by *anabasis* – 'rising' upon the basis of what is common to created and uncreated being, and by *katabasis* – God's 'descending' self-disclosure which comes down in the Judaeo-Christian revelation from the One whom the Letter of James calls 'the Father of lights' (James 1:17).[3]

In St Thomas's theology of God and creation, the two kinds or, if you prefer, *directions* of such knowing – upwards and downwards, anabatic and katabatic, are generally found interwoven. Such interweaving of the two approaches produces, to Thomas's mind, the greatest richness of theological understanding, the maximal fullness of theological intelligibility. That is why we have to agree with those historians of medieval thought who have insisted that Thomas was a theologian who made use of philosophy, not a philosopher who was under an ecclesiastical obligation to say something about faith as well.

On the other hand, St Thomas is also perfectly capable of using the anabatic approach by itself if he thinks it will serve his turn. Entire questions – that is, sets of articles – in the *Prima Pars* of the *Summa theologiae* rely almost exclusively on the ascending approach to the knowledge of God, as do great swathes of the *Summa contra Gentiles*. So those Thomists who have seen Thomas as the fountainhead of a distinctively Thomistic tradition of philosophical – as distinct from revealed – theology also have a case to put. Their claims can, however, be overstated. The purely philosophical Thomas is confined to relatively minor treatises. On a great topic of doctrine like the Creator God and his work, Aquinas does not treat katabatic understanding as something merely to be tagged on by way of an appendix.[4] He does not, that is, treat the distinctively Christian knowledge of God as the triune God, God the Trinity, as though it were an afterthought. The God who creates is, for him, Father, Son and Spirit, and this, the triune nature of the Creator, leaves its mark in Trinitarian vestiges in the world and, in the case of man, in a stronger impression of the Trinity – viz., the created image of God, for as we read in the first Genesis creation account, 'In the image of God he created him' (Gen. 1:27).[5] Why, then, does Thomas begin his account of God with a treatise *De Deo uno*, and only then look to God's *triune* being?

> The fundamental reason . . . for beginning theology with the *unity* of God, rather than with God's Trinity, is 'because the one is by nature principle'. The sequence of topics in the *Prima pars* follows 'the step-by-step derivation of multiplicity from the divine unity'; it moves from the 'simpleness' of God's being through increasing complexity (even in God himself) to the scattered diversity of his creatures. Hence, on the specific question of the relationship between the treatment of God's being and the consideration of God's Trinity, we can say that 'the *de deo trino* communicates with the *de deo uno* in virtue of the gradual development toward greater distinction in the terms of the various forms of self-relation in the divine'.[6]

As, however, I propose to discuss Thomas's theology of the Holy

Trinity and his Trinitarian anthropology in the chapters that follow, I shall largely confine myself here to the anabatic, rather than katabatic, knowledge of God and creation. And this is legitimately Thomistic so long as such division of labour is not pushed too far. Thomas takes thought for the 'order of consideration', taking care to distinguish the two 'methods'. Though theology begins with divine revelation and hence from consideration of the Creator, and philosophy from the consideration of creatures, striving to rise to their First Cause, the two are frequently combined, using philosophical arguments to make more manifest truths encountered on the theological way. As one of the finest living Thomists, the Dutch Verbist priest Leo Elders has put it:

> Faith is non-evident knowledge which uses concepts of the natural order to signify supernatural realities. This is possible, for there is an analogy between both orders, because God is the author of both. Reason must assist faith in the analysis, ordering and further elaboration of what is revealed. This is precisely what Aquinas does: philosophical insights and natural truths are used *within* sacred theology, becoming integral parts of it (without them theology is not possible) and they partake in the nature of theology as long as they are used by it. But they can also be detached from it. One may compare their function to that of the chemical elements and reactions in the living organism. Outside the organism they occur in their own right; but in the organism they are subservient to the principle of life and taken up into a higher unity.[7]

There will be more to say about Thomas's practice of philosophy, and idea of theology, in Chapters 10 and 11 of this book.

The anabatic knowledge of God turns on the real but limited continuity between created and uncreated being. It turns, that is, on the twofold character of natural being as, on the one hand, enjoying a continuity or 'communality' with the uncreated being of God (for both are being, one derived, the other underived), and, on the other hand, as radically differentiated from the divine being on which it totally depends. Thomas's metaphysics of being – his ontology – will inevitably be central to any account of his philosophical theology of God and the world. In his commentary on the

De Trinitate of the sixth-century philosopher–statesman Boethius, Thomas remarks that philosophers consider the *res divinae* – 'divine things', the divine reality – only insofar as that divine reality is the principle of all things.[8] Again, in the preamble to his commentary on Aristotle's *Metaphysics*, he explains that God falls within the study which is metaphysics inasmuch as he is the cause of being – even though in himself he far exceeds what human reason can understand.[9] Since only created being is immediately accessible to man, God is known insofar as he is the cause of such being (here we have the foundation of anabasis, ascent towards God). In any other sense, God is not a possible subject of metaphysics or, then, of philosophical theology. Here Thomas erects a warning sign: 'Thus far and no further!', lest the claims of anabatic knowledge begin to trespass on God's freedom in making the katabatic disclosure of himself. (In his insistence that metaphysics, and so philosophical theology, must be so defined as to safeguard God's transcendence and save us from making God subject to the human intellect, Thomas is quite as passionate a defender of the freedom of God vis-à-vis human enquiry as any modern disciple of Karl Barth.)

And yet the affirmation that God is the cause of common being does open the way to a provisional yet valuable – indeed, invaluable – sketch map of our theme: God and creation. For Thomas claims that, when one analyses common being – the being common to all that exists around us – and resolves it into its causes, one comes to the conclusion that God exists. And this is the primary and indispensable presupposition of *sacra doctrina*, the 'holy teaching' of the Gospel. According to later Thomists of all varieties, we have here *the* great philosophical discovery (or rediscovery) which should have constituted a definitive acquisition of the Western mind. So small a crater, however, did this intellectual bombshell make that, when we reach the second half of the twentieth century at Magdalen College, Oxford, we hear, instead of its continuing reverberations only the tired patrician tone in which Professor P. F. Strawson remarked:

> It is with very moderate enthusiasm that a twentieth century philosopher enters the field of philosophical theology even to follow Kant's exposure of its illusions.[10]

How different from Thomas's conclusion, a conclusion pertinent to poetry and love, to wonder at the cosmos and at other persons, namely, that since common being can be shown to be the effect of a transcendent Cause, in touching the effect – anything that is – one also touches God's causality, for God is present in his effects and active in them.[11]

Some objections

We might pause for a moment here to consider some objections to Thomas's approach. The denial of a philosophical route to the objective knowledge of God as Cause of common being, Cause of creation, is not restricted to agnostic philosophers such as Strawson. Barth was deeply influenced by the Danish Existentialist Søren Kierkegaard in the assertion that God can only be a Subject, an initiator of action, including cognitive action, and never an Object. On this view any attempt to initiate description of God would be idolatrous. While, by contrast, Thomas thinks we can, may and should describe the objectivity of God, he is clear that this divine objectivity is quite different from the object-status of anything within the world. In his terminology, God does not belong to any genus: he falls outside, or stands above, all categories. When, in affirming the objective existence of a transcendent Cause of all things, we call that Cause 'transcendent', we are by that very fact denying that the Cause in question suffers the limitations of any finite thing.

A further Kierkegaardian objection to the anabatic knowledge of God would be that seeking God as Object diminishes the human subject, for the human person only fully finds herself in relation to the living Lord. But – so runs the Thomist reply – the divine objectivity is *not* something outside us, for as the abiding Source of all being, God is present not least in the being of the creature that knows his existence to be the case.

And speaking as widely as possible, we can say that, since Thomas's philosophical theology is based on the metaphysics of being, it is close to reality, which is the work of God, and so cannot be in a state of contradiction with the understanding that comes from revelation or even in competition with that understanding.

Indeed it can be argued that the combination of, on the one hand, biblicist opposition à la Barth with philosophical opposition à la Strawson to any anabatic approach to the God of creation has damaged not only the Christian prospect but also the wider human hope of happy inhabitation of the world. In the wider culture, the rejection of the great discovery or rediscovery of Thomas's metaphysics worked itself out as nihilism, in which the world, once seen as God's beautiful effect, filled with wisdom and goodness, becomes an indifferent or even threatening place where these qualities of created being cease to be present since they are no longer considered as enjoying extra-mental reality. Whereas the American philosopher John Dewey argued that to admit the distinction between caused and uncaused being disrupts the homogeneity – the seamlessness – of reality, and thus devalues the world about us, the disciples of St Thomas argue the contrary. The denial of God destroys the inherent value and meaningfulness of the world. And in the Christian or ecclesial context, when Thomas's understanding of being – 'onto-theology', as its detractors call it – is dismissed, no elements of religious rationality remain to hold out the possibility that the trend towards culture's secularisation can be halted or reversed.

And in any case, *pace* the Christian opponents of 'onto-theology', Thomists maintain that the anabatic understanding of God in the creation relationship which such ontology makes possible is itself guaranteed by katabatic understanding – that is, by divine revelation. The chief source of Thomas's confidence that his ontology was licensed by Scripture was Exodus 3:14 – the disclosure of the divine Name to Moses during the Sinai encounter as 'I am who am'. Although a biblical scholarship more attuned to the nuances of the Hebrew original would want to find more in the revelation of the divine Name than simply metaphysics, it is hard to deny that the biblical author is making some kind of statement about the God of the Fathers as a unique referent of the language of being. To this extent – a considerable extent! – the ancient and medieval exegesis of what is on any showing a key text of the biblical revelation is abundantly justified.

Resuming the thread

It is time to pick up again the main thread of my exposition. On Thomas's reading of the 'metaphysics of Exodus', God's essence is subsistent being itself so that, were one to know God's essence, his existence would appear as something absolutely necessary. Hence, in itself the proposition 'God exists' is necessarily true, for in it subject and predicate are the same. To us, however, the proposition 'God exists' needs arguing for. Its truth is not self-evident, however much it may seem so to those who, from earliest childhood, have been brought up hearing about him.

That is not to say, though, that in some more general sense we lack all spontaneous knowledge of God, all native movement of the mind towards him. Thomas holds that, in a broad sense, the knowledge of God's existence *is* implanted in all human beings by nature – but only inasmuch as we naturally desire happiness, and God has so disposed our nature that he alone is that happiness, that beatitude. But, as Thomas points out in the second question of the *Prima Pars* of the *Summa theologiae*, this is not really to know, in the full meaning of the word 'know', that God exists, just as to know that someone is approaching is not to know that Peter is approaching even though it is indeed Peter who is approaching. As Aquinas explains, applying this comparison to the case in hand, there are many who imagine that man's perfect good consists rather in riches or pleasure or in something else again.[12] Such imaginings falsify truth. The desire, though, remains. Surging up to the first Cause from the depths of the rational soul, it cannot be otherwise because humankind's ultimate happiness lies in seeing God, in the openness of his being. We are disturbed by deep intellectual discontent, fundamentally frustrated in our nature, if at best we are to know him only darkly, in a mirror, rather than face to face.

In his *Sept leçons sur l'être*, the Thomistic philosopher Jacques Maritain distinguishes three kinds of intellectual thirst. The first is the thirst for the water of science. When this particular thirst is quenched, however, one thirsts for something else, and this is thirst for the water of created wisdom – to know being in its various modes, the ontological mystery. But even then the thirst continues and this is the thirst for the water of uncreated wisdom, for the vision of God.[13]

The Five Ways to God's existence

Concretely, as is well known, Thomas sets forth for his readers the pattern of the anabatic movement from the being of the things around us to the being of God in the form of five 'ways' – ways, namely, to show the existence of that transcendent Cause of the world which all human beings call 'God'. The Five Ways have generated an enormous literature, partly because of the extreme concision with which they are expressed, but also because of the fact that Thomas leaves their internal relationships to be inferred.

There is reason to think that the first two and last two of the Ways correspond to the four sorts of causality discussed by Aristotle. Thomas's own metaphysics are far closer to those of the Muslim thinker Avicenna than they are to Aristotle (Christianity and Islam share a foundational belief in creation), but what he received from Avicenna was a theistic understanding of, precisely, Aristotelian philosophy. And so it is here.

First, *material* causality is that out of which something is effected, the potential which, whether suddenly or by a long-drawn-out process, becomes actuality. But *sheer* potentiality cannot be a true starting-point for the world. The First Way argues that the true starting-point is, rather, sheer *actuality*, a reality wholly lacking in potentiality because it is Pure Act.[14]

Secondly, *efficient* causality is that by whose agency something is brought into being, or brought about. Nine times out of ten it is what we have in mind when we use the word 'cause' in ordinary language. What causes hailstones? What caused the sinking of the *Titanic*? If, as regularly happens in human enquiry, we seek after such an efficient cause for some event or development, or for the emergence of some new kind of entity, we cannot be prevented, Thomas argues, from asking after that transcendent efficient Cause which explains the working of efficient causes and their interrelation as a whole. And this is the argument of the Second Way, which reaches, then, the conclusion that deity is at work in all processes taking place in the world.

Leaving aside for the moment the Third Way and coming to the Fourth: the next kind of causality enumerated by Aristotle is *formal* causality. This raises the question of how a particular thing is said to be the *kind* of thing it is – raises, then, the question of its formal properties. Now a very important set of formal properties are those value-laden properties we denote by the terms 'good', 'beautiful', 'true', and the like. Here a concern with formal properties will want to press home the question, How is it that these pure-value 'perfections' (goodness, beauty, truth, and so on) are embodied in the world around us, yet only in varying degrees? This is the approach of the Fourth Way, and it leads to the conclusion that all limited perfections – regarded by Thomas as manifestations or explicitations of the qualities inherent in finite being – share in divine being, which is perfect in the maximal degree.

The remaining sort of causality, on Aristotle's scheme, is *final* causality, which deals with the ends or goals for which all beings strive, whether consciously or not. Whether in a micro-context or in the macro-context of the world as a whole, goal-directedness appears to be a feature of the cosmic process. The Fifth Way begins from this discovery, and it concludes to the divine intellect as the Cause of the order in the world.

I have left out the Third Way, and this is because, on the reading of the *Quinque Viae* I am adopting, it is not by chance that it occupies a central position. The Third Way indicates the ground or basis of the fourfold causality whose role in the relation between the world and God the First, Second, Fourth and Fifth Ways explore. For the argument of the Third Way derives from the fact that the relationship between observable things and their being is contingent, not necessary. Things do not have their being of themselves. Rather, things receive their being – in Thomas's term, their *esse* – and that causality of *esse* lies at a deeper level than material, efficient, formal and final causality and is indeed the root of all of these. So the perspective in which the Third Way, the central way of the Five Ways, attains to God is the most important for Thomas's metaphysics, and indeed for any creation thinking.[15] The Third Way concludes to God as the foundation and source not of this or that aspect of things nor of this or that aspect of the world as a whole, but of the very being of things, the very being of the world.

What, thus far, Aquinas thinks he has shown by anabatic reasoning is the well-foundedness of the popular belief, arrived at by spontaneous insight in pre-Judaeo-Christian religious experience, that there exists a common Cause of all things. This all human beings call God – a formula which goes back to the pre-Socratic philosophers. He also thinks – and this is shown by the fact that the Five Ways are set in a theological context governed by the citation of Exodus 3:14 – that he has gone some way to justify, in terms of rational thinking, the katabatic disclosure of Scripture that in God – to cite St Paul's words to the Athenians in Acts 17:28 – 'we live and move and have our being'.

Reverent exploration of God's being

Having established *that* God exists, we must now consider *what* he is. In the *Prima Pars* of the *Summa theologiae*, St Thomas begins his reverent exploration of God's being by an account of *how* he exists – the mode in which he exists, and this turns out to be a primarily negative account of God's attributes, a study of the ways he is unlike his creation.[16] Then secondly, Thomas offers an account of how God operates or acts – of his knowledge, his will, his power.[17] But Thomas links these two treatises together by an exposition of the Divine Names.[18] Here he explains how, despite that primarily negative character of our knowledge of God – despite, that is, our well-founded belief that his mode of existence is unlike that of creatures – we can still 'name' the divine Being correctly in various ways.

There are, then, wrapped up in the relatively short compass of Thomas's *De Deo*, three distinct but related projects: an account of how God exists, executed as an explanation of the ways in which, in fact, he does not exist; a demonstration of why, nonetheless, basic names for the divine Being do actually work; and finally a study of God's agency, his knowing and loving, which also serves as an *entrée* to Thomas's Trinitarian thought.

The Five Ways and the plenitude of perfection

Thomas's account of the mode of being of God – or rather of what that mode of being is not – follows anabatically from the Five Ways. Katabatically, he regards the conclusions he reaches as essentially already found in revelation itself. Thus, the *First* Way leads to the conclusion that there exists a First Unmoved Mover whose being contains no potentiality at all – and this leads Aquinas to affirm the divine 'simplicity'. In God there is no distinction between his nature and his properties, his substance and his qualities, nor even (and this for Thomas is the most amazing thing about God one can think of) between his essence and his existence. God's being is entirely unique, and we reach our knowledge of it in a negative fashion, when, namely, we understand that his *esse* is entirely different from that of the beings around us. This is especially notable when Thomas comes to consider the divine *rationes* – the ways in which God's inmost reality (his *quidditas*) is expressed. Although the *rationes* of the divine knowledge, say, or the divine wisdom, are, in fact, *more* distinct – infinitely so! – than are the *rationes* of human knowledge and wisdom (because they 'exist in God with their maximal formalities'), *in re*, in the divine reality, such divine attributes are utterly identical. The reason is that in God there is no potentiality which could limit their act. 'His possession of the eminent form of created attribute is not by participation'.[19]

From this starting-point, Thomas goes on with the help of the *Second* Way to speak of the perfection of God, which leads on by a logical progression to an account of God's goodness. Thomas's doctrine of God's perfection is linked to the Second Way inasmuch as the latter argued, on the basis of efficient causality, that God is active (or, if one prefers, so as to distinguish creaturely activity from divine, 'super-active') in all the processes taking place in the world. If God is able to move with efficacy, in the transcendent mode proper to him, all efficient causes at work in the world, then he must himself be absolutely 'achieved' or complete – which is the original meaning of *perfectum*, 'perfect'.[20]

Most Thomists would say, however, that Thomas's profoundest

explanation of this point occurs in the answer to an objector when, in the course of his question 'on the divine perfection', he proposes that this perfection of God follows from God's identification with being itself. As he puts it:

> Being is the most perfect of all things, for it is compared to all things as that by which they are made actual, for nothing has actuality except insofar as it is. Hence being itself is that which actuates in things, even their forms.[21]

Precisely because *esse* realises things, including their forms, it is the source of every perfection. Compare, in the New Testament corpus, the Letter of James, 'Every good and every perfect gift is from above' (1:17).

And furthermore – and here we move on to the *goodness* of God – because things strive after their own perfection, the completion of their form, they strive after God. In this treatise on the divine properties, by calling God 'good' Aquinas is not saying mainly – if at all – that God is kind or generous (which is what in ordinary religious discourse we take God's goodness to mean), but that he is that which is sought for in all the variegated activity the universe shows. Since all things tend to their own perfection, nothing can escape this seeking to become like God. So Thomas's treatise on the goodness of God is a way of showing how the whole universe strives after liberation in him. Again, compare a New Testament writing, this time the Letter to the Romans:

> We know that the whole creation has been groaning in travail together until now; and not only the creation but we ourselves who have the firstfruits of the Spirit, groan inwardly as we wait for adoption as sons, the redemption of our bodies (8:22).

What Thomas is developing in his *De Deo* is, evidently, a rich anabatic account of God that is congruent with the katabatic disclosure of God in revelation.

So too, then, with the help of the *Third* Way, Thomas deals with the infinity of God, on which there follows, in his philosophical theology, the existence of God in all things. The Third Way concludes that there must be being that has of itself its own necessity to be and is the cause of the being of all other things. It is as the unlimited realisation of reality and perfection that God is infinite, and this unlimited plenitude of God's subsistent being is prolonged by his presence in things, sustaining them at their deepest core, and yet by the sublimity of the divine nature raised high above them. God is omnipresent in space and time not because he is in any way spatially or temporally determined but because he continually gives being to the realities that *are* determined in those ways. I have already cited the text from the Book of the Acts which, among the New Testament Scriptures, seems best to sum up katabatically this same thought: God is the One 'in whom we live and move and have our being' (17:28).

Next, with assistance from the *Fourth* Way, as well as a helping hand from the First, Thomas speaks of the immutability of God, and this extends quite naturally into a discussion of God's eternity. From the logic of the Fourth Way it follows that, if God contains within himself the plenitude of the perfections of all things, he can neither degenerate nor advance ('He does not faint or grow weary', Isa. 40:28b). Replying to an objection, Thomas denies that such immutability is the immobility of a crystal. To the contrary: God is full of intellectual life and love. As the First and Second Ways would have it, he is Pure Act, positively bursting with actuality and ceaselessly pouring it out on the mobile things of the world. It is because God is immutable that he knows no succession and so is eternal ('Have you not known, have you not heard? The Lord is the everlasting God, the Lord of the ends of the earth', Isa. 40:28a). But, as Thomas explains, what this principally means is that everything God is, he is simultaneously and altogether. He is his own duration, an entirely actualised 'now'.

Lastly, aided and abetted by the *Fifth* Way, Thomas speaks of the unity of God, a theme that is absolutely central to Old Testament revelation and finds its epitome in the *Shema*, 'Hear, O Israel, the Lord your God is one' (Deut. 6:4), and taken from there into the Trinitarian monotheism of the New. Looking at the same topic anabatically, Thomas argues that the way things in the universe are ordered to one another, and so the way the universe itself can be said to be orderly, is inexplicable unless one supreme Mind brings about these interrelations. And this supplements his arguments from the identification of God as He Who Is: plenary, fontal, *esse*.

Of course, if God is his own nature, and includes in himself the entire perfection of being, he cannot but be one. By closing his treatise on God's being with a discussion of the divine unity in this way, Thomas is preparing his readers for the study of the mystery of the *triune* God which will follow later.

Knowing and unknowing

So what Thomas has done, in his treatise on the attributes of divine being, has been to show – to his own satisfaction at least – the utter uniqueness and pre-eminence of God's being. He started out from the divine simplicity which exemplifies the purely negative characterisation of God, since owing to his total actuality (he is all the qualities he has) God is unlike all beings in the world. He then moved on to consider, by an affirmative way, what God's causal origination of all such beings implies: he is all-perfect and infinite in his being, and so is good and exists in all things. Finally, crowning the negative and affirmative ways, Thomas draws to our attention the fact that God transcends whatever being we know, since he is beyond all process and change, and exists in the simultaneity of his eternal now. Though, with Thomas and the entire Christian Platonist tradition (to which, through Denys, he was indebted), we distinguish between negative, affirmative and transcendent (or 'eminent') statements about God, Aquinas's whole discussion is in a broader sense conditioned by the primacy of the negative way. At all times, we say what God is by distinguishing him from the way creatures exist – by saying, in other words, what he is not. This is the nugget of truth in Victor White's contention that the Five Ways establish the necessity of a positive agnosticism: 'There is an Unknown'.[22]

As always, however, in Christian theology, one must distinguish between the apophatic or negative *form* of discourse about God and its cataphatic or positive *intent*. Mark Jordan writes:

> The danger in an unqualified doctrine of remotion is that the negative will destroy any positive content and so rob the language of sense. This is the danger Thomas underlines in

Maimonides. The Dionysian alternative to Maimonides is a remotion which is tethered to a certain positive intentionality. Dionysian predication by supereminence is an attempt to project an intention through a negative moment, through remotion.[23]

For in the Bible, after all, God has made himself known to humankind in a twofold covenant, the covenant of creation, and the covenant of the saving revelation – a covenant both internally differentiated (there were covenants with Abraham, Moses, David . . .) and yet ultimately unitary, owing to its ordering to the new and everlasting covenant in Jesus Christ. Now for Scripture any covenant brings about a union of mutual knowledge and love. It would be false to regard covenant as chiefly apophatic in purpose, as though it were a veiling, rather than revealing, of the divine.[24] And while with the covenant of the saving revelation we are limited, it is true, to katabatic reception, with the covenant of creation we are free to adopt an anabatic approach, rising up to the 'invisible things of God', as Paul writes in Romans (1:20), 'through the visible things that are made'.

So, lest we should lose hold on this truth, Thomas goes on immediately to speak of our radical God-given capacity for the knowledge of God, and the way that capacity can be exercised through response to the Divine Names as given in and with creation. Though no created intellect can comprehend God, nevertheless our minds do have an aptitude to be elevated to the contemplation of God – a potentiality, though without grace a purely passive one, to be satisfied by the Beatific Vision. Unfortunately, many human beings seem to have no inkling that this *is* the end to which their curiosity about the world or thirst to know reality points them. Thomas, then, moves by a natural progression to a consideration of how we can speak about God to the good pagan or anyone else for that matter. And it is at this point that we reach the treatise on the Divine Names.

The Divine Names

How do we come, anabatically, to be able to speak of God at all? As we have seen, Thomas is profoundly convinced of the primarily negative character of our knowledge of God, yet he affirms the possibility of predicating certain 'Names' of him. We can name God on the basis of creatures inasmuch as creatures represent God, or (we might say) insofar as they 're-present' him. And this they do to the degree that, in exhibiting perfections of intrinsically valuable qualities of one kind or another, they show forth the Source of those perfections in subsistent Being himself from which they come forth.

Such justified linguistic usage may come about in the form of metaphor, as with calling God (as the Hebrew Bible does) a rock or sheltering-place, for this way of speaking co-signifies the ideas of permanence, protection and safety which God exemplifies incomparably well.[25] Or we may find ourselves able to name God in a 'proper' way by means of those Names that signify pure perfections, like goodness, truth, beauty, that of their very nature range over the entire gamut of creaturely being.[26]

But of course the Names we apply to God, signifying as they do 'perfections' as we know them in created things, while at the same time expressing what is, in a pre-eminent and altogether unified way, present in God, cannot be predicated in the same fashion of creatures and of God. Such names are not predicated 'univocally' as though what goodness, truth and beauty mean for creatures and for God is one and the same. Rather are they predicated 'analogically'. We render our concepts and words analogous when we intend to apply them to God by deliberately prescinding from that mode of signifying proper to them when they go about their normal, non-religious business – which is as they describe created things. The analogical use of language is not, as the mid-to-late-twentieth-century 'Transcendental Thomists' liked to say, the expression of an inner dynamism of the mind towards a reality constantly escaping it. On the contrary, analogical thinking is, rather, the adaptation of the intellect to reality. We have a hint of that in Thomas's decision to expound the idea of analogy after – not before – he sets out his understanding of the divine being itself.

Not surprisingly, then, Thomas considers 'He who is' as the best name we have for God. Its disclosure, in the Sinai theophany, is a high point of Scripture. The reasons he gives in commending it to us sum up his entire treatise on the divine attributes. 'He who is' names God as the actuality of all acts and the action of all perfections. It is universal, the founding principle of all names applied to God (a claim also made by the seventh-century Greek father John of Damascus). Finally, the name 'He who is' signifies being in the present – and this above all applies to God, who knows neither past nor future. 'He who is' just has to be accounted the primary divine Name.[27] This is how, as Dom Ghislain Lafont puts it, the Mosaic revelation commands study of God in his essence, while the Gospel revelation will do the same for God in his Trinity.[28]

We note, however, that, in the Thomist tradition, this is no ultra-cataphatic violation of the sanctuary. All classical Thomists agree that what formally constitutes the divine nature – *Deitas* – is utterly unknown to us. What we ascribe to God properly yet analogically – by reference to the naturally participable perfections, with *being* pre-eminent among them – asserts an identity *secundum quid*, after a fashion, yet a diversity *simpliciter*, in the most basic sense.

Being, knowing, willing

But being, Aristotle's *einai*, is not to be sundered from intellection – understanding or knowing, Aristotle's *noein*. By his very *ousia*, his essence, God is plenary activity, *energeia*, and that *energeia* is itself a *knowing*. Of course, if in God 'understanding', *intelligere*, is, in all its comprehensive vitality, identical with the divine *esse* (and this is Thomas's view),[29] then we can no more grasp the 'how' of that knowing – no more think through its 'all-powerful energy'[30] – than we can grasp the 'how' of the divine being itself. However, as the French Dominican Dominique Dubarle remarks, we cannot dispense with some 'functional representation' of that knowing. But how good a one can we find?

In Aristotle, the divine knowing which, by its own inherent nature, is fully possessed of the intelligibility constituted by its *ousia*, just *is* its own richly differentiated universe. In the very understanding the divine mind has of itself, it lives out the understanding of its own intimate being and 'world'. For St Thomas, writing in the light of the biblical revelation, it is not only himself that God sees but all the realities that issue from him. The ontological consistency of creation is itself a consequence of the consistency of the divine knowing, identical as this is with the divine being. Thus the very materiality of things – their 'thinginess' – as well as their configuration or specificity – their 'form' – comes from the divine knowing. That knowing is not only the model for the world, as the Plato of the *Timaeus* already held. It is also the energy that brings the world into being.

We can take a further step as well. 'In God', writes Thomas, 'is maximal life'.[31] And so the divine knowing is inseparable from the divine willing. God's life is a willing life, at once contented willing in the indefectible happiness of his perfect being, and a will to do, to institute something, to govern the world's course and act upon it. God wills not only himself but what is not himself, doing the latter in sovereign freedom. Conjointly with the divine knowing, the divine willing is a cause of things.[32]

Creation by the Trinity

Katabatically, however, we may – and, on the basis of Scripture and Tradition, must – say more.

The analogically derived Names of God, though used to point to the divine in itself – for this is included 'in the intent of those who speak of God'[33] – rest for justification on our experience of the created medium, while the vantage point for Thomas's questions on Father, Son and Spirit in the *Summa theologiae* is set by the very different statement that they cannot be known through any process of natural reason.[34] In the *De veritate* Thomas will explain that these 'proper' Names rest not on the relation of God to creatures but on those of the divine Persons to each other.[35]

Naturally, if anabatic and katabatic are to throw any light on each other at all, there must, though, be *some* possibility of mutual illumination by the Names, both 'essential' and Trinitarian. Thus in the *De potentia*, Thomas will suggest how, if the Son is named

'Word' by Scriptures that are inspired for the sake of human understanding there must be *some* use of that name in human experience
that can serve to bring out its meaning.

> By natural reason we can ascertain about that he is, not what
> he is; similarly, the fact that he has intellectual knowledge, but
> not its mode. Now to have the conception of a word *is* a matter
> of the mode of knowing; so reason cannot develop a conclusive
> proof of this but through a simile based on our own case it can
> form a conjecture.[36]

What, however, allows Thomas to appreciate this 'simile' and weigh
this 'conjecture' as a true if deficient analogy, is the faith-acceptance
of St John's title for Jesus – the *Logos* – as naming in a 'proper'
fashion the coming forth of the Son from the Father in the divine
being. And bringing anabatic and katabatic together, Thomas
argues in question 27 of the *Prima Pars* that, just because God
undertands by one single act and loves by one single act, there can
be in him no succession of intellectual or affective processions.[37]
There can only be one perfect Word, and one perfect Love. And
this, adds Thomas, manifests God's abounding fruitfulness.

God as the triune Lord will be the subject of the next Chapter,
but meanwhile I must at least signal the Trinitarian dimension of
the divine creative action. In the *Scriptum super Sententiis*, Thomas
declares:

> In the procession of creatures there are two things to consider
> with respect to the Creator himself: namely, the [divine] nature,
> from whose fulness and perfection the perfection of every crea-
> ture is both effected and copied . . . and the [divine] will, from
> whose liberality, and not by the necessity of nature, all these
> things are conferred on the creature.[38]

And Thomas goes on to show that these two aspects of the temporal
procession of creatures from God have their exemplary cause in
the two eternal processions within God. He proposes that while the
Son proceeds according to nature, as God's nature's perfect Image,
through whom all creatures have some share in that divine nature,
the Holy Spirit proceeds according to will, as the Love in whom all
creatures enjoy the liberality of God. In this *Writing on the Sen-*

tences, Thomas's inspiration is Dionysian, not Augustinian. Nowhere in this discussion, for instance, does Thomas refer to the procession of the Son as the procession of *Verbum*, 'the Word'.[39] By contrast, when Thomas comes to write the *Summa theologiae*, he holds that, though God's creative action is in fact his own *esse*, which is common to the three Persons[40], creation as the free act of God proceeds nonetheless (or, rather, *accordingly*) via his intellect and will, through which from all eternity there takes place the immanent procession of the consubstantial Word and Spirit.[41]

For Aquinas, it is a general principle of sound ontology that every effect is assimilated to its cause, and yet effects represent their causes diversely. Some indicate no more than the cause's causal power. Others, by virtue of a real mimesis, imitation, manifest something of its nature and form.[42] We shall see the relevance of this distinction for a Trinitarian account of creation when we come to look in Chapter 5 at the imagehood of God in man.

The ontology of creation

Meanwhile, however, we must consider the ontology of creation at large. In questions 44 to 46 of the *Prima Pars*, Thomas considers the divine creative act, the temporal condition of the world's existing, and the origin of the differentiated multiplicity of being, followed by the question of evil and its causal relation to the good and the God who is good itself (briefly, the possibility of a return of created reality to nothingness). And in question 107, under the general rubric of the divine government of the world, Thomas will look at the 'continuing creation' which is God's preservation of the world in being.

The theology of creation is believing metaphysics. It consists in the analogical comprehension of being as participation not simply in *ousia*, 'substance', as in Aristotle, or in the Ideas, supremely the Idea of the Good, as with the Platonic school, but in God himself.

Thomas brings together the Platonic conception of participation with an Aristotelian comprehension of causality at large: no longer confined to 'regional' causality, the causing of certain facets of some sorts of things, but enlarged to the dimensions of a general ontology – to the degree, indeed, that he can think through, in the light of biblical revelation, the relation between God and what is not God.[43] If God is subsistent being, and sovereign goodness, then all that exists by participation will be understood as an *effect* of the sovereign causality of the being of God. God is the agent cause of creation, its primary exemplary cause as also its final cause. Creation is:

> the most extreme expansion (*épanouissement*) of the generosity of [God's] being, beyond the intimate expansion of the divine trinitarian life. It realises as it were 'on the outside', *ad extram*, as theology sometimes says, the supreme cycle of the causality of the Good: the immanence of the Source to itself, the procession or diffusive emanation of its excellence in realizations of all sorts, and to complete the converting return to the Good, in itself and for themselves, things thus come forth from the Source and are sustained by the diffusion of its goodness.[44]

Basic to Thomas's thought is the claim that the creature exists only in the creation relationship – that is, only in its relation to God. Whatever its potential for a variety of relations within the world, this is every subject's ontological foundation. What the creation relationship turns out to look like in time depends on the condition of individual things: for spiritual creatures, highly pertinent here is their freedom and consequent involvement in history. This is a question not of the essential nature of creation, but of the actuality of the physical universe: a point especially relevant, as we shall see, to the mode of being of the angels.

Over against all attempts to deduce the world's plurality (from some kind of single principle), Thomas holds it just to be the case that God has elected to originate a differentiated, radically plural world.[45]

Evil is a problem for Thomas, holding as he does that all that is, insofar as it has being, is good, and this because every 'act' – every being in act – manifests a perfection of some kind.[46] Just by being, it shares in the goodness of God 'in the mode of a certain assimilation, even though this be in a distant and deficient way'.[47]

'Evil', then, cannot signify some *esse* or nature or form. The only alternative left us, accordingly, is to say that, when the term 'evil' is used, what we are signifying is 'some absence of the good'.[48]

Is justice done here to the world's ills unlimited: the experience of pain, or the awareness of wickedness, both within and without? Rational explanation of the facticity of evil runs up against a limit. Kant will hold that what he termed 'radical evil' has a provenance that philosophy is powerless to penetrate. Yet at least it cannot arise from the good God of the human moral hope. Thomas too defends the Creator against this charge, distinguishing *both* between what is inevitable in a world of physical finitude, on the one hand, and fault on the other, *and* between the direct divine willing of something and the will to (merely) permit it. The two distinctions are invoked together when Thomas argues that God has so ordered the world's perfection that it requires the existence of some beings that can fail in regard to the good: if they do so fail, God does not prevent them.[49]

That is not, however, his final word on the subject. As we shall see, he is yet to consider the order of grace, the ontology – once again! – of grace.

4.
The Trinity

The mystery of the Trinity in itself

In this chapter I try first to locate St Thomas's teaching on the Holy Trinity in the perspective of the history of doctrine. Without this, it will be difficult if not impossible to locate the original adjustments he makes at the heart of this theological doctrine. We shall be looking, then, at the genesis of the problematic within which Thomas expounded the Church's Trinitarian faith – at, that is, the origin and interconnection of the major questions on which he pronounced.

East against West?

The day is largely past (one hopes) when theology textbooks trotted out the misleading but influential thesis of the early-twentieth-century French Catholic historian of Christian thought, Théodore de Régnon, to the effect that the Western theology of God begins from a rationally conceived divine unity, while its Eastern counterpart starts out from the historical revelation of the living threefold Lord.[1] De Régnon's case, enthusiastically welcomed by Eastern Orthodox representatives (we told you so!) was misleading not least because the unity of God, rather than God's threefoldness, was the chief problem for all ancient Christian theologies. Subordinationism – where Son and Spirit belong below the Father in a descending hierarchy – which, we might think, leads in the direction of tritheism and constitutes a characteristically Eastern heresy, and modalism – where Son and Spirit are additional ways of being God –

which, we might think, is a half-way house to Unitarianism and so a characteristically Western heresy, simply translate in different ways the same insistence on the divinity of the Father. Modalism saves the Father's 'monarchy' – his being the principle of the entire Trinity – by absorbing the Son (and Spirit) into him; Subordinationism tries to achieve the same goal by making the Son (and Spirit) inferior to him.

Moreover, and this is a second question-mark to be set against de Régnon's thesis, it was in the Greek East that Christians began to reflect on the common nature, *ousia*, of Father, Son and Spirit and to ask the question, What constitutes their *to theion*, their divine reality? A Greek doctor like Athanasius uses the language of *homoousia*, sameness of being, to say that, when we speak of Father and Son, we are not dealing with generic identity, as we should be were we to affirm two Gods. Rather, we are talking about a numerically identical reality that is one-in-two, by virtue of the origin the one takes from the other.[2] This was clarified by Athanasius's successors, the Cappadocian Fathers, who regarded the divine Persons as the expressions – at once distinct yet exhaustive – of the unique, concrete *ousia*. For St Gregory of Nyssa, for example, each divine Person differs from the others only by the way he makes their single *ousia* exist. Hence the search for identifying idioms, characteristics or signs (*idiomata, charakteres, semeia*) which will uncover the *tropoi* or 'manners' in which the Persons let the divine nature be.

Weaknesses among the Greeks

This suggestion that Father, Son and Holy Spirit are distinct thanks to the way their specifying relationships actualise the divine nature, was pregnant with rich implications of what we would now call a 'personalist' kind – without by any means overthrowing that equally valid concept of God's own essence or nature. But this insight – which, as we shall see, is central to Thomas's work as a Trinitarian theologian – was by no means consistently followed up. The Greek Fathers may *say* that 'the Father' is the subject of the act of engendering whereby the Son comes to be, but then it can turn out that they are using the term 'Father' as a synonym for the divine essence itself. The Son, they are fond of saying, is En-gendered Wisdom, *ousia* from *ousia* – or (as we say with them in the Creed of Nicaea-Constantinople) 'Light from Light'.[3] This way of speaking of the origin of the Son derives from the peculiar press-ures and anxieties of the Arian crisis. It was adopted because the alternative, more personal, way of speaking of the Son's prov-enance was open to at least a *semi*-Arian interpretation. Between the Engendered One as such and the Unengendered One as such (and that is a typical use of the more personalist language), there may perhaps be nothing common and so nothing consubstantial! But that misunderstanding is ruled out once we call the Son 'God from God'.

And so this type of 'essentialist' credal language for the Holy Trinity came to exist side by side with the more personalist option of using names that identify in terms of the relations of origin – as when the Greeks speak of the Father in terms of unengenderedness (*agennesia*), the Son in terms of engenderedness (*gennesia*), and the Spirit in terms of procession (*ekporeusis*). Thomas, in his untitled treatise which later generations called the *Contra Graecos*, the 'Treatise against the Greeks', berates this ambivalence in the Eastern tradition, insisting that the divine Persons cannot derive from the divine essence. Only subjects can originate and be originated: as he puts it, 'actions belong to subjects'.

There is also a second caveat which the Latin tradition, not least in Thomas, would enter against the Greeks, and this is its failure (by and large, the Late Byzantine theologian St Gregory Palamas is an exception) to draw on what Augustine had proposed as that psychological analogy for the Trinity accessible by reverent reflection when we think about the image of God in human beings in the line of Genesis 1, 'Let us make man to our own image and likeness'. If, as St Augustine thought, the divine image in man becomes fully actualised in human activity by way of presence to God (*memoria Dei*), knowledge of God (*notitia* or *intellectus Dei*) and the willing love of God (*amor Dei*), why can we not use that fact to speak of the uncreated Archetype of such dynamic spiritual reality in God himself? Can we not, by working back from the Trinitarian divine image in us, under the tutelage, certainly, of revelation, come to a better understanding of what that image is an image of – come to understand more fully, in other words, the Trinity as it exists in itself? And will not this take the chill off the somewhat glacial ontological language for the Holy Trinity to which one is restricted if one speaks of the Persons in terms of their relations of origin alone? As André Malet put it in his *Personne et amour dans la théologie trinitaire de saint Thomas d'Aquin*:

> If, in the Latin way, one conceives of the divine nature as a richness which is not only ontological but also psychological, that is to say, a nature that expresses itself on the level of faculties and acts, in ways that are saturated with the values of awareness and love, then one will have a 'subject' in the modern sense of the word . . .[4]

This is something which Malet, evidently, regards as a self-evidently good thing. By contrast, the Byzantine Church was unwilling to give an account of how the Trinitarian processions are as they are, the *to pos* of those processions, other than by repeating what is said in Scripture, where we learn that the Father has begotten the Son and that the Spirit comes forth from him. Speculatively minded and theologically innovatory thinkers in the later Orthodox tradition, like the early-twentieth-century Russian theologian Sergei Bulgakov, got their fingers sharply rapped when they tried to provide further theological elucidation.[5] Hans Urs von Balthasar, in the first edition of his study of perhaps the last originally minded Byzantine theologian, Maximus the Confessor, comments on this state of affairs. Whereas, he says, in the early Middle Ages, those original elements in Augustine's thought which came to structure the Latin theology of the Trinity produced their finest flower in Thomas's predecessors, the Victorines (canons regular of the Parisian abbey and school of St Victor), Greek Christian thought 'sank into an ever deeper silence before the ultimate mystery of God'.[6]

Weaknesses among the Latins

Given that, of all the non-biblical writers, it is Augustine whom Aquinas cites most frequently, not least when writing of the Trinity, we obviously need to come to terms with the legacy the bishop of Hippo left his medieval successors. It may be suggested that what the medievals drew from Augustine was not, actually, a straight-forward model but a wealth of analogies indicating (a) a special connection of the Spirit with will, love and the ordering and harmon-ising of a moral-spiritual order; (b) a special connection of the Son with knowledge or understanding; and (c) a special connection of the Father as source of the Trinity with being. This was a useful inheritance. But on the issue of the interrelation of personalism and essentialism Augustine hardly made any advance on the Greeks. Indeed, in his study *Saint Augustin et la pensée grecque: les relations trinitaires*, Irénée Chevalier showed that Augustine did not fully grasp the way that, for the Cappadocians, the personal modes whereby it is in Father, Son and Holy Spirit that the unique divine being subsists are *reciprocally* defined, each being named by reference to the others.[7]

Augustine's account of the word *persona* might indeed be termed 'absolutist' in the sense that, for him, to call some reality 'a person' is not, in and of itself, to ascribe to it a form of reciprocity. The word *persona* does not function in the same fashion as, for instance, the word *amicus*, 'friend'. It does not point to relationship, and in that sense is 'absolute', unconditioned by reference to another. Augustine can call the substance – the *quod est* – of the Father his *persona* and indeed remarks of Father, Son and Spirit in the *De Trinitate* that we call them 'persons' *ne omnino taceretur*, 'lest otherwise we should fall silent, finding no words at all for what it is there are three of in God'.[8] And yet, this is not the whole story. When Augustine is preaching about the divine Three, or referring to them in the natural flow of his wider writing, he escapes from the philosophical categories in which he had enclosed the concept of person and gives that concept, in fact, a real relational significance.

Malet's overall conclusion is that all the affirmations we need for a really good theology of the Trinity are found singly in Augus-tine's writing but they do not appear there as a unified whole. His theology is balanced but not integrated.[9] The personalist elements in his thought are not fused into an instrument that could rectify the insufficient personalism of the corresponding Greek Trini-tarianism. For Augustine, the Father loves the Son with a personal love, true; yet that love is also from his essence. The Father loves the Son by the Holy Spirit, true – yet also problematic. Since in God love is not different from being, to say God loves the Son by the Spirit would seem to mean that the Father takes his being from the Holy Spirit, which is absurd. It would be left to St Thomas, with help from his important predecessor Richard of St Victor, to remedy this situation.

What should already be plain, however, is that the overall historical picture with which we began is not as de Régnon described it. We are not faced with a stark choice between a Greek theology of the Persons and an Augustinian theology of the essence. Abelard, who knew Greek teaching thoroughly, fell into modalism; Richard, who was basically an Augustinian, insisted strongly on personalism.

Thomas's immediate predecessors

Still, it is true enough that in the decades immediately prior to Thomas's contribution, 'innovators' (the word is found in Gauthier of St Victor) who were giving the Latin tradition a more personalist stamp *did* appeal to the patronage of the Greek Fathers. Linked to Aquinas via Richard of St Victor are the two main carriers of Oriental influence in twelfth-century Latin theology: William of St Thierry and Gilbert de la Porrée, for though in the *Prima Pars* Thomas disassociates himself from the latter, what he actually rejects is a misunderstanding of Gilbert's doctrine deriving from a Church Council at Rheims which got it wrong, while Porretanus's actual Trinitarian teaching, communicated through various channels, is faithfully reflected in Thomas's work![10] Père Chenu calls Gilbert 'the last avatar of Eastern theology in the West' and believes that the condemnation, in 1241, by a Sorbonne under the hegemony of extreme Augustinians, of ten Gilbertine propositions about the Trinity – propositions strongly apophatic in character and emphasising the primacy of the Persons – was intended as a blow at one and the same time against the Dominican masters who had imbibed this more personalist teaching on God as well as against the self-consciously Orientalising movement on which he had drawn.[11]

Probably the philosophy animating the Parisian condemnation was 'Attack is the best means of defence', for Gilbert's followers had been criticising the memory of the much revered Peter Lombard and notably his calling God *una quaedam summa res*, 'a certain supreme thing'. In Gilbert's teaching the divine essence is presented as that *by which* God is, while Father, Son and Spirit are the three relations that actually are – relations he calls, however, in a poorly chosen word, 'external', meaning, innocently enough, that the Three do not break the numerical unity of God.

Richard of St Victor – so Père Gervais Dumeige shows in his *Richard de Saint-Victor et l'idée chrétienne de l'amour* – began his theological career in an effort to salvage Gilbert's teaching from the strictures of the Council of Rheims.[12] Thomas will accept Richard's reworking of the hitherto classical definition by Boethius of what it is to be a person – 'an individual substance rational in nature' and its replacement by a formula better suited to the Trinitarian Persons, 'an incommunicable existence of the divine nature'.[13] Richard also suppressed the ambiguous Gilbertine language of Persons as 'external' relations from which there had been drawn the erroneous inference that the Persons are extrinsic to the divine essence. He spoke of them, rather, as 'ways of having' (*modi obtinentiae*) the divine nature. Finally and most importantly, Richard treats Trinitarian theology as a restatement of St John's proclamation that 'God is love' (1 John 4:8). Love, he says, subjecting that notion to a thorough subject-object analysis, requires a plurality of persons – not just two but a third also, since perfect love will make a third share the happiness of lovers.

Between Richard and Thomas come, finally, Alexander of Hales, first of the Franciscan Scholastics, and the admirable Bonaventure. In nearly all respects, Alexander's teaching anticipates Thomas's. Though unlike Thomas he distinguishes between *hypostasis* and *persona* (the Greek and Latin terms, respectively, for what Father, Son and Spirit are), like Thomas he defines both *hypostasis* and *persona* in terms of the Trinitarian *relationships*. The word *hypostasis* denotes the relation in question while *persona* is our word for what the relation constitutes, namely, a reality that is different and indeed unique and incommunicable. The hypostases *are* their relations, and these relations bring about the utterly incomparable reality of (each of) Father, Son, Spirit. On Alexander's scheme, we move from considering that by which God is (*quo est*) to what he is (*quod est*), then from what he is to who he is (*qui est*), and finally from who he is to which one he is (*quis est*). And in so doing, we find that the closer we come in this enquiry to what is most intimate in the divine life, the more we are simply confronted with the relations of the Persons. This is why Alexander insists we must not say, Because God generates the Son, he is the Father, as though the hypostasis of the Father could exist autonomously 'prior' to his constitution as Father. Rather must we say, Because he is the Father, he generates the Son.[14] Bonaventure will echo his fellow-Franciscan here.

Such theologians reached their position against the resistance of an alternative tradition of thought moving from Anselm via Abelard to Peter Lombard. In these latter theologies, what we call 'the Persons' are relations all right, but these relations are so presented as, apparently, to issue from the essence, or even to belong to it as quasi-attributes thereof: an approach which would merit the strictures of the Christian East and finds exemplification in a statement in Abelard's *De unitate*: to say God consists of three Persons is to say that the divine substance is at once powerful, good and wise.

Journey's end (for now): the teaching of Thomas

Some commentators on Thomas's triadology would place him squarely in this camp, with the Persons being fructifications of the divine unity.[15] This is perhaps because, in the prologue to this topic in the great *Summa* – namely, question 27 of the *Prima Pars* – so as to link his theology of the Holy Trinity to what he has said of God in his unique being, knowing and willing, Thomas considers first the divine processions – that is, the origins of the Persons; next, the divine relations; and only in last place, the Persons themselves. He pleads that this is, in context, a good pedagogical order. But it can lead the student to misrepresent the strongly personalist cast of his Trinitarian thinking.

In the *De Deo uno* of the *Summa theologiae*, Thomas speaks of the unity and unicity of God as *Ipsum esse per se subsistens* in such a fashion as not to close off the conceptual way to the affirmation of the Trinity of Persons. Understood as self-subsistent *esse*, God does not belong to the genus 'substance' – characterised as the members of this genus are by a one-to-one structure in the relation of subject to concretely existing essence. In his account of the one God, then, Thomas avoids any presumption that the divine nature may have a monadic subject; he leaves quite open the question of the manner in which the divine being subsists.[16]

> The unique and selfsame divine *esse*, identical with its *ousia* and its *energeia* under its three achieved modalities of life, intellection and willing, can be accomplished in the threefold subsistent . . . individuality of three divine Persons . . . [by] the integral communication of the nature to each of these personal individualities and among them . . . [17]

What Thomas is able to show – thanks to the biblical foundations of Catholic belief – is that the God of life enacts his being in vital relational acts. And this breakthrough of ontological perception will eventually be of massive consequence, overcoming the ancient presumption that whatever else reality is, it is not intrinsically relational. Against a background of Thomism, W. Norris Clarke has developed the idea that substantiality and relationality are equally primordial aspects of being in his study, *Person and Being*.[18]

Certainly Thomas is no unilateral personalist, uninterested in the theology of the essence. But, as he himself remarks in his earliest major work, the *Commentary on the Sentences*, to say that 'God engenders God' (which in effect we do when in the Creed we call the Son 'God from God') is only correct in the measure that 'God' here signifies not the divine essence but the Person of the Father.[19] As he will put it later, more carefully, in the *Summa theologiae*:

> The term 'God' signifies the divine essence as possessed by the person, and this mode of signifying gives the term ['God'] a natural aptitude to represent the person [of the Father].[20]

A 'natural aptitude': we can note here that, in Thomas's theology, the notion of the divine nature – subtly different in his usage from that of the divine essence – is a basis for a more fully personalised theology of the Trinity. As in his metaphysics at large, the concepts of nature, on the one hand, essence on the other, overlap but do not coincide. 'Nature' has to do with the active life of essence, and hence, in the context of the treatise on God, already carries a tacit reference to personality since, in the maxim of Thomas already cited, 'actions belong to subjects'. In the origination of the Holy Trinity the role of the divine essence is simply that of an operative principle by which a subject acts. The actual acts of generation and spiration, terminating as they do in the unique reality of Son and Spirit, can only arise from a Person or (if we accept the *Filioque*) Persons.

In Thomas's Trinitarian personalism the Persons are their relations. He speaks of those relations in two ways. There is 'relation as relation' – relation as a formal notion – in which case a relation logically presupposes a procession of the Person. One cannot say who the relation is between until one says who the Persons concerned are. But there is also 'relation as constitutive of [a] divine person' – relation as constituting a Person – in which case relation is logically prior to procession. Here the relation of filiation or spiration wholly produces the Person in the way the divine nature is actualised by the relation signified by its name.

If we bear in mind that, following Richard, Thomas's concept of personhood includes the idea of what is 'incommunicable by nature', we are confronted with an extraordinary truth indeed. If the Trinitarian Persons are their relations, then Father, Son and Spirit are irreducibly personal precisely by communicating their life to each other. Here the incommunicability of subjects is located, amazingly, in their perfect reciprocity.

This reciprocity is in knowing and willing. By the mid thirteenth century in the West, 'person' had come to mean not just any grammatically ultimate subject of attribution (grammatical logic was the context from which the Greek-speaking Fathers originally borrowed the language of hypostasis). Instead, 'person' meant one that, existing in itself, operates by intelligence and love. As Thomas declares in the *Prima Pars*, a person is that which is 'most perfect' in active nature.[21] Now if in God there really are two sets of subsistent realtionships – filiation, which from the side of the Only-begotten is called sonship, and spiration, which from the side of the Holy Spirit is called procession, then the divine nature as personalised in the hypostases who are its ultimate subjects must consist in two streams of distinctive activity welling up from the Father, the *plenitudo fontalis*, the 'fontal plenitude'. And this is convenient, for here Augustine's psychological analogy can be brought into play to explore further what is involved in the triune life. Once we bring together the psychological image of the Trinity in the human being with the names which Scripture, or scripturally based reflection, give to the two sets of subsistent relationships, the Son and the Spirit, as respectively *Verbum*, 'Word', and *Amor*, 'Love', we can – with all due deference to the merely analogous character of discourse about God – say something more about those subsistent relations.

So first, the generation of the Son can be compared with intellectual generation. The Father's eternal act of self-awareness is perfectly fecund. It brings forth a subject who enjoys the divine nature as the very Wisdom of God. And the effect of that generation of the Word can in turn be compared with spiritual love. It is a generation that 'spirates love', bringing forth (once again, so fertile is God's eternal action) a subject who enjoys the divine nature as the Love of God, the Love of the Father for the Word. The Holy Spirit is thus the final cause of the procession of the Word – something which is full of soteriological implications when we turn our minds to the way the processions of Word and Spirit are prolonged in their missions on earth. The Father sends the Son not for his own sake but that the Spirit may come to us.

Moreover, the Spirit as the mutual love of Father and Son introduces into the Trinity the love of friendship, which is for Thomas the most perfect of all loves. The Trinitarian love of friendship is not for him a mere application, however, of some general theory of love. The friendship love in the Trinity is the prototype from which the more or less imperfect realisations of the love of friendship in the universe take their rise.

In conclusion: to say, as an anabatic theology would no doubt wish to do, that, owing to the fullness of the divine being, God naturally knows and loves God, is metaphysically appropriate. In reality, though, it is, as katabatic theology alone can inform us, the *Persons* who know and love each other. Malet, then, can justly remark that Thomas integrates the entire heritage of Richard while giving it a deeper foundation – namely, by including within a 'Richardian' theology of the Trinity not simply the dialectic of subject and object but that of Person and nature as well.[22] As to Augustine's problem of how, if the Father and the Son love each other by the Spirit, we can avoid saying that the Father enjoys his love and therefore his being by courtesy of the Spirit, Thomas incorporates his own version of Richard's solution. The love that is the divine nature is the principle whereby the personal love of God operates, and by that personal love the Father does not indeed *receive* his love for the Word from the Spirit, yet with equal certainty he *manifests* his love for the second divine Person *in* the third.

The Trinity in relation to ourselves

And first, in relation to human subjectivity, to our own awareness of who God is. For Thomas, the sending of the Persons of Son and Spirit is a precondition of the Christian understanding of the divine. This is not to say, of course, that Christians cannot also be natural theologians, but that is not, *ex hypothesi*, a distinctively Christian knowledge of God. The Trinitarian presence in our minds and affections is prior, for Thomas, to theological reflection on the relation between God and man.[23] The Trinitarian missions make possible an awareness of salvation by dilating – expanding – the human subject in her interpenetrating powers of intelligence and will. (Mind and will are distinct, but they must not be pictured, so Thomas Gilby liked to warn, as tentacles twirling out of the soul.) Their interplay is deep and delicate: they mutually contain one another. The Word, and the Spirit of love, are sent to us in such a way that all the words of the science of faith and all affections within divine friendship are echoes and refractions of their presence.

When Thomas wishes to lay his finger on this, he goes to Augustine. He writes:

By grace the soul is made like to God and therefore when a

divine Person is sent there is implied a being made like to him by some sort of grace. Now because the Holy Spirit is Love the soul belongs to him through the gift of charity; consequently love in its manner corresponds to the sending of the Spirit. Similarly, because the Son is Word, not any kind of mental utterance but Word breathing Love, blessed Augustine says that the word he is proposing to consider is conceived in company with love. Consequently, what matches the sending of the Son to us is not just any quality of mind, but that sort of enlightening by which the mind breaks forth into loving affection . . . therefore Augustine remarks that the Son is sent to somebody when he is known and perceived.[24]

Perception here denotes real experience, *experimentalis quaedam notitia*. And this, Thomas concludes, is properly called 'wisdom', as it were a 'savorous knowing', *sapida scientia*.

Well and good. Yet it is not simply as the precondition of this subjective grasping of the Trinity that the Trinity saves us! The Trinity is itself, in its own reality, our salvation. Thomas sees salvation as the plan of God to communicate his own goodness. By teaching and by transmitting the grace of the Holy Spirit, Christ re-actualises the Trinitarian image in us, sterile and inoperative as this had become. God sends his Word to assume full manhood and through his human service of the Father restore to the created divine image that inner dynamism which can bear all creation towards its fullness in God. For Thomas, the life of grace and glory is our adoption as God's sons, heirs to the riches of God. And what are these riches? Nothing less than God himself, possessing his own goodness in the act of begetting the Word that breathes Love forth.

How does the Trinity thus indwell us? Thomas's account – offered in question 43 of the *Prima Pars* – circles around three words from the Vulgate text of the New Testament: *mitti*, being sent; *dari*, being given; *habitare*, abiding. His theology of grace is Thomas's reply to our query. We shall be investigating that in Chapter 7, but we can note here the key statement, 'In knowing and loving the rational creature reaches God himself',[25] with its echoes of Thomas's names (*Verbum, Amor*) for Son and Spirit. Grace is so exalted that it brings about an unmediated union with the divine.

The Spirit enters the soul invisibly in the gift of love, the Word in the gift of wisdom (and there is thereby a manifestation of the Father, the ultimate to whom we return). In due accord with these gifts, a likeness to what is proper to the Persons comes to be in us, and by reason of this reality-in-likeness, the Persons are truly in our souls. 'The whole Trinity, the Persons themselves and not merely their gifts, dwells in man through sanctifying grace'.[26]

It may seem strange that this discussion turns on the *invisible* sendings of the Persons in Uncreated Grace. As we shall see more fully in Chapter 8, Thomas is well aware of the dependence of our faith experience on the *visible* missions – when the Son became visibly present to the creation by his Incarnation as author of our sanctification, and the Holy Spirit at Pentecost in tongues of fire as sign of our sanctification, *sanctificationis indicium*. But for Aquinas the Incarnation and that Pentecostal outpouring of the Spirit are means, precisely, in our return to the invisible Father: that is their privileged glory and pre-eminence. (We may compare here the evangelist John's teaching that the Son's raison d'être is simply to point to the Father, and, in the Book of Acts, the sense that the Holy Spirit is given for the upbuilding of the community – which, for Thomas at least, is a community of grace, continuous, if not completely so, with the community of glory, the blessed in heaven, since deriving its relation to the Father from Christ its Head.) As humans we proceed in our grasp of things from the visible to the invisible.

Very well, then. God has ordered our sanctification according to the pattern of our needs and perception – though it is no mere afterthought when we add that the flesh too – the happy carnal medium of our spiritual life – is to be saved, and raised up.

5.
The Trinity in Man

In the last Chapter, I had occasion to refer to the image of the Holy Trinity which, on the reading of Genesis offered by Thomas, following Augustine, is 'in' ourselves. As we saw, the scriptural understanding of the relation between Father and Son, and Father and Son with Spirit, can be illumined if we take our cue from the names of Son and Spirit as respectively, Word and Love, and consider how these processions may be comparable to understanding and love in us. What are the implications of the *imago Trinitatis* for man's creation?

Vestiges of the Trinity

We can begin by recalling how, whether we are talking about human or angelic beings, or indeed feline or canine beings, or even for that matter arboreal and lapidine beings (trees and rocks), all creation for Thomas is *ex Trinitate*, from God as, specifically, the Holy Trinity.[1]

In evoking the triune life of God in its outflow into the creation, Thomas holds that while the production of creatures is not hypostatically distinctive (the act of creation does not belong specifically to any particular Person of the Trinity but to all three in common), the processions of the Persons – the ways they are divine – nonetheless enter into the very constitution of God's creative causing. Does that mean, then, that we can infer that God is the Holy Trinity from the world around us? Thomas would answer, No. Since the created is necessarily other than the divine and the distinction of the Persons is their most intimate and proper way of being divine, there is no possibility of discovering the Trinitarian Persons by 'ascending' or anabatic theology, in the latter's attempt to move from the effect that is the world to its ultimate Cause which is the Trinity. The only way of knowing the distinction of Persons is katabatically, by 'descending' theology, from divine revelation. And yet this does not mean that the divine creative causality is something other than, or over and above, the Trinitarian relationships. The presence of God in his causal sustenance of creatures is not anything different from the Holy Trinity.

More especially, Thomas connects the depth of creative power in the *esse* received by the creature with the Father. He links the intrinsic order of the creature's constitution with the Word. And he relates the creature's dynamic tendency to move towards its own perfection with the Holy Spirit.

The image of the Trinity

These traces or 'vestiges' of the Trinity – power, order, fulfilment, as we might sum them up – can be found in all creatures without exception. But, emboldened by the sacred texts of Scripture as well as his reading of Augustine,[2] Thomas thinks there is more to be said when we come to humankind. Here we are dealing not with a mere vestige but with the image of God. But what is the difference between vestige and image? Thomas's earliest discussion of the matter comes in his 'Writing on the *Sentences*' where he explains:

> An image . . . represents a thing in a better defined manner, according to all its parts and the arrangement of its parts, from which [arrangement] it is possible to perceive something of the inner characterstics of the thing.[3]

And later on in this 'Writing' (*Scriptum*), Thomas will maintain that in the case of any 'true' image, the form an image takes will always be a 'clear and express sign' of the nature of what the image represents. Where images are concerned, authenticity turns on the way a form resembles its exemplar. In his commentary on Aristotle's *Metaphysics*, Thomas enquires what *imago* means, and replies that, while in a perfect image there will be equality between imaged and image, this is surely not necessary for the *ratio* of an image. What is indispensable, rather, is *similitudo*, likeness. Things that differ in substance may well possess unity inasmuch as they share, albeit unequally, in some common quality in an analogical manner.[4] The key, evidently, is 'proportionate resemblance'. What Thomas has to say about the image of the Trinity in man illustrates this theory of the ontology of images. There is, he says, a proportionate resemblance between, on the one hand, the faculties of the soul, that soul in which the body shares through being enlivened by it, and, on the other, the divine Persons in God. The 'arrangement' of the one mirrors that of the other. In the *Summa theologiae* Thomas will flesh out that same basic idea in the language of form. An image is a likeness that expresses in its own formality the form of another. An image represents its cause *quantum ad similitudinem formae eius*, and hence goes beyond those vestigial signs of the Creator's activity which simply indicate his causal power. Thomas is taken to be the great theologian of analogy, but for him *conformitas* goes well beyond *analogia*. As the Scots Dominican Ian Hislop wrote, 'Image' for Thomas is even more pregnant a term than 'sign'. It is 'a representative likeness necessarily and intrinsically dependent on its exemplar'.[5]

In saying that an image can be distinguished from a mere vestige, thanks to the more defined way it represents the *structured unity* of some really existing thing, Thomas is evidently preparing the ground for the assertion that the image of God is to found where there is a likeness of God that represents the three divine Persons in their characteristics of consubstantiality and hypostatic distinctiveness. And Thomas will apply his definition to the case of the Trinity-and-ourselves by arguing that the image of God is found only in those creatures that reflect the triune divine life in this way through the highest faculties proper to an intellectual nature: understanding and love.

As time went on, however, and Thomas's theological mind developed, he came to place less emphasis on this proportionate resemblance between our faculties and the divine Persons – what we might call the formal, some would say the 'static', aspect of the image, the aspect of structural correspondence. Instead, he put the stress more and more on the active or dynamic aspect of the image, whereby we image the Trinity not just by existing as the kind of unitary but internally differentiated intellectual and volitional beings that we are, but through actually using the faculties which that description identifies so as really to know and love God himself. The soul's memory, understanding and love of itself, it now turns out, are not the image of God in the full sense of those words. They are no more than a *potential* image of the Trinity. Augustine had already written that this image 'is not preserved except it be in relation to him by whom it is impressed'.[6] Only our understanding and our love of God as united to our memory – the retentive capacity which allows knowledge and love to exist habitually in the mind – actualise the image of God in us. If Augustine's treatise on the Trinity, exploratory and even tentative as it is, 'abounds in unexplored reservations and provisos', Thomas could draw on these to assist his move from a structural to a functional account of the *imago Trinitatis* in man.

What, after all, is the function of an image? Surely, any image – from a Leonardo Madonna to a landscape by Turner – exists so as to lead the beholder to actual perception of the deeper character of what it exemplifies. So here too, in Thomas's mature theology (as for that matter in Augustine's), the *raison d'être* of the *imago Trinitatis* in us is union with God. The image is unactualised without the life of grace. In the 'Disputed Questions on Truth', Thomas can already be found inferring that the image of the Trinity is primarily *mens* in its knowing God, and only very secondarily in its knowing self – and even then principally when the self is known *as* image, and thus 'as something *through* which the gaze of the beholder passes on to God himself'.[7] By the time he wrote the *Prima Pars* Thomas realised that the main question for sacred doctrine here is, How, at our own level of creaturely reality, are we actually to participate in the Trinitarian processions – in the conception of the Word, the hypostatic equivalent of the divine knowing, and the breathing forth of the Spirit, the hypostatic equivalent of the divine willing? How are we to image the Trinity precisely by sharing its life? In Thomas's three attempts to expound this mystery – the 'Writing on the *Sentences*', the 'Disputed Questions on Truth' and the *Summa theologiae* – he realises with ever greater clarity that, while the basic foundation of our own Trinitarian imagehood is given with our distinctively human being itself, that basic foundation has to be built upon, and the relation of imagehood itself augmented or elevated if we are ever to come efficaciously to God. Realised conformation to the Trinity by grace rather than the formal analogy which relates our nature to that of the triune God is the principal cause of the likeness that constitutes the *imago Trinitatis* in the world.[8]

And this fits with Thomas's ongoing references to the image – and indeed, the vestiges – of the Trinity in the second and third parts of the *Summa theologiae*. There Thomas develops his account of the supreme theological rationale for the creation's *exitus* from God in a creation that bears on its face a myriad traces of the triune God in non-human creatures and, as their crown, the image of God in men and women. The reason why these vestiges and images exist is so that the creation can play its part in the *reditus*, the return to God. By the Father's sending of Son and Spirit, in their public missions in saving history at the Incarnation and Pentecost and then in their invisible missions in our souls, we are to be con-joined to the divine being itself. In our first birth, our *exitus* from God in creation, we were possessed by God. In our second birth, our *reditus* to him in redemption, he is to be possessed by us.

The Christological image

We must not neglect, however, the way in which the imagehood is not only, in wide terms, Trinitarian but also, in more specific fashion, *Christological*.

In his commentary on the Letter to the Church at Colossae, Thomas notes (in the typical fashion of Scholastic exegetes) how the apostle divides into three parts what he asks the Colossians to hold in faith about Jesus Christ and his work.

> Having recalled the benefits of grace, particular and general, he [Paul] here exalts the author of this grace, Christ, first com-paring him to God, then to all creation, and finally to the Church.[9]

We may compare with this the prologue to the 'Writing on the

Sentences', where Thomas speaks of the key role of the Word of God in, first, the 'manifestation of divine things' (it is by his Word that God knows himself fully and so it belongs to the Word to manifest not only the Father but the entire divine Trinity); second, the 'production' of creatures (God possesses a knowledge that is not just speculative but operative, and the Son is the *creative* Word, inasmuch as he is the invisible God's Image according to whose form all has been formed); thirdly, the 'restoration' of God's work (accomplished by the Son when, made man, he repairs the human state and at the same time repairs all creatures 'in some manner'); and fourthly, the perfect completion of the divine work, preserving things for their final goal by 'introducing us to the glory of the Fatherly inheritance'.

Compared with God, then (returning to Thomas's scheme in the Colossians commentary), Christ is the image of the invisible God. As the plenitude of being on which all creation draws, God is unknown – but the Image of the Invisible can represent the Source and mediate the Father in creation.

Compared with creation, creatures are in the image of the First Born:

> The procession of creatures, imperfect images of the perfect divine nature, leads back to the perfect Image containing the plenitude of the divine perfection, namely, the Son ... He is the exemplar and *ratio* of the quasi-natural procession of creatures issued from the God whose nature they imitate.[10]

(It is a feature of Thomism to emphasise not only their mimesis of the divine ideas, as found in the Son as *Ars Dei*, the 'Art of God', but also their likeness to God through the gift of *esse* – again through the Word who is their immediate principle of union with the Father.) And here the human person must be said to be in the Son by a specific likeness, sharing in the light which he is as the Word of God.

Compared with the Church, the grace of divine adoption has its own exemplary cause in that image of God that is the humanity of Christ. God's providential plan enables the natural image of the divine, inscribed in man's being, to become an image that is deiform, really 'God-shaped'.[11] The likeness to the Son by grace and charity is what constitutes the divine adoption of the redeemed, since the beneficiaries of this gift really have a title to the Father's eternal inheritance. The spiritual rebirth whereby one becomes a child of God presupposes the infusion of the *esse gratiae*, the root in us of deiform living, imperfect under the regime of faith but perfected in the condition of glory.[12]

While it is true that the *esse naturae* furnishes the human person with her primordial, natural being, whereas the *esse gratiae* is only 'modal' (it is a *way*, the *gracious* way, of inhabiting our being), still, when all is said and done, it is, unlike our 'being of nature', deiform. The divine *esse* of the Son imprints its likeness on the humanity of Christ with the infusion of the *esse gratiae*, and the unique (then) *esse* of the Word incarnate has exemplary value for us: our grace follows his own 'as splendour does the sun'. So Thomas in the *Tertia Pars*.[13] This *conformitas gratiae* brings about in us the recreated image – *imago recreationis*, exceeding in beauty the *imago creationis*, the image that is ours on the basis of creation.

And finally the full 'similitude' to our Redeemer implies the perfect, unloseable habit of knowing and loving God. It is the glory of the blessed, the image now found *secundum similitudinem gloriae*.[14] Basically, for Thomas, the *imago recreationis* mediates between the *imago creationis* and the *imago similitudinis*, and the mediation happens through that multiplicity of ways the theology of graces considers: the grace of the sacraments for their particular purposes, sanctifying grace in the soul's essence, the infused supernatural virtues in its powers, modulated as these can be by the Gifts of the Holy Spirit. Grace is not only 'Christic', coming from Christ; it is also 'Christoconforming'.

Clearly enough, these aspects of Christological – and Trinitarian – imagehood are bound up one with another. They are so many interrelated moments in a single spiritual itinerary. The end, our return to God, is joined by divine developmentalism to our beginning, our *exitus* from him. Père Louis-Marie de Blignières writes:

> In a Pelagian or Molinist perspective, one thinks of the return as a movement disjoined from the procession. One imagines the first movement – the one under the divine influx – terminated, and the second starting up in a kind of dissolution of

continuity. In the case of the second movement, we pay honour exclusively to man, exalting his autonomy. But then we are forgetting that everything proceeds from God *including the return*, i.e., in the case under discussion, our human actions. For the more creatures are rich in being and action, the more they depend on God.[15]

6.
Angelology

If we consider the final conclusion of the last Chapter too anthropo-
centric a view of creation (in the world of the Resurrection Thomas
finds a place only for the human and mineral, not the animal realm),
Aquinas's concern with the destiny of humanity is in itself unsurprising. This is, after all, the chief topic of Scripture, and we saw
in the second Chapter of this book how for him the primary task
of the theologian is to expound the revelation laid out in the Bible
and summarised in the Creed. In any case, even if we had no special
divine revelation through the *lumen propheticum*, just by dint of
the *lumen naturale* we should be, as all men have been, fascinated
by our own human mystery. As Alexander Pope declared in a con-
centrated flurry of non-inclusive language, 'The proper study of
mankind is man'.[1]

Why angels?

If we ask why St Thomas is so interested, then, in angels, the
reply is actually isomorphic with the account just given of his
interest in man. On the one hand, the Bible is full of angels, and on
the other, one accepts their presence in the world by some kind of
rational necessity. It was, Thomas considered, unthinkable that the
God who has unlimited power to bring into existence such reflec-
tions of himself as he chooses, would not have created intelligences
vastly less limited or restricted than our own. Or, more strongly,
God intends to produce a goodness that consists in a likeness to
himself. The universe tends to completeness of God-likeness in
respect of kinds of being. But since God causes precisely by his

intellect and will, a creation that did not include sheerly intellectual-volitional creatures could only be incomplete.[2]

Their creation

The *Summa theologiae*'s treatise on the angels is one of the fullest accounts of the angelological thinking of medieval Christians we possess. Its opening question, on the creation of the angels, already indicates that fullness.

Thomas begins by asking whether the existence of the angels is caused. He replies that it must be, since only God is essential being while everything else exists by participation. Every being, every limited thing, is of its nature derived being, received being, shared-out being. Since an angel is a limited thing, a particular kind of thing, it cannot be the ultimate mystery. Only plenary being, fullness overflowing, is sovereign being. Everything else that exists is its beneficiary and dependant.

Nowadays it would not occur to many people to wonder whether angels were created or not. This is because we find ourselves at the tail end of the process whereby the angels were cut down to size – and, all too often, reduced to cardboard cut-outs at that. In biblical religion it was not always so. The Old Testament includes strata of great antiquity where the angel of the Lord is a dynamic expression of the Lord himself, and so the question as to whether he was created with all the other things that are is a real one. Even older than these strata, probably, are others where the name of God is the plural *Elohim*: 'God stands in the divine assembly', says the Psalmist (Ps. 82:1), and we should suppose that the angels are his interlocutors. In such texts the divine world is a pluralistic world where the Lord of Israel is the central and sovereign power but does not stand alone. There is a dynamic interplay of powers, God coming forth out of his unity into multiplicity. Though the ancient Hebrews did not, as did the ancient Greeks, pose the problem of 'the One and the many' philosophically, they worked at it through the modifying of their imagery for God and his angels.

In this respect, the history of Greek thought from, say, Hesiod to Plotinus, is quite parallel to the history of Hebrew religion from the earliest times to Second Isaiah. In both, polytheism – at least in the sense of belief that there are many gods, though in Israel only one may be worshipped – is gradually transformed into monotheism, in the Old Testament of a fully personal, in the Platonist tradition a quasi-personal kind. What the Greek struggles to express rationally, in concepts and arguments, the Israelite deals with mythopoeically, in stories and images. In later Hebrew religion, the angels are God's messengers in the sense of his functionaries. They are not his powers, aspects of his overwhelming being. They are simply his powerful servants. And so Thomas appropriately cites as the opening article's *sed contra* (in any article of the *Summa* the cue for Thomas's exposition of what he takes to be the truth of a question) a psalm text: 'Praise him all you angels' (148:2), which in Old Testament language places the angels firmly on the created side of the infinite abyss between Creator and creature. In biblical language only God is praised and only God cannot himself praise. Praise is adoration, the confession of the incomparable Lord of Israel and all the earth. So without a word of philosophy, a simple liturgical text says all there really is to say on this subject.

As always, much of Thomas's positive doctrine is found in thinking through answers to objections. In the *ad primum* – his response to the first objection – Thomas gives an interesting suggestion for the absence of any reference to the angels in Genesis 1, Scripture's account of the act of creation. Why did not Moses include the angels in the opening chapter of his work? First, because people in that ancient time would not have understood the idea of sheerly mental being, and secondly, because awareness of such tremendous beings might have tempted them to idolatry, a vice to which they were only too prone. It is true that the idea of purely mental reality is a highly sophisticated one, deriving as it does from our grasp of our own consciousness as the ability to reflect on ourselves reflecting. We are only aware of mind when we have (so to speak) got outside our own skins and taken a good look at ourselves taking a good look at something. It was not to be expected that a crowd of escaped slaves in the third millennium BC would get hold immediately of this idea. And as to the avoidance of idolatry argument: even in the Apocalypse of St John, the closing book of the biblical Canon, the seer of Patmos is tempted to fall down and worship the angel of the Apocalypse, until that angel gently raises him, explaining that he (the angel) is his fellow-servant (19:10) – an incident that perhaps suggested to Newman the beautiful line in *The Dream of Gerontius* where the soul of the dead Gerontius is greeted by its angel guardian, 'All hail, my child! My child and brother, hail!'[3] But if John the Beloved Disciple was tempted to adore an angel, there was little hope, so St Thomas evidently thought, for the worshippers of the golden calf. Thomas's decision to explain Moses' silence by the need to inoculate people against paganism raises the question as to whether the 'gods of the nations' may not be misconstrued angels. The intuition of natural religion that the world is full of gods may derive from awareness of angelic presence.

The *ad tertium* concerns itself with a point of Thomistic metaphysics: it is true that angels do not come to be something through a natural process, actualised by the determining principle called form in the way that, for example, a fertilised ovum is formally actualised as a human being. But that is not to say they were not created! Their existence as a whole has still to be accounted for and such an account is what the doctrine of creation is for.

The angels are created in time, but they are not in time in the way we are. Thomas argues for the multivalency of time. Time is a measure of change in reality, and if reality has a radically differentiated structure – which must be the case if it includes things as different as ants and angels – then there cannot just be one sort of time. One o'clock has no meaning in their realm, but this is not to say that the idea of before and after baffles them. 'In their realm': it is, for Thomas, of great importance that we do not replace that phrase by 'in their universe'. There is only one universe, a single, integrated and unified cosmos of which all are citizens, albeit with differing roles. The total good of the universe consists in the interrelationship of things, *ordo rerum ad invicem*, 'the ordering of things to one another'.[4] Ultimately this is not just an aesthetic question – a matter of the *pattern* of the world, the 'rich and complex' tapestry God has made. More than this, it is a question of the *purpose* of the universe, and the way in which all the beings which constitute the world in their inter-relation conspire, whether consciously or not, to serve the final purpose of God, his saving plan.

Our distance from Thomas, intellectually – or, rather, scientifically – speaking, is gauged when he goes on to ask whether the angels were created in the 'empyrean heaven'. As educated thirteenth-century people saw the cosmos, the earth is surrounded by a series of concentric spheres in which the sun and moon, planets and stars, are embedded. The furthest of these spheres, the *primum mobile,* carries no luminaries. What it does is to impart movement to the other spheres, each of which was reckoned to have its own periodic revolution. The interaction of the two kinds of motion was held to account for – among other things – the change of the seasons, and the so-called epicycles which resulted were handy in explaining a good deal of genuine astronomical observation (although, as it turned out, incorrectly). Above the *primum mobile* lay the empyrean, corresponding to the 'highest heaven' of the Hebrew Bible. Medieval students computed its distance from earth in millions of miles. Dante's *Paradiso* has the literary structure of a space journey from earth to the empyrean. Only the journey would have been regarded as a theological device. The space traversed was contemporary science.[5] The empyrean was useful to theologians who needed a point, as it were, where our universe could shade off into the world of the Resurrection, with the risen (or assumed) bodies of Christ and his Mother and perhaps the saints. Dante's account of the empyrean explores a metaphor of light, at first blinding but then revealing: *lume in forma di rivera/ fulvido di fulgore,* 'light in the form of a river pouring its splendour forth'.[6] It is here, claimed the ninth-century monastic writer Walafrid Strabo, that the angels have their dwelling. We can sense that Thomas does not want to commit himself too strongly to this, but he allows himself the remark that it is fitting to think of the angels as created in the supreme region of the cosmos, for are they not to preside over the world of creatures as instruments and functionaries of God's providence? There is a symbolic appropriateness in at least the *arch*angels occupying the empyrean – and that is about as far as he wants (sensible man!) to go.

Their knowledge

It is chiefly as intellects that angels appear in Thomas's theology. Of the 15 questions devoted to angels in the *Summa theologiae*, as many as a third are concerned with their power to know.[7] The English Dominican Dante scholar Kenelm Foster commented on this salient fact:

> Knowing seems the most knowable of spiritual operations to mixed spirits like ourselves – the most accessible to reflection and analysis. So it seemed, at any rate, to the Greek philosophical tradition with its Arabic affiliations, from which St Thomas derived as a philosopher: it is symptomatic that Aristotle's treatise on the soul, the *De anima*, is very largely an account of cognition. And though as a Christian St Thomas was more sensitive to problems involving the will and the affections, he remains exceedingly Hellenic in this respect; his gift for introspective analysis is most readily and fruitfully exercised on the experience of knowing.

And alerting us to the significance of this for angelology, Foster goes on:

> This experience was, of course, the human one of understanding by way of sensation, and it still had to be his starting-point when he aspires to know how a pure spirit knows. There was, and of course is, no other available model. Hence his teaching on angelic knowledge might be described as a series of answers to the question, What would thinking be like with no sensations to think about?[8]

But, as always, with Aquinas, epistemology follows on ontological enquiry: we know in the way we do because of what we are. Now angels, for Thomas, are *matterless forms*. In his writing, *form* is normally that factor in the structure of something that makes it this kind of determinate thing and not any other; matter, by contrast, is that which form determines. But by extension of meaning, 'form' can also denote a matterless actuality in which what is realised is *the mere potentiality to exist*, rather than matter itself. Unlike our nature, angelic nature is purely form. But unlike the divine nature, it is *not* purely act. On the contrary, its nature is in potency to the actuality which is its existence (it is, to repeat, *participated* being). It is because angels are actualised potentialities that they differ *toto caelo* from God. In another sense, however, an angel can be said to be an infinitude. For it is, by form, sheer intellect, and thus utter openness to all being.

Humans lack such an infinite grasp of the whole realm of the real. That, however, does not tell us something about what knowing is like in and of itself. It simply instructs us in what happens to knowing when knowing is embodied in such animals as ourselves.

The most striking aspect of the difference lies in its implications for self-knowledge. Our self-knowledge must be extricated laboriously from awareness of our activities; the human self has no sign, and yet human beings move happily as knowing agents only in a world of signs. An angel's knowledge of its own angelhood is very different. The angel's self-possession is an act of immediate and total self-knowledge. As Kenelm Foster wrote:

> Free from matter it is free to be self-determining, to deploy its activity 'immanently' and so vitally to possess itself.[9]

But the object of this effortless, transparent act of self-knowing – to that degree, a reflection of God's way of knowing himself – is only the limited actuality of this particular angel. And there's the rub.

> His intellect, essentially correlated as it is to actuality and being as such, cannot rest in himself but only in the infinite perfection and actuality of God.[10]

Limited as it is, the angel's essence cannot reveal the whole of being to the act of knowledge which results; yet it is this fullness of actuality that is the proper term of mind as such. So the angel must needs receive knowledge from what is other than himself, through likenesses of other things. Something that is alien to the knower yet apt to be known by him – and in that way not alien but congenial – comes to be actually known by a kind of presentation of itself in the knower's mind. How, then, do angels come to know of the richness of the divine being expressed in a multiform, material creation? For Thomas this can only come about when God infuses into the mind of the angel the whole range of intelligible forms requisite for grasping the realm of finite being.

There can be no question of angels disengaging these forms, as we do, from material objects. That would need imagination, which implies a sensuous grasp of things proper only to the embodied. So what is natural knowledge for us is utterly beyond – because beneath – their capacities, whereas what in us would be mystical knowledge is second nature to them.

Their fall

The fall of the angels is not only a problem for Milton studies. (Question: Why, in *Paradise Lost*, did the poet present the fallen angels as so attractively plausible when his aim was rather to show their choice as lethal – not least for ourselves? Answer: In order to warn us that sin after their fall *is* plausibly attractive, so we must be on our guard.) The fall of the angels is a metaphysico-theological problem of the most daunting order, at least on the presuppositions about the goodness of being and the openness of intellect to truth which Thomas, in the twin light of revelation and the Hellenic heritage, made his own.

For Thomas the angelic creation, like its human counterpart, was created in a state of grace, but not a condition of beatitude. It belongs to the dignity of free spirits, and the corresponding delicacy of the divine action in its dealings with them, that created liberty should play its part in the raising of any creature to its own ultimate perfection: concretely, to bliss in the enjoyment of God's glory. By contrast to human, however, it is characteristic of angelic nature to reach its completeness by a single act, rather than as with us, a long-drawn-out process. As sheer intelligences, angels grasp whatever they understand immediately, not by ratiocinative thinking whose materials are laboriously educed from sensuous experience.[11] And so each angel that reaches bliss does so immediately after meriting it with his first act of charity.[12] By virtue of their creation, all angels know God reflected in their natural essence, but not, unless they are so elevated, by 'glorious knowledge', in the divine essence itself. This distinction enables Thomas to approach a solution of the difficulty which the proposal of angelic evil entails:

> It belongs to an angel's nature to turn to God in love as to the source of his nature's existence; but to turn to him as the source of a supernatural happiness, this comes of a love received as a grace; and such love could be rejected, sinfully.[13]

The megawatt level of angelic intelligence – by comparison with which Professor Steven Hawking is a dimwit – makes it impossible to see the fall of the angels as resulting from a metaphysical mistake. The distinction just drawn, however, enables Thomas to present it as the result, nonetheless, of pride.

> It was that the devil aspired to be as God. Not that he desired godlikeness in the sense of an absolute pre-eminence in being; for that would have amounted to desiring non-existence, since no creature can exist except as holding existence under God. But he desired godlikeness in this sense, that he placed his ultimate bliss in an objective to be obtained by the force of his own nature alone, rejecting the supernatural bliss which depends on the grace of God.[14]

The fallen angel's hallmark is his insistence that 'the good must not be a gift'; he 'aspired to be absolutely autonomous, not indeed directly in existence, but in respect of the fulfilment of existence that is joy'.[15] For Thomas, however, self-existence in joy is only possible through divine grace and that deiformity which comes from the theological virtues. So this seems a good moment to pass on to that subject.

7.
Grace and the Virtues

A natural coupling

For Thomists, grace and the virtues form a natural coupling. Indeed, the Irish Dominican theologian Colman O'Neill could declare roundly that 'the significance of grace lies primarily in the moral order'. But as he explained, he did not mean thereby to deny that grace

> makes us sharers in the divine nature, reproduces in us the image of God, brings about the indwelling of the Blessed Trinity, and thus pertains to the mystery of God.

(This is the theme of the ontology of grace, to which I shall return.) Rather, what he wished to assert, following Aquinas, is that, precisely because grace has this divinising effect, reintegrating and fulfilling the image of God in us, it

> raises up the essence and faculties of the creature so that he or she can *act* in a divine fashion, knowing and loving God supernaturally . . .

and because grace, then, is concerned with the way we act, and especially with the way our powers of understanding and loving are exercised, it is a moral matter.[1] As to the relation of grace not just to morals in general but to the virtues in particular, perhaps I can anticipate my eventual response by saying that for Thomism, while the theology of grace raises the question, 'How does grace create in us the necesssary and sufficient conditions of enjoying God not only naturally but supernaturally?' the theology of the virtues –

natural and supernatural – helps to provide that question with its answer.[2]

If it sounds slightly depressing to say that grace is really about morals, we can invert the proposition and say that, by the same token, the only proper context for morals is grace. On Thomas's view, the vision of God in heaven is the unique overarching end or goal of the human person to which all human action – all moral action – needs relating if it is to be accounted, in the last analysis, good for man.

Here the Thomist position is today under challenge from an influential – and otherwise admirable – school of Catholic ethicists, centring on the formidable figure of the American layman Germain Grisez – for which moral decision-making has no single super-ordinate ultimate end. Both schools – Thomas's and theirs – accept that human nature displays *finalitas*:

> To say . . . that human action is teleological is as much as to say that it is 'responsive' in structure; it is called, summoned, evoked and provoked, rather than launched, projected, cast out into a world which is otherwise a void of unmeaning and purposelessness . . . Our deciding is finally a kind of accepting, because it happens within a vision of the meaningfulness of being.[3]

And, introducing the key word 'nature', Fr Fergus Kerr points out (with help from Shakespeare who, perhaps via Hooker, shares this vision)[4] how

> Being human is . . . essentially a matter of responding to the normative appeal issued by nature; there is a law inherent in reality, some 'supervening orientation' which confers meaning and purpose on human life. Response, correspondence, is the fundamental structure of being human.[5]

The problem lies not here – for this is common ground – but in the disparity disjoining two aspects of Thomism's fundamental picture of the morality-grace relation from the positions of the Grisez school. In the first place, the members of the latter deny that the natural end of man becomes strictly subordinate to his ultimate supernatural end. In the second place, they do not regard the contemplation of God in his works in the creation as the correct answer to the question, What unifies on the natural level the goals for which human beings should strive in moral effort on earth?

Owing to the importance of the issues raised, it seems worth delaying a little on these points. The *first* denial of the Grisez school is that man's final natural end, received with his creation, becomes relativised by the final supernatural end received with our ordination to glory by the further, supplementary and gratuitous act of God. By the very nature of our humanity, created as it was in the image of God, human beings have always in some sense tended – so the tradition of Thomas's disciples maintains – toward intimate union with God, even though that union was (and is) unachievable without grace. Setting aside, for the purposes of the argument, the super-natural economy of grace in which our creation was always located, human nature was from the first moment of its creation, in the phrase of the Latin Fathers, *capax Dei*, 'capable of God': meaning, it was a fit subject for God's divinising action should such action in fact take place. As the American Dominican Benedict Ashley has put it:

> Human nature is *capax Dei* because it is personal-intellectual, and hence open to enter into a union with a personal, spiritual God if he graciously chooses to invite it to this union and empowers it by transforming grace.[6]

There was no necessity which obliged God to re-contextualise our nature in the supernatural, but there was a basic congruence in his so doing. As Ashley goes on, with reference to Pius XII's encyclical *Humani generis*, which dealt with this and other issues:

> Hence, as *Humani generis* taught, no impossibility appears why God could not have created human persons in a merely natural state, although in fact we were not so created. In such a world, humans might be led by 'natural desire' of their intelli-gences to wonder if perhaps God would call them to perfect beatitude as sharers in his inner life. Nevertheless, when they found no signs that this was God's will, the virtuous would be humbly content with and grateful for the imperfect but marvel-lous beatitude proper to their own nature, an imperfect

happiness specified by and culminating in the contemplation of God's glory in creation.[7]

When, in point of fact, God does confer on our human nature a supernatural finality, ordaining it to a life of friendship with the Trinity, this does not annul the basic integrity of human nature but places that nature in a new context which radically changes its meaning. As Ashley has it, our nature still retains its own finality, its ordering to the contemplation of God in his works, but this goal for our humanity, remaining as it does ultimate in the natural order, is now itself relativised or instrumentalised by the supervening of the supernatural order where we have an ultimate goal of a different sort, the very vision of God in his own inner life.

> To know *Ipsum esse per se subsistens* is only connatural to the divine intellect, and that is above the natural faculty of every created mind, since no creature is its own *esse* but has a partici-pated *esse*. Thus created intellect cannot see God by essence except in the measure that God joins himself by grace to created mind, making himself intelligible to it.[8]

And this way of putting things seems the more impressive in that, as an exegete of Thomas's texts, Ashley – along with many disciples of Thomas – takes a more sceptical view of the idea that our human nature is itself ordered to the supernatural than did, for example, the French Jesuit and later cardinal, Henri de Lubac.[9] Rather than holding that, for St Thomas, our nature was itself made for the supernatural, Ashley thinks that Thomas did not argue directly that the natural end of man lies in the supernatural order. More modestly, he hoped to show that a perfect knowledge of the First Cause of ourselves and the world, such as the vision of the Trinity superla-tively – amazingly – provides, far from contradicting human nature, or even being unfitted to it, or going against its grain, fulfils a 'desire' of that nature.

Human intelligence – for Thomas the power that specifies the way all other powers operate when they are functioning in a distinc-tively human, as distinct from animal or even vegetable, fashion – tends to seek to know the ultimate cause of things as perfectly as possible. The supernatural vision of the triune God, accordingly, fits in perfectly with nature's own tendency.

Such intellectual desire is, to be sure, solidary with a desire for happiness that is fuller than the aspect of intellectuality if the latter be taken in isolation. When writing as a theologian of beatitude – *eudaimonia* – Thomas likes to refer to Aristotle. But whereas for Aristotle the contemplative operation is the supreme and sovereign moment of the whole felicity of spirit, his description of *eudaimonia* – the 'daimonic' or superhuman form of the goodness of existence – exceeds in connotative richness the contemplative act of laying hold on the intelligible. Thomas too identifies the natural desire for understanding God as the central and most sublime facet of the natural desire for beatitude on the part of the human being in her total – and not least fleshly – reality. To this extent – in part, then – the gulf between his approach and the Grisez school's can be bridged. But the introduction of a more explicit anthropological maximalism would leave Thomas's radical theocentrism untouched. 'My heart and flesh sing for joy to the living God', confesses the Psalmist (Ps. 84:2), and again, 'My body pines for you like a dry weary land without water' (Ps. 63:1).

So our ultimate natural end becomes, with the coming of the supernatural order, auxiliary or instrumental to our ultimate supernatural end – a change which, evidently, must have tremendous consequences for our natural humanity. And this is the first Thomistic claim which the Grisez school would debate.

Their second departure from the tradition of the angelic doctor concerns the unity of our last end within the purely natural order itself. For they maintain that our nature has no single ultimate goal. Rather, it has several co-ordinate goals, multiple goals, then, that are arranged in a non-hierarchical fashion. Because, they argue, such basic goods of natural living as self-integration, friendship, health, religion, knowledge of truth, appreciation of art, skilful work or play, are incommensurable – they cannot be measured against each other by reference to some further criterion which transcends them – Thomas and his later disciples were wrong – simplistic – to say that the contemplation of God in his works is what ultimately achieves the integral fulfilment of our humanity on the level of nature. Our nature has no one goal.[10]

The contrast with Thomas here is marked. Take, for instance, these lines from the *Summa contra Gentiles*:

> All other human activities are ordered [to the contemplation of truth] as to their end and goal. For the fulness of contemplation presupposes bodily integrity, which in turn presupposes the production and use of consumer goods. One also requires respite from the turbulence of the emotions, and one attains to this through the exercise of the moral virtues and good sense. One also needs respite from external disturbances, which is the *raison d'être* of civil government and life. If we look at things aright, therefore, we see that all human activities subserve those who contemplate the truth.[11]

Were we to agree with the alternative, 'polyteleological' approach, we should, however – so Ashley contends – destroy the harmony which otherwise exists between our natural end, so understood, and the supernatural end of enjoying God as the blessed Trinity which, as we know from revelation, is actually ours. If we are to keep that harmony intact we must say that it is God himself who is the final cause of every morally good act even in the purely natural order, since it is God himself – even naturally – who is our final end. Grace is needful because, for the end to be possible, the person must be put in an adequate *condition*. Grace is not in any immediate sense the final achievement of a person's being, but it is what sets in motion the historical *entrée* of the spiritual creature to that fullness – for that can only happen through a history produced by the operation of the human subject in the condition of grace. Grace places the intelligent creature in that condition where the achievement of its being is possible. And it likewise places her in a condition of liberty where the choice of this possibility can be made.

The place of the virtues

But where do the *virtues* enter into all this? Aristotle – and in his debt to the pagan thinker here Thomas is at his most full-bloodedly Aristotelian – maintained within his natural philosophical account of the human goal that without the moral virtues disciplining our sensory appetites, feelings, emotions, we lack the necessary preparation for developing the intellectual virtues which modulate our understanding and will. And without the intellectual virtues contemplation is impossible. The setting in which Aristotle imagines that process taking place (or not taking place) is conceived in a patrician fashion, in a polis where there is not fundamental epistemic equality among people, equality of access to resources of meaning and truth. Thus Aristotle considered that those engaged in manual labour would always lack the basic human cultivation – the *paideia*, the education – necessary for acquiring the moral virtues and so would not be able to get underway in this whole project. For St Thomas, by contrast, the setting for the process, now understood as simultaneously natural and supernatural, is the ecclesial society of medieval Christendom, where, to be sure, people did not have equality of access to education in a technical sense, but where they did enjoy such equality – through the Church – in the kind of cultivation that led at a more foundational level to human flourishing.

According to Aquinas, exclusion from the free and happy life is the result of sin, both original and personal, and the light of faith, by making possible for all and sundry without exception that supernatural knowledge of God which embraces the natural knowledge of God, also opened the door to the practice of the virtues for everyone.

Thomas, however, agrees with Aristotle that while we can come to know general moral principles by a process of reasoning,[12] assisted by a sound cultural inheritance, the use of moral reason does not by itself ensure that people will lead a truly moral life. For that we need the virtues, which are dispositions – abilities, tendencies, capacities – that help us to act in ways that contribute to our flourishing, our happiness, and ultimately, then, to our beatitude, which is happiness in, with and through God. Virtue, so Thomas declares in the *Prima Secundae*, is a 'habitus that is always for good', a disposition whereby a person acts well.

And here ethics for Thomas implies anthropology, an account of human nature as embodied in persons. Every virtue, he claims, always involves some perfecting of a human power, some power of human nature itself. This could be a sensory power, an appetite bound up with our feelings and emotions, since these require 'moral' (in Thomas's technical use of the word) virtues for their functioning well. Indeed, the unity-in-complexity of a human personality is made most manifest by the presence of true virtues in sensual appetites. Thomas rejects the Stoic doctrine that passions are alien to reason. Human passions, he holds, can share in reason and are frustrated when they fail to do so. Sense appetites cry out for rational shaping, spiritual habituating, not mere repression by the will.[13]

Or again it could be our intellect or will that needs attending to. Thomas calls the virtues that perfect these powers the 'intellectual virtues', since for him our exercise of will is always that of an intellectual animal that seeks things out under the aspect of the good – even if we mislocate where the good for man is. Of the moral virtues the most important – the cardinal, literally the 'hinge' virtues – are: justice, which concerns our ability to deal rightly with others; temperance, which concerns our being subject to physical desires; and courage, which concerns our fear of danger, and, at the limit, death; as well as – and this is crucial to Thomas's scheme as a whole – prudence, called by Aristotle *phronesis* and by Jane Austen 'good sense'. This is the virtue whereby we recognise when and how we should bring the other moral virtues into play. Accepted by the Latin Fathers as the first of the cardinal virtues, its primacy was reinforced by such key words of the Vulgate Bible as *discernere*, *disceptatio*, *discretio*, themselves major stimuli to the asceticism of monastic teachers like Cassian, Benedict, Bernard. They found in 'discernment' the salt of the moral virtues, without which they go to waste. Treating the 'old wine as good', Thomas extended their teaching till it took on the dimensions of a Christian ethics at large.[14] Here prudence forms the bridge between the moral and the intellectual virtues because, though not a virtue of the speculative intellect, it makes possible – not least through the 'fields and spacious palaces' of memory[15] – correct judgement about what actions should be carried out if the overall good of the agent is to be secured – and so includes the operation of the strictly intellectual virtues.

The latter Thomas names as, firstly, the virtue of understanding, which deals with basic principles in knowing reality; secondly, the virtue of 'science' which concerns how we use those principles so as to arrive at truth regarding the different kinds of thing there are in the world; and, finally, wisdom, which deals with the way we arrive at a true knowledge of God – vital as that is to disposing all our activities toward their final natural end.

For the sake of completeness I should add a reference to the virtue of art, found in use when we act rightly in making things – from pots and pans to Picassos, from devising a school curriculum to drawing up a constitution for the State. This virtue of art is for Thomas the close neighbour of prudence, being as it is a virtue of the practical mind.

Thomas's account of the virtuous life in the human city as a friendly *consociatio* is especially fine, and must be seen as the proper context of what is called by moderns his 'political philosophy'.

> In the vision of St Thomas, self-fulfilment, the goal of man's striving, is essentially other-directed, con-genial, co-subjective, co-relative, con-joining, co-operative, co-aptive, co-venantal, 'amical'.

In this context, constitution-making is a very secondary issue:

> The fact that [Thomas] expressed this insight in terms of a non-despotic, constitutional monarchy is far less important than the insight itself – with all its rich suggestiveness of the somehow *intrinsic* and reciprocal relationship between individual and society, and so with its potentiality for 'demythologization' and redevelopment in terms of other culture-contexts.[16]

It is in this context, then, that we must see the significant principles he underlined for civil society in an age when (as argued by Burckhardt, at least) the State as a 'work of art' was first created.

- The right of political authority to command derives from social needs in human nature as such, and is not postulated merely because of corrupt proclivities due to original sin. Law is not restricted to a criminal code; power has the positive function of encouraging human excellence as well as the negative one of checking vice.
- This authority, at least when considered abstractly, in its essential

nature, as distinct from the concrete historical form in which that nature is enacted in different epochs of human time before God, does not depend for its consistency on the sacramental community of the Church. Thomas analyses the just condominion of two 'dignities' – *sacerdotium* ('priesthood') and *regnum* or *imperium* ('kingdom' or 'empire'). He distinguishes two sets of social obligations without merging them under the direct control of either the ecclesial or the civil power.[17]

- It follows from the above that civil power is immediately concerned only with temporal affairs, though its purpose is to promote social virtue and its just commands oblige in conscience. The foremost task of government is to establish those objective conditions, principally matters of justice, that allow citizens to lead the good life. The ordinances of human law should be kept to the minimum consonant with the needs of the city. Legislators must not be fussy; laws must be sufficiently stable for subjects to know where they stand.
- Government and legislations are functions of *ars*. Sound political judgement must in some cases decide between alternatives each of which has good moral reasons in its favour, and reach a resolve by a kind of poetic freedom, not the determinism proper to deductive sciences.[18]

The moral virtues, then, unified among themselves by prudence which also links them to the intellectual virtues whether pure or applied, lead through these intellectual virtues to a life of contemplation, of enjoying God in his works – to which matters political must be subordinate. So far as this goes, that is fine, if only it actually happened! But how far does it go? Only as far as our natural finality extends. At the level of our supernatural finality – the enjoyment of the Holy Trinity – such virtues, even when including the specifically theocentric virtue of wisdom, do not suffice. Here we stand in need of virtues which will dispose us rightly toward the God who is not only the God of our creation but the God of our salvation as well.

Elevation and repair

For Thomas, two things are involved in that divine work of salvation that is made known to us not through the natural light of reason but by way of the prophetic light of revelation. Salvation entails the elevation of the entire natural order in which we live to a new supernatural end: we can call that salvation as transfiguration – our receiving that kind of wholeness, integrity, health that go with becoming transformed creatures. Salvation also entails the applying of medication to whatever in our natural condition needs doctoring: we can call that salvation as redemption, our receiving back the sort of wholeness, integrity, health that befits creatures of God who are (in this formal perspective, then) not so much transformed as healed. For Thomas, saving grace is both *gratia elevans*, grace that raises (from the natural level to a level beyond it) and *gratia sanans*, grace that heals (heals, namely, the wounds of created human nature).

So in the supernatural context we are going to need two kinds of virtue corresponding to elevating grace and healing grace. We need virtues that directly dispose us toward the God of our salvation in not just his medicinal but also his further, transfiguring capacity in our regard. And here, Thomas singles out the virtues of faith, hope and charity, taking his cue from St Paul's Corinthian correspondence as well as the tradition of the Latin Fathers and subsequent divines. It is because faith, hope and charity dispose us directly towards the God of salvation as not only healer but transformer of our condition that Aquinas calls them 'theological' virtues, virtues that create an immediate bond with God. Such is their importance that Thomas felt able to structure his *précis* of the faith, the *Compendium theologiae*, by reference to them. He wrote in the preamble:

> The apostle taught that the whole perfection of this present life consists in faith, hope and charity, as in certain brief headings outlining our salvation: 'Now, there remain faith, hope and charity' [1 Cor. 13:13]. These are the three virtues, as St Augustine says, by which God is to be worshipped [*De doctrina christiana*, I. 35]. Wherefore my dearest son Reginald, receive

from my hands this compendious treatise on Christian teaching to keep continually before your eyes. My whole endeavour in the present work is taken up with these three virtues. I shall treat first of faith, then of hope and lastly of charity. This is the apostle's arrangement which, for that matter, right reason imposes. Love cannot be rightly ordered unless the proper goal of our hope is established; nor can there be any hope if knowledge of the truth is lacking. Therefore the first thing necessary is faith, by which you may come to a knowledge of the truth. Secondly, hope is necessary, that your intention may be fixed in the right end. Thirdly, love is necessary, that your affections may be perfectly put in order.

But in addition we need virtues that augment those natural virtues which we should have acquired simply by living in the world around us but which, in the state of sin, we do not so readily acquire in point of fact. We need those virtues augmented in a form fitting to people who are morally ill and need healing from God. In other words, we need 'infused' and not merely acquired or learned versions of the natural virtues, because experience has shown we do not always acquire, we do not always learn. On both counts, we need to receive resources for good living – for both natural living and supernatural living – from the grace of God.

Grace and sin

The grace of God, as it enters on the scene, profoundly modifies the Aristotelian picture. Of course, simply to state what the actual end of man now is (even while prescinding from the virtues as ways to attain that supreme good) requires some reference to grace. The revelation of our final end as the supernatural enjoyment of God the Trinity is already in itself the work of divine grace. But Thomas could hardly confine grace to simply the disclosure, by the *lumen propheticum* to the prophets and apostles, and the *lumen fidei* to the members of the Church built thereon, of our supernatural ultimate end. Over and above the *lumen gratiae*, if we are to attain to that supernatural end, and the natural end which is now its instrument, we have need of grace to penetrate and affect our being, both as individuals and as a corporate body.

It is, clearly, far from the case that human life in this world as we now experience it consists in an unbroken process of acquiring moral and intellectual virtue, all directed towards not only the natural enjoyment of God in his creation but the supernatural enjoyment of the Trinity, and at all points assisted by the helpful efforts of society and its members. Against the background of the true finality of human living, we have to say that human beings, individually and corporately, are in a condition of disorientation and discord. This disorientation and discord can only be grasped philosophically when we see them as the privation of an antecedent state of integration, just as they can only be grasped theologically when we see them as our loss of the original creation relationship with God, that original justice or righteousness the loss of which we call 'original sin'. It is no longer the case that our intellect is subject to God, nor the lower powers of the soul to the intellect, nor the body to the soul.[19]

On the personal level, it is the unruliness of our feelings that brings this home to us. According to Thomas, our appetite for sense objects is not only capable of but positively calls out for the controlling care of reason. Appetite is not simply to be repressed by the action of the will, for owing to the nature of the human being as a complex unity of which intellect is the superordinate function, our passions are frustrated unless they share in rationality.[20] Our appetites are perfected in their human quality by finding contentment in their own proper scope – by loving limited objects for neither more nor less than what those objects are worth. And owing to original sin, ratified by personal sin, this cannot happen without the healing of these powers by the infused moral virtues, while the fact that we are now placed within a supernatural order where such virtues are called into play in order to subserve a more-than-natural goal means that the theological virtues are likewise relevant to how our emotions function in a Christian sensibility. Thus for instance, we may need fortitude not just to withstand giving way to self-pity in sickness but in order, if called upon, to die for the faith of the Gospel as carried by the Church.

On the corporate level, the breakdown of the ordered unity

which should characterise human life is most notable for Thomas in injustice which he discusses in a thoroughly realistic way, touching on such topics as discrimination, homicide, physical injury to the person, theft, robbery with violence, unjust judgement, slander, calumny, detraction, ridicule, fraud. As this catalogue of failures in the virtue of justice indicates, injustice – differently from what much modern political theology insinuates – is not only a matter of the actions of a community relating through its government towards the members of that community (what Thomas calls 'distributive justice'). It also concerns the actions of one member of that community towards another one ('commutative justice'), and of one member towards all the rest ('legal justice').

Thomas would not undervalue the improvement that can be effected when, through the exercise of the virtue of justice, some people manage to change what would now be called the 'structures' of society so as to rectify such behaviour externally. But he would argue that, inasmuch as our behaviour stems from our emotions, it cannot in fact be rectified without the practice by each individual of the moral virtues at large, since it is their business to bring our passions into alignment with the good. Most fundamentally, what needs to be decisively affected by grace is our most basic passional drive, which for Thomas, as for Augustine, is *amor*, a 'love'-drive, but one that is specific to man as a rational creature. It is the key feature of this love-drive that it tends to ever greater comprehensiveness – both exteriorly, in the sense of loving human beings more widely and all-embracingly, and interiorly, in the sense of an increasing pacification and rectification of our discordant and disoriented feelings. But this love-drive of the rational creature with its tendency toward universality constitutes, Aquinas maintains, an instinct – his own word, *instinctus* – for a final beatitude which can be found only in God.[21] As the final goal of this process of universalisation, God is the implicit end of our social relations just as much as he is the tacit goal of our personal fulfilment.

The ontology of grace

For Thomism, grace is divine movement, and the divine dis-posing of created being.[22] It is the divine *energeia* enabling the creature not only to perceive (as revelation) but to do (as salvifically relevant action) what of itself it could neither do nor perceive. Grace has an ontology because it causes the being of the person to be disposed in a new way, thanks to a

> special dilection, according to which God draws the rational creature to a participation of the divine good above the con-dition of nature . . . a dilection by which God wills concretely and simply that eternal good for the creature that is none other than himself.[23]

What is thus infused is more than a virtue, it is the principle of deployment of the entire organism of the supernatural life. Made interior to the soul's essence, grace is ontologically prior not only to virtue but to the very powers of souls themselves.[24] While for Thomas the being of a creature – any creature – is as such a participation in the divine *esse*, what we are speaking of here is a sharing in the divine *nature* – this is the unique privilege of the spiritual creature in a state of grace.

The consequence of grace's being is our 'pneumatic' existence: life in the Holy Spirit. For Thomas, the distinctive characteristic of Christianity is a new inward principle or power active within us. He defines this principle or power as the grace of the Holy Spirit given through faith in Christ. In comparison, the written text of the New Testament is secondary – as indeed is the Gospel's oral procla-mation. The point of evangelical writing and preaching is either to prepare us to receive the Holy Spirit or to show us how his grace should be utilised in acting. No fuller set of spiritual responsibilities can be envisaged this side of heaven than those brought by the Spirit in the mode of his coming at Easter and Pentecost, fulfilling the Old Covenant and placing us in right relation with God. Objec-tively heavy, they are subjectively light since the grace of the Spirit manifests itself by faith working through love, and love makes light. Though the inner Kingdom of the Spirit has its corporate context, in the sacramental life of the Church and the deeds of love that must flow from it (and supernaturally tend to do so), pneumatic existence has its energising centre within.

Grace and freedom

Human nature is so wounded by sin that the will must be healed by grace even to attain the good that belongs to natural happiness, never mind the supernatural good that goes with beatitude. When a person tries to emerge from sinfulness he does so by a decision which is really his own yet at the same time is made possible by the ground-preparing grace of God itself. (Thomas's shocked discovery of the fence-straddling of the Semi-Pelagians ever after inoculated him against shilly-shallying on this point.) The upshot is justification, the victorious grace of the Spirit setting us right with God: forgiveness of sins, union with the Father. Subjectively, this appears as faith working through love; objectively, it is God converting us to himself. The transformation is instantaneous, no matter how long prepared. In this moment we become adopted sons to whom the inheritance of heaven belongs by right. It is meant to be an abiding possession of the Christian, qualifying – indeed, transfiguring – the soul that receives it. Just as the seed of a tree has enough potency to make one day the whole tree, so in our present condition the grace of the Spirit is equal in power to the grace of glory, to what will (unless we apostatise in mind, heart or behaviour) bring us finally before God.

So the grace of God is God in action and the change that makes in us. Our part is first to consent (that is, not, negatively, to withhold consent) and then, on the basis of grace appropriated, to share in forwarding the gracious life.

Amor Dei, writes Thomas, *est infundens et creans bonitatem in rebus*: the love of God infuses and creates goodness in things.[25] To act well as Christians is to let the primary action of God spread out in us the divine being, the divine life.

The place of charity

What this means for Thomas is that the virtues which were once united on the level of prudence alone now – in the supernatural context – need unification at a higher level. In his theology it is the task of charity to achieve this. For Aquinas, as for Paul, charity enjoys pre-eminence when compared with both faith and hope, its sisters. Faith and hope, considered as theological virtues, enable us to reach God as, respectively, the source of the knowledge given us in revelation and the provider of that ultimate gift which the Gospel promises hold out to us: the life everlasting. Charity, however, enables us to attain God even now as he is in himself, making us rest in God without looking for further reward. Such enjoyment of God is our chief and ultimate end, which is why, without charity, no act can be fully good. Without charity an action lacks due reference to this final goal of our being.

Though Thomas is at his most theocentric in his account of charity, he does not define it in such a way as to exclude the Christian love of neighbour from its ambit. Far from it! Arguing that charity can be understood on the model of companionate friendship, with God as the Friend *par excellence*, loved for his own sake in a common life project, Thomas points out how, for the sake of a friend, we typically also love, as he puts it:

> Those belonging to him, be they children, servants or anyone connected with him at all, even if they hurt or hate us, so much do we love him.[26]

Charity, accordingly, loves all those whom God loves for God's sake, even hardened sinners, though it loves more still, Thomas would add, the saints in whom God has communicated his beatitude, since in them more of the divine life is invested for us to share.

Thomas holds that charity comes to be in us as a new form conferred on our will, enabling the love the Spirit spreads abroad in our hearts as healing and elevating grace in our justification and sanctification to be really ours – so that we are not just passive recipients of divine charity or mere channels of it but are active mediators of it. Since it is a kind of love, the locus of charity will be the will, but because for Aquinas the will has an affinity with reason – it is 'rational appetite' – charity is not to be counterposed to the virtues that have their seat in the mind. It differs from such virtues in being ruled not by human reason but by a higher rationality, the wisdom of God.

Seated in the will as a divine gift in human form, charity can grow, but only in the sense that it can become that much more deeply rooted in our will. It can gain a deeper hold on us, thus bringing it about that our soul becomes more like the Spirit who is *Amor*, 'Love', in God himself. In this life, there can be no limit to such growth of charity. If we think of the specific form of charity, it is a sharing in the infinite charity that is the Holy Spirit. If we think of what causes charity to grow, it is God himself with his infinite power. And if we think of the subject of charity, namely our will, there too development can be endless, owing to the will's capacity to increase its range and strength by willing its own capacity to will. To increase charity is to increase the capacity of charity for further growth. In all other loves, writes Thomas, it is right to ask after the just measure by reference to which we can love too little or too much. With charity there can be no question of too much. 'The more God is loved so much the better is the love.'[27]

For Thomas such love generates four effects: joy, because of the lover's awareness of the unchangeableness of God's goodness; peace, because the concord of those united in charity harmonises their desires and appetites in the good; mercy, because when the friendship which is charity loves others as friends for the sake of the primordial Friend, God, we grieve for their misfortunes as though they were our own; beneficence, since, as friendship always entails willing the friend's good, the actions that flow from charity will include deeds of goodness.

Here the disorientation and discord which afflicted both the inner city of the soul in the state of sin and the outer city of the social commonwealth find their remedy, and the natural powers that the life of each expresses are raised up beyond themselves in a way possible through divine agency alone.

Natural love already loves God above all things since in the natural order of things that is where God ranks; and in charity we love our friend's world because we love him [God], and that means loving ourselves and our fellows as ourselves and not only as *we* love ourselves but as *he* does.[28]

Whether at the level of the passions or of the will, love stands revealed as rooted ontologically in God as its first co-subject as well as author, and only derivatively in ourselves. In the dispensation of grace, charity, joining us to God, stands forth as the all-shaping virtue.

8.
Christ, Church, Sacraments

A theology of history

The regime of charity can only be ours, though, creatures subject to radical evil as we are, by dint of divine re-creating. The pedagogy of the Hebrew Bible, the instructive leading of the God of Israel, points to a new covenant between the Creator and fallen humankind, whose agent will be, by amazing grace, at once a saving presence of God in person – Emmanuel – and the provision of a perfect human instrument of that presence, the 'anointed one' of Jewry's expectation. Though Thomas did not possess the quantity or quality of data concerning Old Testament history available to the modern exegete, he grasped the need for such data if the literal sense of the ancient Scriptures were to be respected.[1] But he also understood, along with many – but by no means all – practitioners of 'biblical theology' in the modern period that historical investigation here subserves a properly theological purpose. Judaism and Christianity are two different religions because they have two ways of understanding the Scriptures of Israel. The Christian way sees the testimony of those Scriptures to the divine revelatory activity among the Jews as oriented to its fulfilment in the Gospel. What this means in specifically 'Thomasian' terms is that Israel is divinely drawn towards the constitution of a community of charity in and through the supernaturally intimate union of God with man in Jesus Christ.[2] It is via the epoch of Torah, the *tempus Legis* or 'time of law' that humankind is brought by God from the 'time of nature' – deeply wounded nature, ontologically disordered nature – to the 'time of grace'. Where, as with Thomas, the Incarnation of the Word is understood as the key event in making possible the movement of creation to its own perfection, a 'theology of history' just has to be implied.[3]

Christ

We saw in Chapters 3, 4 and 5 how for Thomas creation begins with the Trinity. It is the Trinity – and not some undifferentiated Godhead – that is the Creator. The *exitus* of the divine Persons of Son and Spirit in their unity of essence with the Father is the cause of the *exitus* of creatures in their diversity of essence from the Father. What happens with the Incarnation, for Thomas, is that God, in an utterly free fashion, assumes a human nature into the unity of one of these Persons, the Person of the consubstantial Son. Which is to say, at one level, the level of the history of doctrine, that Aquinas is a Nicene Christian whose interpretation of the teaching offered by the Fathers at that assembly is that of the great Tradition. It is also to say, in terms of his own theology, that for Thomas the intelligibility of the Incarnation is rooted in speculation about, or contemplation of, the triune God. To which we must add that the Incarnation also requires a doctrine of creation, without which the human nature assumed cannot be theologically described. So the dogma of the Trinity and the doctrine of creation are two poles between which his theology of the Word incarnate moves. It is for this reason that we typically find Thomas dealing with Christology in third place – in the third book of the *Scriptum super Sententiis*, in the *Tertia Pars* of the *Summa theologiae* – after dealing, then, with the Trinity and the created world, and notably within the latter, with humankind. And that is so even though he cannot speak about God the Son in his Triadology, nor about evangelical ethics in his theological anthropology and moral theology without anticipating *something* of what he will say in his Christology proper.

Before embarking on his formal Christology, Thomas has already shown – in the 'Writing on the *Sentences*' at greater length than in the *Summa theologiae* – that the Word is the *raison d'être* of creatures insofar as creatures proceed from God by way of understanding: the Father utters all the things that are by his 'word' which is also his 'art'. And similarly he explained how the *raison d'être* of creatures can also be said to be the Holy Spirit inasmuch as creatures proceed from God's wholly free will: God gives loving existence to the things that are by the Holy Spirit. But these eternal processions in God will not suffice to show how we are to return, enriched by our experience of the created order, to our Alpha, our Beginning, the Father, now approached in this new context of our destiny as our Omega, our End. Of course, the Son and the Spirit whose being and activity condition our coming forth from God will have to be involved in our return to him, since they are the enduring principles of our continued existence, our being sustained in existence by God. But the resources they cause us to have by creation, the natural goods that they give, are not enough to carry fallen creatures to an end situated in the supernatural order. Hence the need for the temporal and not simply the eternal processions of Spirit and Son – the need, that is, for 'missions', 'sendings' of Spirit and Son in history. We have need of their presence and action in our lives in a new way.

What, for Thomas, we have to do with in Christology is the temporal or visible mission of the Son. The Incarnation is its coming about in time that a human nature, involving the existing of a human being, was assumed by a divine Person who remained unaltered in his divine nature. As Thomas explains, with the Annunciation the Son is not sent to dwell in man in an invisible manner, as is the case with his simple presence by grace, but in a visible manner, for now he is actually to become man as well. The Greek Fathers chiefly responsible for the development of Christological doctrine had spoken of the divine and human *ousiai* of the Word incarnate. It is sometimes suggested that we cannot do justice to the dynamic quality of the 'Christ-event' if we restrict ourselves to those 'static' terms.[4] But at Thomas's hands the language of the 'natures' is altogether dynamic, since for him nature is the essence of a thing as directed to its distinctive activity, for no reality lacks its specific operation.[5]

Thomas offers an entirely orthodox interpretation of Chalcedonian faith:

Divinised in Jesus Christ, man remains man; made flesh in

Jesus Christ, the Word of God remains God without any alteration.[6]

Nature is what informs each reality according to its specific difference.[7] That is why it cannot be the case that in Christ divine and human natures form a sort of hybrid, by way of fusion; nor can one be said to absorb the other. But nature is not all there is to a reality. We do not, after all, say that this particular man *is* his humanity. There is always a *subject* (*suppositum*, or in the case of a rational creature, *persona*) which, for Thomas, is 'the whole that has the nature as its proper formal and perfective part'.[8] It is because everything that belongs to someone, be it by virtue of his nature or not, is united to him in his person that the human nature of Christ, if united to the divine Word at all, must be *personally* so united. Though the nature assumed by the Word is not human nature in general but individualised human nature (a stress Thomas borrowed from John Damascene), it does not exist of itself but in the Word's own person.[9] In Cyril of Alexandria's famous phrase, there is a hypostatic union.[10] The grace of union joining the Word to the human of Christ is 'nothing other than this personal being given gratuitously to human nature in the person of the Word'.[11]

Reference to 'being' there should alert us to something novel. What, in fact, Aquinas adds to the orthodox interpretation of the Chalcedonian Formula is his own metaphysics of being. As he presents things, the *esse personale* of the Son, the personal act of being by which the second Person of the Godhead exists, comes to be the *esse personale* of a human being as well.[12] As the Swedish Thomist scholar Per Erik Persson sums up:

> The uniqueness of Christ is thus that the *esse* of the pre-existent divine Word becomes the act through which, from a particular moment of time, a human nature also exists in union with this Word . . . We may speak of God's presence in Christ as a *missio visibilis* precisely because a fully human nature possessing body and soul was united to God in the hypostatic union. Through the mediation of the soul even the body of Christ co-exists with the eternal *esse* of the second person of the Godhead.[13]

Such is the intimacy of this union that the way Christ's human nature exists is itself divine – this is the nugget of truth in Monophysitism. But on the other hand, and here we come to the nugget of truth in Nestorianism:

> *Esse est personae subsistentia* [this being is the subsistence of a person], and since it is therefore really distinct from human nature, the latter remains at every point a human and created nature, despite its union with one of the persons of the Godhead and in spite of the fact that it was assumed to subsist in the eternal and uncreated *esse* of the Son.[14]

Though for Thomas the Incarnation is utterly real – it is not a fancy way of speaking about the working of grace in the man Jesus – nonetheless it involves no change in God, no process of any kind. The change concerned takes place in a particular part of the creation which begins to enjoy a new and unique relation to the transcendent First Cause, the triune God. To say that the Father sends the Son into the world is to say that an *effectus temporalis* begins at a certain moment in history to accompany the Son's eternal procession from the Father and from then on will never cease to do so.

It is, Thomas thinks, entirely congruent with the hypostatic specificity of the Son within the Godhead that it was this divine Person and no other who in that way became incarnate. And this for two reasons related to those distinct healing and elevating aspects of the divine saving activity we explored in the last Chapter. First, just as a craftsman repairs damage in something he has made by reference to the idea of the thing which is in him, his creative conception of it, so it is fitting that God repairs humanity by means of the Son who is humanity's exemplar. And secondly, since those who are to reach through Christ their supernatural goal in God receive a heavenly inheritance fitting only to sons, it is appropriate that 'through him who is a Son by nature we share by adoption in a likeness to his Sonship'.[15]

The rationale of the Incarnation

In later centuries, conflict between the Thomism of the Dominicans and the (rather less official) Scotism of many Franciscans led Thomas's brethren to narrow somewhat his account of the purpose or purposes of the Incarnation. His discussion of the Incarnation's *rationes convenientiae*, the reasons for thinking it fitting that there should have been an Incarnation at all, by no means wholly exclude the possibility that its purposes went beyond simply repair of the damage done by sin.

Though in the *Summa theologiae* Thomas stresses that reparation is indeed the clearest explanation of the matter the New Testament offers, and so must be central to what we say on the topic, in the *Summa contra Gentiles* he had taken a wider view. There he suggests that the Incarnation happened so as to give mankind the possibility of seeing God. He cites in this connection the wonderful Nativity Preface of the Roman liturgy which prays that through love of what is seen we may be swept up to love of what is unseen. Thus the purpose of the Incarnation was to revive in human beings hope for their own beatitude, their own happiness in, with, and through God. In the Great *Summa* – and the timing of the *Tertia Pars* at the end of his life suggests that this must be his maturest thought – Thomas emphasises the *concrete manner* in which the Incarnation did this.

The Son of God gave man and all creation a model, at once exemplary and reparatory, to be followed in the crisis of created liberty – that is, the fallen state. Jesus made the choice of our true destiny in perfect conformity of his human will with the divine. 'For the joy that was set before him he endured the Cross' (Heb. 12:2). After his discovery of the anti-Monothelite Council, Constantinople III, Thomas, like Maximus the Confessor before him, was passionately insistent on the reality of Christ's human will.[16]

The grace of union

As we have seen, the Incarnation is more than the union of a creature with God *secundum gratiam*, 'according to grace'. Uniquely, it is a union *secundum esse*, 'according to being' – in Thomas's technical sense of the word, meaning: a union brought about in terms of the very act by which God and the creature exist. (This is, however, not to deny that Christ was in a singular way graced, for the effect of the union *secundum esse* is precisely an unheard-of outflow of grace onto the humanity of Jesus, first of all, but then, in dependence on him, into the humanity of all those who are to be redeemed.) Drawing inspiration from, in particular, John Damascene, Thomas so presents the distinction of person and nature in Christ as to show him endowed with a perfectly individualised human nature that is not, however, an hypostasis.[17] Since person and nature are not on the same level, there is nothing less in a human nature without a human suppositum than there is in a nature possessed by such.

Indeed, the free and loving, and in that sense gracious act whereby God has united the humanity of Christ to the Word – the *gratia unionis* – has as its consequence the fullest possible perfecting – natural and supernatural – of that humanity, for, as we saw in the last Chapter, it is not only the case that human nature can be perfected as nature since, being as it is *capax Dei*, our humanity can also attain through grace that further perfection which lies far beyond its own capacities. All this came about 'for us men and for our salvation'. The life of Christ can be our salvation history because God has filled and super-filled the being of Christ with graces, graces meant not least to overflow from the Church's Head to the Church's members.

The plenitude of grace which belongs to the humanity of Christ by virtue of the hypostatic union exists not only as personal, habitual grace in its maximal form (entailing so full a perception of the realities of faith and so ample an enjoyment of God that the tissue of faith, hope and charity, which makes up in Christians the life of the theological virtues, exists in Jesus as charity alone). His fullness of grace takes the further form of 'capital' grace, meaning: the grace of Christ as *caput*, 'head', of the Church. 'From his fullness', so the Johannine Prologue has it, 'we have all received, grace upon grace' (John 1:16). God alone is the source of grace but grace reaches us via the mediation of Christ and so bears his imprint. Though Thomas is far from denying the importance of the imitation of Christ, learning from not only his words but also, and more especially, his deeds, how to live ('Christ's action was our instruction'; Aquinas cites this adage of the fifth-century Cassiodorus), his emphasis lies not on the imitation of Christ so much as on Christ's role in our deification – that way of under-standing grace often presented in textbook histories of doctrine as peculiarly Eastern and Orthodox but which in fact puts in a major appearance in Thomas's Western and Catholic teaching.[18] What God is by substance is to be realised in the mode of accident in the soul that shares in the divine Goodness, for if we are really to be conformed to the First-born Son, and so be in God's image and likeness, we shall need not only healing grace but also, and yet more radically, elevating grace.

Thomas speaks of the humanity of Christ as playing its pre-destined mediatorial role in our deification in what he calls an instrumental way, but, as time goes on, he stresses more and more that this instrument is not like a tool used by God – like a pen or a pair of secateurs. Nor is it even just a 'conjoined' instrument, as the hand or the leg for a human being, without further qualifying nuance. For Christ's humanity is itself not only animated but also free. It does not just pass on the divine action like a conduit, a canal. It has its own action, issuing from its own liberty, as well as that which derives from the principal agent, God himself.[19] And the upshot is that the grace of the New Covenant bears a 'Christic' character.

Christ in his mysteries

But how does Christ manifest the grace that is not only God's but also his in a salvific manner? Thomas's account emphasises the way Christ expresses the fullness of grace which was his as our Head through a series of actions which in some sense – in quite what sense is disputed by interpreters – *endure* for our salvation. One of those actions, or sets of actions, his Passion and Death, was crucial (even literally so, since it took the form of crucifixion!). But none of the keynote actions of the Word incarnate described in the Gospels, from Annunciation to Ascension, is without significance in this regard.

For Thomas, those actions fall into four categories. There is, first, the Word incarnate's *entry into the world* – which includes Jesus's conception (and there is where we find Thomas's theology of our Lady; he has no other Mariology than a theology of the divine motherhood), Jesus's Nativity and its manifestation in the Epiphany as well as his Circumcision, all culminating in the Baptism of Christ. Next, there is his *life on earth*, which more or less corresponds to what we call the public ministry, the teaching and miracle-working activity of the Saviour, though this is framed, on Thomas's version, by his Temptations at one end, his Transfiguration at the other. Thirdly, there is Christ's *'exitus' from the world and return to the Father*, comprising his Passion, Death, Burial and Descent into hell. Lastly, there is his *exaltation*, made up for Aquinas of four moments – the Resurrection, Ascension, Session or 'seating' at the Father's right hand and, finally, his being given the power to judge (Thomas's equivalent to the 'kingship' of Christ). Each and every one of the actions which Christ carried out as expressions of his mission were and are of saving efficacy for us.

Thomas did not think it enough simply to offer an account of the metaphysics of the hypostatic union – the constitution of the single Person of the Word incarnate in his two natures – as the means whereby the Incarnation was set in motion and leave it at that. Rather, the Incarnation makes possible the acts which the Word incarnate posits for our salvation, posits by not only his divine but also his human volition. For Thomas, these mysteries have an abiding impact on those who are to receive the Christic grace of the healing and elevation of their nature: our rejoining our first principle now approached as our last end.

But just what kind of 'abiding impact'? Surely, considered as past actions, these events are over and done with? Unlike the in-fluential early-twentieth-century Benedictine theologian of the Liturgy, Odo Casel, Thomas does not go so far as to say that Christ's actions, as the actions of one who was God, not only occur in time but also fall outside it. The terse style of what Thomas *does* say, however, has meant that his interpreters, abhorring a vacuum on this topic, have perforce rushed to fill it. One suggestion is that, since any effect produced by an instrumental cause (in this case the humanity of Christ) will be conditioned by the nature of the principal cause (in this case God), we are dealing here with past actions which can be so supported by the divine power as to possess a *continuing* instrumental effect. The Swiss Thomist Cardinal Charles Journet initiated an astronomical comparison. Take the analogy of light from an actually existing but invisible star reaching the earth through refraction from some planet which itself no longer exists.[20] Just so, the Baptism of Christ, say, or his Transfiguration are not still happening, and yet the grace of God in Christ reaches me in a form that is profoundly affected by those events. Père Congar, however, prefers to speak of what he calls

> the mysteries lived out by the Saviour [remaining] in his glorified humanity as a disposition of eternal value, properly equipped to produce in us the saving effects which correspond to each of those mysteries.[21]

Here, then, the events in question are eternalised as permanent dispositions in the soul of the God-man, salvation's instrumental cause.

Naturally, pride of place belongs in this context to the Passion, Death and Resurrection of Christ. But Thomas's soteriology is not simply staurological, a matter of the Cross, or even purely Paschal, a matter of the Cross and Resurrection together. All of the *acta et passa Christi in carnae*, everything Christ did and underwent in the flesh, is relevant to the way God saves us.

The mission of the Son, then – one with, but not the same thing as, his eternal procession from the Father (the doctrines of the economic and immanent Trinity are unified but not identical) – finds its expression in the mysteries of the life of Christ, which mysteries extend to our lives too, for when those lives are considered lives of Christian grace, these mysteries can be said to determine and structure them.[22] As the German Thomist scholar Gerd Lohaus puts it, the *gratia unionis* in Christ (the grace of the hypostatic union) entails, since Christ is Head of the new humanity in the Church, a *unio gratiae*, 'union of grace' for us – a union, namely, with God in Christ via his mysteries.

> If the grace of the human being Jesus is the being united of his human nature with the eternal Son of God in fulness, so our being graced is our being bound up with Christ as a participation in his likeness to God.[23]

To use more Scholastic categories, the work of Christ is not just the efficient cause of grace, it is also grace's exemplar cause. Grace in us takes the form of a real participation in the engraced being of Christ, a sharing in that being through an indrawing into the form of his mysteries.

The Church and her sacraments

Were we now to ask, By what media – concretely, visibly – does the capital grace of Christ, of which the mysteries provide the inner form, come to us?, then we should be raising the topics of the Church and her sacraments.

It is rather disconcerting that Thomas, unlike a modern Catholic dogmatician, does not at this point move first into an account of the Church of Christ, the Church that flows from the missions of Son and Spirit in the era after Easter-Pentecost, but instead turns directly to speak of the ritual sacraments.

St Thomas never devoted any treatise or even part treatise to the topic of ecclesiology. Not a single question of the *Summa theologiae* deals *ex professo* with the Church. However, if Thomas were confronted with this fact he would surely have replied that all the elements necessary for ecclesiology can be found in his work. As we saw when looking at the question of revelation in Thomas – and notably at the role of the pope in adjudicating disputed questions from Scripture, it is not as though he has a low doctrine of the Church! But what sort of doctrine *does* he have? The Church in Thomas's corpus is first, human life oriented to God in Christ – and hence the ark of salvation, the gathering-place of all men of good will whom grace has set on the road to God. Secondly, the Church is for him the corporate possessing of God in Christ – and hence the commencement of the heavenly city in faith and hope: only a commencement it is true, and yet there is found in her life a real enjoying of God.[24]

Thomas's key term for the Church is *congregatio fidelium*, 'the congregation of the faithful', but owing to his high view of faith this option has exalted consequences. For Thomas faith, so we noted, is the beginning of glory. It is a disposition or capacity that has no rationale other than God himself considered as uncreated Truth, the God who plants in us, precisely by faith, the seeds of his own self-knowledge, seeds which will come to flower in the face-to-face vision of him in heaven. Thomas's view of the Church as *congregatio fidelium* leads him to treat her as homogeneous with the universal or cosmic assembly of the elect, those who will see God – including even the elect angels. Angels and men are ordered alike to the same end: the glory of enjoying God. So the Church's mystical body consists not of humans alone but also of angels: Christ is the Head of this entire multitude, the whole caboodle.[25]

Secundum statum viae, in her pilgrim condition, the Church is the *congregatio fidelium*; but *secundum statum patriae*, in her heavenly homeland, she is the *congregatio comprehendentium*, the 'assembly of those who understand', who lay intellectual hold on, God himself.

Inasmuch as the Church is a wayfaring Church, however, she cannot be a purely spiritual reality. She must exist in the conditions of incarnation, by a regime of embodiment, where spiritual gifts are communicated and exercised in both corporate and corporeal forms. Only this will serve the needs of humans as embodied creatures still learning through the senses. On earth, the *congregatio* exists as a *populus* – which implies, as Congar showed in his studies of Thomas's ecclesiology, a body with authority and organisation, law and discipline, what he terms *un emboîtement des communautés*, 'a Chinese box of communities', ranging from the parish right up to the universal Church and with a multiplicity of different members rendering various services to each other.[26] The relation between *congregatio fidelium* and *populus christianus* in St Thomas has aptly been compared with the duo of terms used by the influential nineteenth-century ecclesiologist Friedrich Pilgram for the same bipolarity in the Church's make-up. She is a communion in the form of a society, a *koinonia* taking the form of a *politeia*. She is attached to her Head by a twofold connection: the invisible influx of his grace and the visible hierarchy whose ministerial acts are signs of that gracious 'flow'. *Decor Ecclesiae principaliter in interior-ibus consistit*: the Church's beauty is chiefly within.[27] Still, her 'powers' (note the 'political' term) are needed in various ways to prepare souls for the Eucharist: the centre on which the sacraments converge,[28] and whose *res* or ultimate reality is the unity of the mystical body.[29] Exterior ecclesial acts are required for manifesting and supporting that interior life and worship in which her beauty resides.

But what for Thomas joins together *via* and *patria*, the historical and the eschatological aspects of the Church? The answer is: the divine missions, for the Church can also be described as God's saving and divinising humanity by the mystery of Christ. She is the mediation of Christ's capital grace, and so the sub-mediation of the Mediator in his mysteries.

For the question also arises, How are we to be united to the saving causality of the mysteries of the life of Christ? And Thomas's answer to *this* is, By faith and the sacraments of faith, a frequently encountered formula in his work. It is on faith and the sacraments of faith that the Church is founded. That twofold basis corresponds well enough to the double-sided ministry of Christ who worked for our salvation *per modum doctrinae*, 'in the mode of teaching', but also *per modum operationis*, 'in the mode of action'. Now for the communication of faith and the celebration of the sacraments of faith ministers are needed. For Thomas such ministers act *in persona Christi*, playing Christ's part or role on the visible, public stage of the Church. As a visible enterprise the Church is a body structured by the apostolic ministry of Word and sacraments. Though Thomas stresses that this ministry is that of a *dispensator*, a 'dispenser' whose task is to give things, not that of a *dominus*, whose job is to hold onto them, he nonetheless maintains that, precisely as the authorised dispensers of Word and sacraments, the ordained ministry enjoys an eschatological efficacy, opening the gates of heaven.

Thomas characterises the time of the Church, between Easter

and the Parousia, as the time when the cause of all the ultimate gifts of God – what he calls 'heavenly' goods, the good things of our final intended destiny – has already been put in place. It has already become operative through the redemption won by Christ. But also defining of the Church's time is the fact that this cause has not yet brought forth all its effects, its fruits. The time of the Church is an epoch when the grace of the divine life is already being conferred, but only by a regime of sensuous signs, through a world of sacraments. As he puts it in the 'Writing on the *Sentences*', citing Denys the Areopagite's *On the Ecclesiastical Hierarchy*:

> The status of the New Law is intermediate between that of the Old Law and that of the heavenly fatherland. And therefore those things which pertain to the New Law are both truth when compared with the signs of the Old Law and also figures when compared with the manifest and full knowledge of the truth which will be in the fatherland. And thus it is still appropriate that in the New Law some figures would remain; but in the fatherland there will be a plenary perception of the truth, and all figures will cease [30]

In the *Summa theologiae* – by the time, then, of his mature writing – Thomas will define sacraments as at once signs and causes.[31] They are sensuous signs of invisible realities whereby man is rendered holy. Along the lines of this general definition, he is happy to speak not only about sacraments of the Old Law, the Jewish ceremonial observance, which was a commonplace in medieval assessment of Hebrew religion, but also – and this was more unusual – about sacraments of the law of nature, rites and gestures in which the human instinct for beatitude came to expression even under paganism. The 'sacraments' of the Old Law and those of the law of nature resemble the sacraments of the New Law inasmuch as they too depend on the principle that no saving efficacy is possible except by way of the one Mediator between God and man, Jesus Christ. As Aquinas remarks, after sin no one can be made holy except through Christ. But if God could give grace in view of the overflowing merits of Christ on the occasion of such Jewish and even pagan 'sacraments', then what is the difference between them and the sacraments of the Church? The difference is,

Thomas explains, that the sacraments of the New Law really are in their own right – by the institution of Christ – instrumental causes of grace. They bring it about that grace comes to Fred or Margaret in this or that respect, even though their instrumentality is only that of 'separated' instruments, not that of a 'conjoined' instrument as is the sacred humanity of the Logos. The sacraments are like the felt pen used at the whiteboard, rather than the hand that holds it, and yet the felt pen truly writes.

At the time when he produced his 'Writing on the *Sentences*', Thomas was sufficiently impressed by Peter Lombard, the Master of the *Sentences*, to suppose that the context in which these sacraments are set to work is that of *gratia sanans*, healing grace, for Lombard had argued that the sacraments are essentially medicines which Christ applies to wounded humanity. But by the time he wrote the *Summa theologiae*, Thomas had gone beyond this, ascribing to the sacraments their due role in the economy of transfiguration or transformation and not just that in our nature's restoration or repair. One can see that in the wonderfully lyrical texts he composed in honour of the Blessed Eucharist, both in the Office *Cibavit* and the Mass *Transiturus*, composed at the request of Pope Urban IV, and in the devotional hymn *Adoro te*, best known in English-speaking lands through its translation by Hopkins.

For Thomas, the sacraments are at one and the same time the worship we give to God and the holiness we receive. They are *protestatio fidei*, the confession or expression of faith, but precisely as such they are also, at the same time, *signa sanctificationis*, efficacious signs of our sanctification.[32] It is because they are worshipful expressions of our faith that they are liturgical, and it is because they constitute liturgical signs effective for our sanctification that they can be the media of the continuing work of the Son through the power of the Spirit. The sacraments mediate the salvation which the humanity of the exalted Lord has won for us as the conjoined instrument of the Godhead, the salvation achieved on the Cross in which all the other mysteries of the life of Christ culminate, the salvation manifested in the Resurrection.

Thomas does not, however, separate the sacraments from the wider Christian life. Though the role of the Holy Spirit in the sacraments is somewhat obscured in the *Summa*'s design by the way

Thomas places his sacramentology immediately after his Christ-ology, we have here no 'Christomonism', no unilateral, exclusive reference to Christ over against the Spirit. The same 'power', *virtus*, of the Holy Spirit which in the *Secunda Pars* Thomas describes as active in the lives of the faithful through the Gifts of the Holy Spirit – Gifts he presents as at the service of theological virtues, to perfect their functioning – this same power of the Spirit is also operative in the sacraments of the Church. As the French Dominican theologian Père Albert Patfoort wrote, there are in the *Summa theologiae* 'great zones of pneumatological concentration'.[33]

The unity of the mystical body, the aim of the Eucharist as the sun of the sacramental planetary system, is made possible through receiving from Christ's plenitude that Holy Spirit who is 'numerically identical' in Head and members as he descends from the one to the others. The 'created grace' this brings about in us (a concept that occasionally alarms Eastern Orthodox Christians) is altogether secondary though nonetheless important. It is only the principle of our *specific* – species-like – unity in redeemed human nature (as Plato and Socrates are united in human nature *tout court*). To be the *numerical* principle of our unity is far more radically unitive, for it is the unity in one trunk of numerous branches. In Thomas's theology, *reditus ad Deum* always comes under the rubric of pneu-matology for, as he emphasises, it is the same Holy Spirit who is in both Christ and ourselves.

Part Three: *The Aftermath*

9.
Thomas in History

Thomas began a *tradition* of Christian thought. So we must consider 'Thomas after Thomas' or 'the posthumous St Thomas': Thomas in history.

The rest of the Middle Ages

In University cities in the West, the response of the episcopate to Thomas's demise was not always encouraging.[1] If the rector of the Sorbonne and its masters of arts sought the custody of his remains, both physical and literary, the bishop of Paris proved less enthusiastic. The condemnation of certain theses in Christian Aristotelianism carried out at Paris by Etienne Tempier and at Oxford by Robert Kilwardby (the only Dominican to be archbishop of Canterbury) was widely interpreted as implicating the deceased divine. But within a couple of generations the flux of opinion had consolidated in a very different pattern. In 1325 at Avignon Thomas was canonised by pope John XXII, the king of Naples being present at the ceremony. Costs of the gastronomic side of the occasion were defrayed by Thomas's nephew.

For this sea-change to come about, two things had been necessary. The rallying of non-Dominicans to Thomas's cause was evidently one. No less important was a conversion experience on the part of the Dominicans themselves. After all, two generations of Dominicans had come to maturity before Thomas began to write, and, if we leave aside the commanding figure of Albert the Great, their theologians and philosophers constituted what the French medievalist Pierre Mandonnet called the 'Dominican Augustinian school'. In Order terms, Kilwardby's intervention at Oxford was precisely a defence of that school which had especially zealous partisans, it would seem, among the English friars. Kilwardby's intervention, however, proved counter-productive. Two friars of the Province of Toulouse were sent to penalise those in England who had spoken ill of Thomas's writings, while in 1286 and 1313 General Chapters recommended his teaching, the latter on the grounds that it was 'saner and more common'.

Not that the result was to sweep the board either of alternative theologies or of continuing criticism of Thomas among the Preachers. In Germany there were Ulrich of Strassburg and Meister Eckhart, Augustinians influenced by Arabic Neoplatonism, and the Avicennian Thierry of Freiburg; in France, Durand de Saint-Pourçain, generally regarded as a precursor of Nominalism; and in Italy the less placeable Ubertus Guidi of Florence and, more spectacularly, a successor of Thomas on his Neapolitan chair, his namesake Thomas of Naples. It should not be thought, however, that none of these writers had learned anything from Thomas's work. In these matters historians of theology often distinguish between what they term 'orthodox' Thomism and a more 'eclectic' use of his writings.

Outside the Order, the same picture can be discerned. The reputation of Aquinas was quickly established, but that did not guarantee conversion to his thought as a whole. Still, soon after Thomas's death, Henry of Würzburg, like the saint a curial professor (*lector Curiae*) under pope Urban IV, declared he had set philosophy on a better foundation than even the ancients, while around 1300 Godefroid de Fontaines, who opposed Thomas on certain points, claimed that by and large his teaching excelled that of all other doctors in usefulness and value, rendering their work more tasty and succulent by the salt of the Gospel. At the time of the canonisation, accordingly, bishop Etienne Bourret of Paris would revoke Tempier's condemnation insofar as it in any way implicated Thomas's work. In the course of the fourteenth century, Thomas acquired the sobriquet *doctor communis*, to which was added in the course of the fifteenth the title *doctor angelicus* as well. A notable sign of his emerging pre-eminence was the translation of his philosophical works into Hebrew by rabbis, and of the *Summa theologiae* into Greek by Byzantines.

That, however, did not foreclose the possibility of continuing disagreement, especially marked among the Franciscans, whose 1282 General Chapter had already agreed that the *Summa theologiae* should be studied only by the most gifted of Greyfriar lecturers and then always accompanied by the critique – to give it its proper name, the *Correctorium* – of the English Franciscan William de la Mare. The Oxford Dominicans who had, evidently, undergone a rapid change of heart since Kilwardby's day, dubbed the *Correctorium* the 'Corruptorium' in their reply which – as so often with these things – gave William's criticisms a far wider currency than would otherwise have been the case. Franciscan doubts would soon find a more egregious rallying-point in the work of John Duns Scotus, to whose name among later medieval critics of Aquinas we should add those of the secular priest Henry of Ghent and the General of the Augustinian hermits Giles of Rome. There was, then, plenty for defenders of Thomas to do. The chief names are all fifteenth century: John Capreolus, the 'prince of Thomists', with his *Defensiones*; Peter Niger, co-founder with the Hungarian king Matthias Corvinus of the University of Budapest, and author of two versions of a *Clypeus thomistarum*, the first, in 1481, 'against the moderns and Scotists', the second, in 1507, 'against all the objectors to the doctrine of the angelic doctor'; and Christopher Columbus's protector Diego de Deza who defended Thomas more specifically as a commentator on the *Sentences*.[2] (In Iberia, Thomas remained best known for this work.) Thomas's disciples also worked at producing concordances and indices to facilitate access to his work (the modern computer-generated *Index Thomisticus* being only the last of a long line). Less appealing to our eyes is the genre of writing which aimed to show how, despite variations in different periods, Thomas's thought was really a unity at all points.

Wide-ranging philosophically-minded theologies like Scotism and Ockhamism were certainly meant as alternatives to Thomism, the first use of which word, *Thomismus*, comes from the fourteenth century. Thomas was fortunate that the doctrinal tradition in its development coincided with his position at various points. Mandonnet wrote:

The progress of Thomist doctrines and the manifest favours

which the Roman church accorded them slowed down the movement of polemics as the mediaeval period ended.[3]

He had in mind especially the definition of the unity of the human person in terms of the intellectual soul, unique form of the human composite, by the Council of Vienne in 1311 – a truly striking example in that Thomas's denial of polymorphism had been high on the list of charges earlier laid by such conservative thinkers as Kilwardby. On the issue of religious poverty, the Holy See supported Thomas's moderate position over against that of the Franciscan Spirituals. At the fifteenth-century Councils of Basle and Florence which dealt with, respectively Conciliarism and reunion with separated Eastern Christians, Thomists like John of Turrecremata and Henry Kalteisen at the former, Andrew of Rhodes and John of Montenero at the latter, were foremost in reiterating the high doctrine of the Petrine office which would receive its supreme vindication at the First Vatican Council. Then again, with the resurgence of Latin Averroism in the Italian renaissance, the Fifth Lateran Council reaffirmed in 1515 the stand Thomas had taken against denials of personal immortality. In a somewhat arcane controversy that troubled late medieval people – the question of whether the precious Blood of the Lord in its sacrificial spilling remains hypostatically united to the Godhead – Thomas and the papacy were again at one in answering 'Yes'.

The one point at which the doctrinal tradition departed from Aquinas is, as is well known, in the matter of the original righteousness of the Mother of the Lord, her Immaculate Conception. Even there we can usefully note two points. First, the *debitum culpae* Thomas ascribed to our Lady is not, strictly speaking, original sin but Mary's belonging to the order of those who need redemption – and in this the 1854 dogma told no different story. Secondly, Thomists who explicitly denied that the Virgin could have been sanctified in the very moment of her conception were always going beyond the letter of Thomas's text. (Indeed, Thomas appears actually to teach the Immaculate Conception, *theologoumenon*, in his Lenten homilies for 1273.[4])

The Renaissance and the 'Second Scholasticism'

After the age of Thomas himself, historians of the Thomist tradition are apt – not unreasonably – to home in on the late fifteenth and sixteenth centuries (the so-called Second Scholasticism) as the next *Blühezeit* or time of flowering. In that epoch, Thomism was practised in settings more thoroughly incorporated into University milieux than had hitherto been normal – and the University of Salamanca with its long list of distinguished names (Vitoria, Cano, Soto, Medina, Bañez) was paramount in this regard. Also, the *Summa theologiae* now became – especially but not exclusively in faculties where Dominicans were prominent – the chief textbook for basic theological education, ousting the *Sentences* from Rostock to Louvain, Valladolid to Trier. Increasingly, the task *par excellence* of self-confessed Thomist authors was to produce commentaries on part or all of the *Summa theologiae*. Francesco Silvestri of Ferrara (known as 'Ferrarensis') was unusual in preferring to comment on the *Summa contra Gentiles* in 1534. A number of the Renaissance Thomists are famed for the beauty of their Latinity, and also for their ecclesiastical erudition, but they are generally less esteemed as metaphysicians. They display the virtues and vices of the humanism by which they were affected.

In general, however, the age of humanism was a time when the standing of Scholasticism sank. The role of philosophy *vis-à-vis* theology was queried; the value of medieval biblical exegesis questioned; the Fathers preferred to all later divines. Around 1500 the Carmelite prior-general Baptista of Mantua ('Mantuanus') in his *Opus aureum in thomistas* criticised the Dominicans for always wanting on principle to defend the views of Thomas. Striking a modern-sounding note, Mantuanus remarks that it is not to be expected that God, who is the infinite fountain of truth, and communicates some aspect of that truth to all, should reserve truth in its entirety for one school. This would be too unlike Nature, who prefers variety and diversity in her works. Our enthusiasm for Mantuanus's espousal of theological pluralism, however, might be tempered by accounts of his epistemological scepticism. Except for the truths of faith, he held, no other truth is more than probable. Here he was influenced by the 'Academic' sceptics of the ancient world.[5] Despite these assaults, however, Thomas retained considerable prestige among the lay philosophers and scholars of the Renaissance (Pico della Mirandola and Marsilio Ficino exemplify those who, while not citing Thomas frequently, agree with him in key respects – notably his anthropology and metaphysics of participation). As the chief student of these matters, Paul Oscar Kristeller, remarked, after the mid sixteenth century Thomas became what he would remain for a typically modern reader until twentieth-century historians of medieval thought got to work, viz.:

> The representative thinker and almost the only thinker of the Middle Ages that people were disposed to read or to cite, or of whom at least the name was known.[6]

Kristeller has in mind a world of laymen. We should not, however, suppose Thomas's influence in the clerical realm of professional theologians to be, at this time, rather marginal. In the Italy of mid century, the Dominicans had turned Thomas to the service of Catholicism in its struggle with its Protestant rival – something not unconnected with the elevation of Thomas to the status of Church doctor by Pope Pius V in 1567. That action was a recognition of the role his thought had played in the deliberations of the Council of Trent.

The early modern period

Quite how thoroughly the Dominicans and others stuck to Thomas in the rest of the early modern period, and up to the French Revolution, is not that easy to judge. The last overall history of Thomism, that of Werner, was published in 1859 and republished, significantly, as late as 1963, even though in between those dates, as well as since, a variety of figures in the Thomist succession have been the subjects of historical monographs. The problem seems to be that medievalists, and theologians who believe in 'going back to the sources', only study what the French call *thomasien* and the Germans *thomanisch* thought – that which derives directly and absolutely authentically from Thomas himself, whereas the wider *thomiste* or *thomistisch* tradition is of much less interest to theological historians. As Kristeller comments:

> Thomism, just like Platonism and Aristoteleanism, represents one of the great traditions of Western thought, and . . . it has undergone the fate of other philosophical or intellectual traditions, that is, it has known in the course of the centuries developments and transformations more or less profound. The philosopher who follows the authority of a master (it little matters whether he is called Plato or Aristotle, saint Thomas or Kant, Dewey or Wittgenstein) is strongly inclined to understand and interpret his master with the aid of his own ways of seeing and according to his own conception of the truth.

As Kristeller explains:

> He has to clarify the ambiguities, obscurities and incoherences that he discovers in the text and thought of the master, fill in its gaps, apply its principles to the solution of new problems and the refutation of new rival positions which the master did not know or did not study.

And as he adds, somewhat wryly, there is also:

> The temptation to attribute to the master all the other truths that have been drawn more or less consciously from different kinds of argument or different sources and yet appear compatible with the central idea and fundamental principles of his work.[7]

All of which is entirely natural for a tradition of thought and yet may be intensely irritating to the historian of that tradition's source. The only proper procedure, so historians studying some later period may aver, is to separate out the real St Thomas from, shall we say, the positions taken by those whom Pascal dubbed the 'new Thomists' in the struggle against Jansenism, or to distinguish, in another example, the probability ethics of a Bartholomew de Medina from Thomas's own position in such matters. To treat ideas like, for instance, sufficient grace or probabilism as new buds that might in this or that regard render fruitful in fresh ways the old Thomist stem, would strike many historians as a departure from the principles of sound scholarship.

We can also note the possibility that when – *res miranda!* – a writer is equally interested in Thomas and 'Thomisms', an ideological construal of the tradition and its source cannot be ruled out. Thus for instance, in Géry Prouvost's *Thomas d'Aquin et les thomismes*,[8] two incompatible strands are alleged to co-exist both in Thomas and among his successors: the one excessively cataphatic, and leading, unconsciously but ineluctably, to rationalism and thus the direr aspects of modernity (atheism, nihilism); the other duly apophatic, if also biblical, and, conformably to the wishes of Heideggerians and Post-moderns, capable of 'exploding' the later Greek metaphysics of being. Here too, where truths Aquinas held together are forced asunder, and the ranks of later Thomists set against each other as heroes and anti-heroes, the dogmatician and the philosopher desirous of an historical overview must suffer.

Gaining a fair perspective on the history of Thomism is not, then, easy. However, for the Dominican general chapters of 1871 and 1885 to take steps to *recall* the Preachers to the study of Thomas would at least suggest that the cue given by Pius V had not altogether been followed in the succeeding 300 years.

The 'Third Scholasticism': the nineteenth-century revival

But the origins of the 'Third Scholasticism' are a good deal farther flung than simply the members of Thomas's own Order. Indeed, their earlier rival, the Society of Jesus, played a notable part in Neo-Thomism's emergence. The single biggest player in the game was, though, the papacy itself. If Pius IX had been laudatory in a formal sort of way, Leo XIII was passionately determined. In the year of his encyclical on the need to revive the study of Aquinas, 1879, he created the Roman Academy of St Thomas. In 1880 he declared Thomas the patron of Catholic schools and Universities. In 1881, he founded a chair of Thomism at Louvain. In 1882 and 1898 respectively, he commended him to both the Jesuits, many of whom remained attached to Suarez, and the Franciscans, who were still, often, devoted to Scotus. His prescriptions were renewed by his successor, Pius X, and reached their apogee under Pius's successor, Benedict XV, a decree of whose Congregation for Studies in 1914 required teachers in seminaries and religious study-houses to adhere to 24 theses deemed basic to Thomas's thought.

Why then around the turn of the nineteenth and twentieth centuries *did* the papacy act so energetically to proclaim Thomism the 'most secure' philosophical and theological underpinning of the faith? The attraction was above all to the *objectivity* of Thomism. Thomism is a philosophy of objective being, and as a theology it sees grace – transfiguration, the resurrection life – as objective reality likewise, a further form or dimension of being. Thomism is able to be in this sense 'objective' because, where our capacity to get in touch with reality in its very pith is concerned, it is not afflicted by the doubts that many epistemologies are heir to. It takes it as axiomatic that the human mind can only grasp what human minds are made to grasp, but it still maintains that, nonetheless, minds were made to know truth. They are inherently open to reality just as reality is inherently open to them. Using those minds, we discover how we live in an ordered universe with different levels of received participation in being – a *created* world, then, whose particular possibilities of being were transformed by the Creator's eternal Word when he assumed human nature and so offered human beings a new mode of participation in God – this time, in God's own personal inner Trinitarian life.

At two moments of papal history, this vision of things seemed irresistible. For Leo XIII, Thomism's attraction lay in its ability to give citizenship rights to both reason and revelation, nature and grace. Not only could it distinguish between each term in these two couplets, permitting neither to seize or suppress the prerogatives of the other, it could also lend the world of rationality and nature a theologically orderly description. Thomism gave Catholic theology something to say not just to rational ethics but, as the early Louvain school would stress, to natural science as well. The nineteenth century, after all, was the century of Darwin, and so of the first full-scale attempt to treat human origins in systematically scientific terms. It was the century of Auguste Comte, the founder of positive sociology, and so of the attempt to treat human behaviour in society in a purely naturalistic way. It was the century of any number of attempts to treat morality as founded on accident or custom or irrationality or the power of a ruling elite. And, not least, it was in the Church the century of somewhat forlorn attempts to pre-empt all of this by, in effect, doing away with philosophy altogether and basing faith purely on tradition or, again, spiritual intuition. Leo saw in Thomism not simply an *ad hoc* solution to a limited number of specifiable threats to the integrity of Catholic doctrine – from such movements as traditionalism, which was fideistic, or ontologism and a theologised Idealism which tended, rather, to a monistic rationalism – in the nineteenth-century Church. More than this, he held that, by means of Thomism, Christian revelation might be restored to its rightful role in the integration of culture, and Catholic ethics given back their proper place in the social, economic and political organisation of the modern world. Thomism offered a philosophy which, though distinct from theology, was ordered to it, and yet remained accessible on the natural level to all, offering people a universal standard of truth by which anthropology, ethics, aesthetics and the philosophy of science might be judged.

Though the Leonine project would later be criticised as a Canute-like command to the North Sea of modern thought to retreat to whence its waves had flowed, the scholarly aspect of Leonine revival – the Leonine edition of the works of Thomas, still proceeding – met, unsurprisingly, with easier acceptance. Based for much of its existence on the fringes of the small town of Grottaferrata, outside Rome and home to an ancient Greek-rite monastic community, the siting of the *editio leonina* was a nice touch of Providence. The issue of reunion with the Greeks dominated the last weeks of Thomas's life, while his love for the Greek Fathers had led him to say he would give Paris itself for a manuscript of Chrysostom on Matthew.

Under Pius X and his successor Benedict XV, the impetus to tie the ark of the Church to a Thomist lightship came from a perception of reefs and shoals within Catholicism rather than in the secular or Protestant world beyond. That impetus was (theological) Modernism. The Modernist movement is not a simple affair. In part, it was a revival of Gallicanism or Cismontanism, a movement of protest against papal or curial hegemony. In part, it was an appeal for critical freedom in studying the origins of Scripture and Church teachings by the historical method. In part, and this is what interests us most here, it was the application to Catholicism of a philosophy of religion that appeared to make Catholic Christianity more acceptable to contemporaries but at the cost of largely emptying it of truth value. That philosophy is often referred to as 'immanentism', and because its clearest statement, in its application to the Catholic religion, appears in the papal encyclical *Pascendi* which condemned it, it is sometimes described as an intellectual system wrought by the pope's imagination (or that of his professorial advisers). But considered as a philosophical tendency, immanentism, as the Baron Friedrich von Hügel ruefully admitted in retrospect, was certainly around, in and among the main Modernist authors. The basic presupposition is that the human spirit possesses a subliminal contact with infinite reality (with God), and that in different cultures, societies, epochs, that spirit throws up symbols which orientate us toward the divine, thus giving expression to that contact. Newman's doctrine of development was in some danger of finding itself stood on its head. For the Modernist mind-set, that the Church has adapted her doctrine shows how, subconsciously, she has always understood her credal statements to be symbolic – gestures towards the infinite. In the Church of the future, the figure of Christ will remain dominant, as the supreme symbol of divine-human unity. But just how people understand the Creed will be a question of what humanity's evolving spiritual needs require. Modernists could remain Modernists and still recite the Creed. Indeed, they could celebrate the Liturgy of St Pius V. What they could not do was be Modernist and Thomist at the same time. This was why the early-twentieth-century papacy wanted seminary professors to accept the characteristic theses of Thomist ontology.

Dark days, and promise of dawn

Why, then, was there a revolt against Thomism so general that, until recently, except in limited circles, it seemed almost to have sunk without trace? There were several reasons. First, the rise of modern biblical studies made people want much more in the way of explicitly biblical categories and themes in their theologising. After an initial fact-finding phase of Catholic biblical scholarship concerned with authorship, dating and historical milieux, came hard on its heels a second, fuelled by the discovery that Scripture itself is full of theology. This report led some to believe that 'biblical theology' could legitimately become the whole of theology. After all, it was a recognised possibility in Catholic dogmatics that everything the Church propounded as revelation might be found *implicitly* in Scripture. But the attempt to create a purely biblical theology foundered in striking two rocks: the realisation that there is no one theology in the Bible but a plurality of theologies, only reconcilable by reference to subsequent tradition; and the recognition that not all relevant questions were already asked and answered by the biblical writers. What remained of the biblical theology movement was the conviction that biblical themes and motifs should play a large role in the construction of theology. The deficiencies of some Neo-Thomists on this score obscured the fact that Thomas himself passes such a test with flying colours.

A second reason why Thomism began to look somewhat fly-blown was the movement of *ressourcement*: go back to the Fathers! Twentieth-century interest in patristics on the part of Catholic scholars was to some extent the result of the 'clamp down' on the more adventurous varieties of biblical scholarship until the pontificate of Pius XII (in England the career of Dom Cuthbert Butler of Downside illustrates the point). Anxiety about the ecclesiastical ill effects of saying the wrong thing about who did or did not write the Pentateuch led some to switch to the safer territory of St Athanasius or the Syriac Fathers. That led, by a happy chance, to the rediscovery of patristic theology as a prayerful theology, saturated in Scripture and the Liturgy, and centring on the main themes of Christian believing: the triune God, the God-man, the sacramental life, the Age to Come. The texts and studies that followed were not intended simply to give people access to ancient authors but to renew the Church by recreating the patristic golden age. That this should constitute grounds for disdain of Aquinas is from one point of view bizarre. The Anglican Tractarians, after all, had in 1841, at the height of their campaign to recall English churchmen to the Church of the Fathers, contrived to translate for the first time Thomas's

Catena aurea, a commentary on the four Gospels put together precisely from the patristic sources.[9] In large part Thomas's output had been patristic synthesis. But even were that conceded, objectors could still argue, why not 'cut out the middle man' and go back to the originals themselves? Whereas for Thomists Thomas had improved on the *modus operandi* of patristic thought, for the neo-patrologists he had introduced a method that was too systematic and over-intellectual. What was wanted was a more poetic, holistic theology full of person-to-person appeal.

The thought might cross our minds that the patristic revival sometimes viewed the Fathers through rose-tinted spectacles. But its criticism of Thomism brings us to a third movement which helped to precipitate the fall of Thomas's star. The aim of 'kerygmatic theology' was to produce a preachable theology, one that could be translated immediately into the Sunday sermon by any and every parish priest. The idea was to extract the essence of New Testament preaching and then to re-state it in a way obviously relevant to contemporary life situations. And once again, Aquinas was found insufficiently biblical, excessively philosophical and simply too complicated to be a model. On the other hand, kerygmatic theology itself resulted from a certain desperation – desperation that dogmatic theology would ever inspire anybody.

Fourthly, in any explanation of the downward curve in Thomism's fortunes, we must reckon with the understandable feeling that all essential truth could not have been stated by 1274. Surely the philosophers of later times had occasionally got *something* right! The debts of transcendental theology (the German Jesuit Karl Rahner at its undisputed head) to Kant, Hegel and Heidegger were incurred under this rubric.

Finally, and perhaps, at the end of the day, most importantly, we cannot neglect the off-putting mode of pedagogical and literary presentation in which Thomism was often cast. Though one relies here chiefly on hearsay, its communication in many seminaries and Catholic philosophy faculties appears to have become dessicated and ahistorical. The actual texts were rarely read (by the average professor, never mind student!), and, when they were, the potency of such reading was usually limited by such factors as: feeble understanding of historical background; insufficient grasp of alternative

systems to enable people to appreciate the liberating and evangelical charge that Thomas's key notions could possess; a want of
the imagination that alone could translate these ideas into other
idioms of reflection and experience. The potted Scholasticism frequently on offer bore as much relation to the actual St Thomas as
the summary of a Shakespeare plot in a school English crammer
bears to the Shakespeare play.

Though of course Thomism never disappeared – it retained
significant centres of diffusion in the United States, in Rome, in
France, in Poland – only in the pontificate of John Paul II did it
bounce back to the point that some now speak of a Fourth Scholasticism, a new Thomistic renaissance. While generalisation here
could be misleading, one can say that distinguishing features of the
new movement include a self-conscious guarding against 'wooden-
ness' in expression, and a desire to integrate the philosophy more
thoroughly within an essentially theologial vision.[10]

To some extent – but only quite a small extent – this is a matter
of the return of Thomist ideas to papal favour – at any rate in
the domain of theological ethics (something particularly clear in the
survey document of the Roman magisterium on fundamental ethical
principles, *Veritatis splendor*). This has served as a reminder that
the Second Vatican Council did not propose to abandon Thomas
but, to the contrary, singled him out as the oustanding post-patristic
thinker of the Catholic tradition – albeit within a philosophical and
theological culture now more broadly conceived. The new renaissance (if the phrase be not premature) proceeds most
characteristically by laymen and laywomen finding out certain
qualities of St Thomas for themselves. In search of intellectual,
moral and spiritual coherence, they find that his writing has a
winning power to keep together things that most people either
separate or confuse.[11]

Here are some examples. First, theology and spirituality. The
exitus-reditus scheme whereby St Thomas shows all things as
issuing from God and returning to him corresponds to the basic
structure of personal spirituality. The artist Paul Gauguin has a
canvas that shows South Sea islanders in postures of contemplative
wonderment. Its title is *Where have I come from? Where am I going
to?* This is the question of Everyman. Or again, we could say

that the *exitus-reditus* scheme provides a satisfying metaphysical rendition of the basic question and answer found in biblical revelation: How can I, as a creature and a sinner, get back to God?

Secondly, revelation and ethics. Christian ethics have often been sundered from revelation by being treated as bare statements of the will of God, without much rooting in this same God's loving plan for us. Alternatively, ethical imperatives and their legitimation have been cut off somewhat from human nature by being related solely to Christ's teaching in, for instance, the Sermon on the Mount. Contrastingly, Thomist ethics are an integration of natural and supernatural in which the virtues become the concrete ways grace fits us for life with God.

Thirdly, the social and the individual. According to Thomas, all right human action must be informed by two principles: justice and charity, for these, at different levels – charity's higher than that of justice – unify the whole moral life. On his view, both charity and justice are inescapably social, to do with my neighbour, and also inherently personal, as relating me to God. Justice relates me to God when, as a worshipping being, I give my Creator what is rightly his; and charity does the same only more intensely for it is a share in the love of Father, Son and Spirit.

Fourthly, philosophy and doctrine. In Thomas's work, philosophy enjoys what we can call a subordinate autonomy in the expression of doctrine. It is subordinate inasmuch as it serves doctrine, and does not attempt to re-make *sacra doctrina* in its own image. At the same time, and here is where autonomy comes in, philosophy is respected as a discipline with rights of its own. Moreover, the realism and sobriety of the Thomist metaphysic – that is, the particular way in which the Thomist philosophy exercises those rights – enables the doctrinal theologian to speak to the common man (or at least the common reasonably well-educated man!) with some well-founded expectation of being heard.[12] Its clarity is refreshing in a post-modern world where parodistic allusiveness, randomness and incoherence are frequently erected into pseudo-virtues that make reflective life an intellectual mess.

It remains to look at how Thomas saw the activities of philosophy and theology – a crucial clue to his success.

Part Four: *The Tools*

10.
Thomas and the Practice of Philosophy

The continuing value of Christian Scholasticism

Ever since the first Ecumenical Councils, the Church has made her own the language of classical ontology – an historical fact which requires, at least, that its concepts (nature, person, and the rest) be regarded as serviceable, illuminating. It seems contradictory for someone to defend the dogmatic definition of Nicaea on the divinity of Christ while opposing root and branch the language of 'substance' actually used by the First Ecumenical Council to state the Son's sharing the Godhead of the Father. But that is, or at any rate was until recently, exactly the position of a spirited opponent of ontological theology – a theology couched in terms of being, divine and human – the French lay theologian Jean-Luc Marion.[1] The ancient philosophical language of patristic and medieval Christianity runs like a river through the dogmatic tradition – from the 'consubstantiality' of the Son with the Father at Nicaea to the 'transubstantiation' of the Holy Gifts at Trent. And like the Nile to the soil of Egypt, this is an indispensable river, for there can be no more vital question than the one the language of substance raises – what *is* this Jesus?, or, What *are*, after the consecration, the Eucharistic Gifts? – if it really is the *truth* of our Creator and Redeemer that we would seek.

Moreover, Church authority has pronounced directly on a number of philosophical questions closely connected with revealed faith, and on these some characteristic theses of Thomism are splendidly compatible with her *parti pris*: one thinks of the Council of Vienne on the soul as form of the body, or Lateran V on the natural knowability of the immortality of soul, or Vatican I on reason's ability to approach the existence of God. All this is barely thinkable without something very like, at least, the 'perennial philosophy'.

Not surprisingly, then, the American Jesuit theologian (and now cardinal) Avery Dulles has opined that 'for the sake of progress the Church needs a relatively stable philosophical tradition'.[2] And he cites approvingly Pope Pius XII's declaration that Catholicism has taken into its patrimony a philosophy that

> safeguards the genuine validity of human knowledge, the unshakable metaphysical principles of sufficient reason, causality and finality, and finally the mind's ability to attain certain and unchangeable truth.[3]

It is, actually, a moot point whether Thomas himself recognises a 'principle of sufficient reason' (that is rather a seventeenth-century notion). However, Catholic appeal to a *philosophia perennis* can hardly bypass Thomas, its classic exponent *par excellence*. Highly pertinent, therefore, to this study is Dulles' defence of the place of such a flower in the garden of the modern Church – and that, notably, against five objections.

- The Council (that is, the Second Vatican, 1962–5) preferred matters of praxis to abstract speculation – but (we can reply) the pastoral can never be played off against the doctrinal, as Pope John XXIII's speech opening the conciliar gathering itself indicates.
- The Council opted for intellectual freedom – but (we may say) in a situation where Scholastic theology was seeking excessive support from magisterial authority. Today, in the context of widespread indifference to doctrine, the need is for 'Catholic intellectuals to argue strenuously for philosophical positions that they regard as contributing to the right understanding of faith'.[4]
- The Council sought modernisation – but (we can interject) the living tradition cannot renew itself by neglecting the classical

and Scholastic sources, on pain of surrender of both identity and direction.

- The Council privileged ecumenical outreach, to which Scholasticism is at best an irrelevance – but (we must surely add) ecumenism entails not only a readiness to learn but a willingness to give from the resources of one's own tradition.
- The Council asked for the manifold inculturation of the Gospel in a myriad cultures – but (we have to insist) this should not be taken to imply a failure of confidence in the Catholic philosophical heritage which has 'achieved insights of abiding validity'.[5] An inculturation-conscious schoolmaster would need to make the natural scientific discovery of a heliocentric planetary system intelligible to other 'methods or idioms' than those of Western astronomical physics: that hardly calls into question the validity of the discovery itself!

Thomas's metaphysics: (1) The nature of metaphysical enquiry

What, then, is the substance – suitable word! – of St Thomas's philosophy? While his anthropology and ethics are important (we have touched on them in Chapters 5 and 7 respectively), his view of philosophy is commanded by a metaphysic.

Thomas accepts the insight of Aristotle that the proper object of metaphysics is *being as being together with its properties*. But in the prologue to his commentary on Aristotle's treatise *The Metaphysics*, he goes to some pains to clarify the shifting and overlapping conceptions the ancient Greek writer entertained of what this might involve. For Aristotle, metaphysics is not only the science of being *qua* being. It is also the science of first causes or principles, as well as the science of that which is 'separated' from matter – since physics (the philosophy of nature) and mathematics (in its concern with quantification) have objects that always retain some mode of materiality.

Thomas clears up the resultant confusion. What these three concepts have in common is that they focus on the highest degree of intelligibility we encounter in the realm of the real. Thus:

- From the viewpoint of the inter-relation of mind and sense, the distinguishing mark of intellect in its differing from sense is its comprehension of universal principles – pre-eminently being, and what naturally accompanies being, namely: unity and plurality, potency and act: in other words, being as being along with its native properties. The science which deals with these can surely claim to be the science of the most intelligible, the most germane to intellect. In the school of Plato, being was a somewhat secondary notion, rather overshadowed by the Good and the One. Aristotle had returned here to the inspiration of Plato's pre-Socratic predecessor, Parmenides: being is prior to being one or being good, crucial though these latter are. (For the sake of historical accuracy, however, we should note that Neoplatonism will go on to treat being as *aph' henos kai pros hen*: 'from the One and towards the One', and that 'henadological' account of metaphysical science will have some influence on Thomas through the Christian and pagan authors of that school.) Metaphysics so understood is not, admittedly, the discipline most suited to earthlings (that, for Aristotle, was physics); nor is it as perspicuous as mathematics. But its 'mode of considering' being – ampler and more synthetic than these – is nonetheless what determines, philosophically, the meaning of these kinds of knowledge.[6]
- From the viewpoint of the ordering of knowing, knowledge that is so well-founded as to be certain – which knowledge through causes is – can surely count as the most intelligible variety of the same. What is known *in se* by way of a principle is thoroughly grasped by our minds; here we can speak of real understanding. So here a second, complementary, approach to the subject matter of metaphysics is validated.
- Lastly, from the viewpoint of the intellect's own knowledge, creatures are endowed with intellectual power to the degree that they are not immersed in the material. A mongoose will never make a mathematician, just because cognitive capacities of a mongoosian kind are suited only to exploring materially relevant aspects of the mongoose's environment. Among the ancient philosophers, Aristotle agreed with Plato that *episteme* – scientific knowledge – calls for a principle of stability and even necessity

(identified by Plato with the Ideas). True, he did not seek this principle in a separate entity (like Plato's 'The Form of the Good') but in a material reality which for him was not *just* matter but matter-and-form. Nevertheless, he rejoined forces with Plato in thinking that, to be fully intelligible, an object has to be educed ('abstracted') from its material matrix. The more immaterial an object is, the more intelligible it is. That is why there has to be a science that goes beyond – *meta* – physics and even mathematics.[7] Those realities that are separate from matter in their very being (here Thomas, as a Christian, will think of God and the angels) turn any science that treats of them, and the primary concepts needed to do so, into the most sheerly intellectual discipline of all. Notice, however, that whereas revelation-based – katabatic – theology treats of God (and the angels) as its own immediate subject matter, the philosopher's 'theology' – anabatic thinking – treats of them only as the 'principles' of *its* subject, spiritual being.

Thomas's metaphysics: (2) The analogy of being

Since everything in reality, whether actual or only possible, falls under the concept of being, this will constitute what the mind judges of, first and foremost. Being is the first and most universal object of thought, and it is also the most foundational in reality. The *something that is* (*to on*, the Greeks called it; *ens*, the Latins) has, evidently, two aspects: the 'something' – essence, *essentia* – and its actuation as indicated in the words 'that is' – existence, *esse*. The two terms are correlative. Essence cannot be conceived except in relation to existence; in turn, existence calls for determination by essence. Though each calls for the other, Thomas's contribution to ontology has often been thought to lie in the forcefulness with which he treats *esse* as dynamic, energising act. In an attempt to capture – albeit somewhat impressionistically – Thomas's conception of the 'act of existence', G. B. Phelan wrote:

Things which 'have being' are not 'just there' . . . like lumps of static essence, inert, immovable, unprogressive and unchanging. The act of existence (*esse*) is not a state, it is an act, the act of all acts . . . *Esse* is dynamic impulse, energy, act – the first, the most persistent and enduring of all dynamisms, all energies, all acts. In all things on earth the act of being is the consubstantial urge of nature, a restless, striving force, carrying each being (*ens*) onward, from within the depths of its own reality to its full self-achievement, i.e. fully to be what by its nature it is apt to become.[8]

If this be somewhat too Lawrentian for comfort, we can return to more sober prose in a consideration of that serviceable intellectual tool, *analogy*. For Thomas, there are no real differentiations of things that are not themselves being. But how could we suppose that God exists in the same sense in which, say, a hydrangea exists? If we cannot do so, then how may we create distinction within the concept of being without going outside it? The answer, for Thomas and the Thomist tradition at large, is the use – later, the 'doctrine' – of analogy.

Analogies fall into two kinds. The less important, though the easier to grasp, is what the tradition came to call the 'analogy of attribution'. Here the idea or 'formality' signified by the analogous term is intrinsically realised only in the 'prime' or 'principal' analogue. Thus, to take a stock example, health exists formally and intrinsically only in an animal body. However, by an extrinsic denomination – which turns on some relation of causality or symptomatic manifestation – food, medicine and a good complexion are called 'healthy' as well.

This, though, cannot be the heart of the matter, for formally and intrinsically, *all* modes of being *are* being. That, after all, was the starting-point from which our interest in analogy was aroused! And so we come to the 'analogy of proportionality'. Here analogues are unified on the basis of proportion to each other, inviting us to see one structure in terms of another. A typical expression of the analogy of proportionality might be: as seeing is to the eye, so understanding is to the soul. In this statement, what the analogous terms denote occurs formally and intrinsically in each analogue. How can that help us?

We recall that, in Thomas's fundamental ontology, the being of something – essence, *essentia* – is that whose 'act' is existence, *esse*. So what is common to every being will be *the proportion of essence to existence*. And this – insofar as mere metaphysics may procure it – will be the key to the difference yet continuity between created and uncreated being: hydrangea and God. Being will be predicated primarily of God who is self-existent being – he whose essence it is to exist, and only secondarily of creatures which are being only by dependence on God. As Thomas remarks crisply in the *De potentia*, between God and the creature is a *diversa habitudo ad esse*,[9] a lack of common measure, and this is something that the uniqueness of the Creator's activity confirms. The act that God exercises as *Ipsum esse subsistens* distinguishes him from all other beings, indeed from being in general.

God is thus above the discourse on being precisely because he is not beyond being. No being, no God.[10]

Thomas's metaphysics: (3) The transcendentals

But (we may now go on) if all that is is being in some way or another, are there no predicates at all that add to being in any sense? For Thomas, in a way there are: oneness, truth, goodness – the 'transcendentals', qualities that 'transcend' the divisions between classes of things – and given to our understanding, at any rate, *in principle* when being itself is given to the apprehension of mind. As Thomas explains in the opening question of the *De veritate*:

Nothing can be added to being as though it were something not included in being in the way that a difference is added to a genus or an accident to a substance – for every reality is essentially a being. The Philosopher has proved this by showing that being cannot be a genus. Yet in this sense some predicates may be said to add to being, namely, inasmuch as they express a mode of being not expressed by the term 'being'.

And Thomas goes on to specify that

> This happens in two ways. First, the mode expressed is some
> particular manner of being; for there are different grades of
> being, according to which we speak of different modes of exist-
> ence; and conformably to those modes the different genera of
> things are drawn up. Second, something is said to add to being
> because the mode it expresses is *one that is common and
> consequent upon every being.*[11]

In other words, being can only be differentiated by modes intrinsic
to itself, and that in two ways – predicamentally, in particular modes,
as in the 'substance' of a bird-of-paradise or the 'accident' of the
brilliance of the plumage of the male; and transcendentally, in uni-
versally necessary modes of which, as already mentioned, oneness,
truth, goodness are those highlighted by Thomas (later Scholastics
will add a more explicit reference here to beauty).[12]

The transcendentals are properties inseparable from being that
designate being under another aspect. They are 'transcendental' in
the same sense as is being itself – which occurs in all that is and
so transcends any category of it. It is because they are as universal
as being itself that such transcendental modes are spoken of as
'convertible' with being.

The discovery of the transcendentals, so understood, is a major
philosophical achievement of Latin Christian thought. Thus we find:

- **Unum** St Thomas distinguishes transcendental unity from
  numerical – the sort we deal with when insisting to our green-
  grocer that we want only one globe artichoke, not two. Unity
  designates being conceived as undivided. So metaphysical unity
  is not in the order of quantity at all; rather, it consists in the
  absence of a division. In that way, then, adding nothing real to
  being, it follows that *unum* and *ens* must be logically convertible
  one with the other.
- **Verum** Truth is not only logical or formal – found in judgements
  whereby our intellect comes into possession of truth as a known
  or recognised conformity of mind with the real. (For Thomas
  there is also a tacit conformity of our sense faculties with their
  objects in the act of sensation.) More than this, truth is also

ontological (which is why, of course, it comes up in this context). Truth is the conformity of things to the divine mind, since all things were preconceived by him and fashioned according to his knowledge. The dependence of an artwork on its maker illus- trates – deficiently but not unilluminatingly – the dependence of creation on the Maker of all. Since nothing escapes the creativity of divine causality, ontological falsehood is impossible. A thing can only be said to be false when its appearance invites mis- conception of its nature, as with that aberration, the plastic flower.

- **Bonum** In the *Summa theologiae* Thomas argues that the good is what all things desire, but a thing is desired inasmuch as it is perfect.[13] It is perfect, however, insofar as it is in act, and it is in act in the measure that it is being. For the tradition of Thomas, the primary meaning of the good is 'perfective' good – what the Latin classics call *bonum honestum*, a good that is the desired end of human beings, granting them, in whatever measure, their happiness. Only secondarily do we have in mind the good that is a means to this end, *bonum utile*, 'useful good', and the com- plement to *bonum honestum* that is *bonum delectabile*, the good that is restful delight in the attaining of some desirable thing. (But what a civilized idea the latter is, suggestive of a friend and a wineglass at a table in Provence.) Evil for Thomas is the absence of a modality of being which *should* be present, given the nature of what is under review. Appetite can be directed to incidental evil, or apparent evil, but not to evil for its own sake: that is part and parcel of how Aquinas understands the divine declaration in Genesis that creation – including, then, our fundamental human capacities (not, of course, our fallen use of them) – is essentially good.

The creature's share in the transcendentals has, naturally, the same structure as its share in being, since the transcendentals are the constant properties thereof. It is by participatory dependence on the divine unity, truth and goodness that created reality shows these features for itself. Since God is his own being, concepts drawn from such perfections as are found in creatures (philosophically, the inevitable starting-point) can only be defective likenesses of him. And yet, as the *Summa theologiae* puts it:

> Nothing prevents one sole essence from responding to all these
> conceptions, though it be imperfectly represented by them.[14]

The absolute simplicity of the divine being (there is no *potentiality*
to existence in his essence, he is all act) is the root of all perfections
and their supereminent realisation. And if, then, it is by his being
that God differs from every existing thing,[15] we can see how far off
the mark are those opponents of 'onto-theology' who cannot see
that Thomas's ontology serves his theology of God rather than
distracts from it.[16] God's being, Thomistically understood, is 'the
guardian of his transcendence'.[17]

Thomas's metaphysics: (4) Causality

Thomas's account of the transcendentals – and the relation
between God and the world that they imply – would scarcely be
possible without his philosophical account of *causality*. In his commentary on Aristotle's *Physics*, Thomas looks (with Aristotle) at
how natural changes are caused. Here is the humble rooting of that
analysis – in terms of 'material' causality and 'formal' causality, and
causality both 'efficient' (a broadening of the Greek philosopher's
'motive' causality under the influence of his Hellenistic and Arab
commentators) and, most important of all, 'final' – which we have
already seen Thomas bringing to bear cosmologically in his proofs
of the existence of God. The *Physics* commentary hints, indeed,
that a doctrine of a first cause, in the fullest sense of the words,
remains to be provided, in 'first philosophy'.

Fundamental for Thomas's interest in causation are the interrelated concepts of causal likeness and causal participation.

> The experience of the likeness between cause and effect which
> is had naturally in the sequence of generations and intentionally
> in human craft, points to the hierarchy of ontological sharing
> which secures that likeness.[18]

The notion of causal likeness can be taken in a literalistic fashion
that renders it absurd. A 'Turner' (a canvas covered with paint) is
not in any obvious sense 'like' the Turner (Joseph Mallord William)

to whom we are indebted for it. But a sane version of this (philosophical) doctrine is grounded in Thomas's account of causal participation, indebted as this is to the *Liber de Causis*, that selection of paraphrased extracts from Proclus's *Elements of Theology*. Thomas's commentary on this Neoplatonic text treats causal likeness as a precondition of the intelligibility of the cause-and-effect nexus in the world. The cause is ever present in the effect *under the aspect relevant to its causation* – which would be, in the example chosen, Turner's creative vision, of colour and line as well as theme, in *The Fall of an Avalanche in the Grisons* or *The Angel Standing in the Sun*.

All causality – this is, for theology, the most important burden of 'first philosophy' – depends on the one Cause that is unconditionally first, grounding as it does the subsistent efficacy of all other causes. Yet, as Mark Jordan cautions, the effects of that Cause 'do not give anything like a complete account of its nature'. And so by a very proper application of the cataphatic and apophatic ways to the principles of causal likeness and participation,

> the principles of causal likeness and participation are at once affirmed and denied. They are affirmed in so far as an ontological ground is secured for them in the luminous causality of the First Cause. They are denied for human knowing in as much as it is blocked in its approach to the originary Cause.[19]

Thomas's metaphysics: (5) The structure of the finite

What, then, can be said of the *make-up* of created things thus known as caused? The French Jesuit student of Thomas, Joseph de Finance, considered that:

> The idea of a metaphysical structure in things is born entirely from the need to trace back to their ultimate rationales the antinomic aspects of reality.[20]

'Antinomic' may be going a little too far, but we can at least say that the metaphysical structure of things appears as a system of reciprocal relations. Thus we find such complementary principles as: matter and form, for matter 'desires' form,[21] being intrinsically ordered to it; form and *'suppositum'*, for all form belongs to the same subsisting individual thing; potency and act, for the measure of what a thing can be is found in its full realisation; and essence and existence, for even essence, so we have seen, is in potentiality to existence.[22] Without for a moment dissolving the wondrous particularity of creatures into a cosmic soup, Thomas was deeply concerned with the dynamic character of things, the way their being structured as they are passes over into congruent activity.

According to the 'intellectualism of St Thomas'[23] truth enjoys ontological priority over goodness. Truth relates to being absolutely, goodness to being insofar as being is perfect. But, by way of counterbalance, we can notice too the 'resolutive' character of Thomas's general metaphysical method. He proceeds to ever more proper determinations of what is given in direct apprehension, and this is, I believe, the hallmark of a metaphysician who is also an artist.

How does that work? From (1) the principles of things – *esse* and *essentia*, form and matter – Thomas moves to (2) the substance of things constituted from those principles, and then (3) to the determination of a thing in its own proper species, according to its form; (4) from form we become aware not only of something's specific being but also of its proper action and end; and (5) taking things in relation to each other, we grasp finally how the diversity of beings, each with some perfection to call their own, belong in a unified order which makes the world precisely a *universe*. Thomas's is never an abstract intellectualism; to the contrary, it is always an *intellectualism of the concrete*.

Thomas on man: (1) The human mind

What I have called Thomas's 'concrete intellectualism' makes it very likely that knowing will be high on the list of his priorities where human activity is concerned, though this will not at all be knowing sundered from the sensuous inhabitation of environment. The humble *conversio ad phantasmata*, the turning of the intellect to the things of sense, already has a salubrious potential for troubled minds. In *The Botany of Desire* the American environmental historian Michael Pollan writes:

> Psychiatrists regard a patient's indifference to flowers as a symptom of clinical depression. It seems that by the time the singular beauty of a flower in bloom can no longer pierce the veil of black or obsessive thoughts in a person's mind, that mind's connection to the sensual world has grown dangerously frayed.[24]

And not just, Thomas would add, its connection to the sensuous world alone, for it is the senses that present to us, in the first instance, the sharing of participated being in the transcendentals. Truth, remarks Thomas in the *De veritate*, is 'in sense' though 'not as something known by sense'.[25] In knowing proper, knower and known join to become a common principle of the act of knowing.[26] Thomas Gilby puts it with his customary vim:

> The knower becomes the known without ceasing to be himself. It is at once an act of nature and an intimation of immortality.[27]

We would, however, mistake Thomas if we thought a philosophy in his image need in any case begin with an epistemology, for he takes it as read that the human spirit finds itself already oriented to being and truth.[28] Still, for sensate animals, knowing can be hard work. De Finance wrote:

> The non-intuitive character of our knowledge means that the human 'word' is not only a luminous tracing of the thing [known], but a 'conceived', 'formulated, 'excogitated' likeness, translating in its structure not just the ontological structure of the object but the law of exercise of the power that construes it as well.[29]

'Luminous', de Finance's adjective for what is transparently effortless in our encounter with the world, reminds us that Thomas is not Kant – who thought that whatever shape we find the world to have is one the human mind itself confers upon it. At the back of our minds is a sunburst in which even the most opaque objects can stand forth for what they really are. In the words of an Irish student of St Thomas:

> For St Thomas the intellect is a light which participates in God's own light and 'beams down', as it were, on the phantasm (image) presented by the senses to uncover or discern the content of intelligibility contained potentially therein and render it intelligible in act. In as much as the object of knowledge is complex, the intellect has to do a certain amount of 'work', moving to and fro between the different aspects of the object, comparing and separating them, or combining earlier insights, until the object is grasped as a whole in the act of understanding. Work, the work of reasoning, *ratio*, ceases then and truth 'dawns' gratuitously on the mind which gazes on its find and enjoys it.[30]

For Thomas *ratio* is compared to *intellectus* as moving is to staying still, or acquiring to having. *Intellectus* is to grasp the intelligible truth *simpliciter*.[31]

This is the knowledge of an ensouled body – which is also, however, an embodied soul. If the language of soul is forced on us by dint of our seeking out a 'first principle of life in vital organisms',[32] nevertheless through that power of soul which is intellect man 'can know the natures of all bodies',[33] and that would be impossible unless mind were immaterial. (The proper formal notion of a stone is in the intellectual soul; that does not make it stony, though its judgements may be lapidary!) Intellect can reflect upon its own act, and the 'proportion' of this act to things, so coming to a degree to know its own truth. The interior space where the mind knows itself through itself may be comparatively shadowy and restricted.[34] Still, enough light comes through the shutters to permit us to say that, on this point, Augustine – that great master of speculative intuition – was right.[35] Our ability intellectually to 'return to ourselves', to become spiritually self-possessed, makes us transcend the animal creation. Evidently, biologism and spiritualism are being combined here in an extraordinary way.

For Aristotle, soul had been the inseparable form of the body and in the same way as with any other form-matter composite there could be no question of any disembodied, separate existence of the form. Only the impersonal (because memory-less) immortality of the 'separable reason' would survive death or, rather, function irrespectively of any individual human life. For Thomas, as a Catholic Christian, the human soul is not only the form of the body, it is also a complete spiritual substance capable of independent existence. He reconciles those two statements by the principle that a higher reality can act as form to a lower whilst having a complete fully substantial existence of its own.[36] Soul and body are more closely united than for any Platonist and yet Thomas manages to preserve the soul's essential substantiality. Thomas's emphasis on not only the naturally enlightened but also – and especially – the industrious activity of mind, did not prevent his writing of the Beatific Vision that, in it, the 'divine essence itself becomes the form through which the mind understands'.[37] When God himself becomes the 'intelligible form', the vision of him must be so 'immediate' that the mind will be, in the light of glory, deiform.

Holding together in this way the two ends of the chain, Thomas's account of mind does justice – extraordinarily – to both biology and mysticism, to the elements of truth in both the materialists and Descartes.

Perhaps at the end of his life Thomas relished the contrast in its sharpest form: Aristotle and Glory. Fergus Kerr wrote:

> Students of Aquinas sometimes talk as if his great interest lay in developing a proto-empiricist theory of knowledge in the wake of Aristotle for its own sake – into which he then, perhaps with some reluctance and a certain amount of massage, had to squeeze the abnormal case of beatific vision. But, given his deepening commitment as the years went by to reading the Fourth Gospel in tandem with the works of Aristotle, it seems more likely that he wanted the relatively down to earth 'empiricist' epistemology in place precisely to highlight the extraordinary nature of the consummation of the human mind in the eschatological gift of 'deiforming' knowledge. The utterly grace-given character of 'beholding and reflecting the glory of the Lord' (cf. 2 Cor. 3:18) could be located in an Aristotelean theory of the economy of human *knowledge* far more pointedly

(pregnantly even) than in the Augustinian Neo-Platonism which Aquinas inherited.[38]

Thomas on man: (2) Language

Mind's privileged instrument is language which, for Thomas, has as its centrally defining task the telling of truths. Words are, as Mark Jordan remarks – by way of comment on Thomas's commentary on Aristotle's treatise *On Interpretation* – crafted forms imposed on sound by the ingenuity of man. They are:

> tools for speaking within a community. Their division and their properties are to be explained by going back to their having been crafted. The genesis of language lies in the intention of social craftsmen.[39]

Modern linguistics undergoes painful intellectual contortions to explain (or, in the case of Post-modernism, avoid explaining) the presence of the signified through the signifier: how language works. But Thomas can safely ascribe this to human skill without incurring the danger of nominalism, the accusation of mere arbitrary labelling.

> Will and ingenuity depend ultimately on the place of the human soul within the hierarchy of creation, which hierarchy is itself a communicating order established by the Creator. As soon as one admits the conventional character of sign-systems in human speech, one must also recall that the distinction between convention and nature is transformed by virtue of the doctrine of creation.[40]

Thomas on man: (3) Man in time, cosmic and historical

The knowing life thus ascribed, not least through language, to this sensate animal, man, throws him open to a wider world. It enables him to position himself in terms of that intelligible pattern of the cosmos, and his own being within it, which the Latin classics called *lex naturae* (and even *lex aeterna*), the Chinese sages *Tao*, and ancient India *rta*. Insofar as humans know the truth, they can know a kind of reflection of, and participation in, the eternal law. More specifically, they can know it as the rational counterpart of the natural tendency towards *telos*, a goal or end. Where lower animals have mute tendencies, 'instincts', rational creatures can make such teleological ordering their own in articulate ways, recognising these goals as participations in the divine intelligibility.[41]

Such is the richness of natural law, with its imperative to us to act rationally – that is, virtuously. But there is also its poverty too. The generality of natural law means that, where many concrete, real-life cases are concerned, positive law – whether human or, by revelation, divine – is sorely needed to specify the right thing for us to do. The long experience of our race – whether in the trial and error of accumulated natural wisdom or the divine pedagogy of salvation history – must come to our aid.

To what extent do evolution (in nature) and development (in history) enter Thomas's account? To ask about *evolution* in this context may seem anachronistic. After all, Thomas lived well before Darwin and Dawkins. But that is not to say he – and indeed his source theologies and philosophies – did not meet anticipations of evolutionary naturalism and in particular the claim that it is 'all by chance'.

As Thomas was aware, Augustine had seen no difficulty for Catholic orthodoxy in the notion of self-evolving powers in nature: he considered that, in part, creation continued via the *rationes seminales*, 'seminal reasons', a code embedded in matter, enabling the latter to become both more differentiated and more complexly organised as time went on.

> According to Augustine, all things that in the course of time have come into being as the effects of divine providence working through created causes – trees and animals and so forth – all these things were produced in the very beginning in certain forms which were so to say the seeds of their later development.[42]

Chance is a more difficult nut to crack. Thomas could read

how Aristotle noted the way the pre-Socratic philosopher Em-
pedocles relied on chance to explain the otherwise
inexplicable concatenation of organs in organisms. That, considered
the philosopher, was counter-intuitive. A cause that fails to
explain the mutual coherence and co-operation of heterogeneous
parts is a non-starter. For Thomas, what is vulgarly named 'chance'
is in fact the intersection of two causal chains, not a gaping hole in
the tissue of causal operation. Darwin, no metaphysician, hardly
raised the foundational issue at all.

> Darwin's . . . conception of chance cannot help us, because that
> conception simply expresses the statistical notion of causality –
> the notion that outcomes are distributed along a curve of prob-
> abilities on which extremes are always possible. Darwin did not
> think that variations were spontaneous in the sense of being
> uncaused, only in the sense of being unpredictable, and was
> willing to leave it at that. *On the Origin of Species* is actually
> silent on the question of origin.[43]

Thomas's views on the providential government of the world (a
katabatically grounded truth, not an anabatic gleaning from
philosophy) would have made him look kindly on the approach to
evolutionary theory of Professor Keith Ward who writes:

> The apparently random element [in genetic change] is in fact
> the best way of achieving a goal-directed outcome . . . The
> process is purposive, in the important sense that it is an elegant
> and efficient law-like system for realising states of great
> value . . . [But] natural selection alone . . . is unable to predict
> what is likely to happen, and gives no reason for expecting any
> trend towards complexity and consciousness.[44]

A 'cosmic mind of immense wisdom' is a thesis of which natural
science – via first philosophy, so Thomas would add – has need.

What of *human historicity* in Thomas? Thomas speaks of
history as *narratio rerum gestarum*, a 'narrative of things done',
and regards it accordingly as one source of truth. But it would be
going too far to say that he gave much thought to the unity of all
human beings in the temporal process. Nonetheless, his theology –

and notably his anthropology – offers some bases for a more generous account of man-in-history.

To begin with, there is the *exitus-reditus* scheme itself, the axe of the Great *Summa*. The scheme implies history and the freedom of spiritual being, as well as its perfectibility through suitable response under grace. The *Prima Secundae*, after all, explores the *movement* of the rational creature towards God. Thomas speaks of the co-operation of man with divine providence in the government of the world, for 'human nature is not immobile as is divine'.[45] In the *Secunda Secundae* he describes the sequential character of the divine economy which works itself out in great epochs: 'before the Law'; 'under the Law'; 'under grace' – though that, admittedly, is a theological not a philosophical construct.[46] In many places he writes of the graduated progress of humankind in its slow march toward the acquisition of truth, both speculative and practical.[47] 'Little by little does human wit seem to have proceeded in investigating the origin of things.'[48]

The historical process of man living out his life in the midst of nature is not for Thomas to be equated with the solvific process which takes place under the impulse of grace.[49] That sort of perfecting of human endeavour which we can aim at by our natural powers (nothing wrong with that, Thomas says robustly; a creature, being the sort of thing it is, cannot help desiring the actualisation of its capacities) can be called 'beatitude' only 'in a measure'. It is not to be confused with the supernatural happiness whereby we shall see God as he is.

Conclusion on philosophy

Philosophy, natural though it be, composes a wisdom: a wisdom that works, assuredly, by the light of natural reason, simply, and yet has as its object God himself regarded as the inferred cause of things, as their (in this sense) supreme principle. In a Christian perspective, this will scarcely be able to compete with the theological wisdom that has for its object God in himself and for its immediate foundation divine revelation. Much less could it compete with the infused wisdom whose basis is charity, a wisdom that enables the soul to judge in the light of a knowledge that is, by grace, connatural with God's own. But why should we think in terms of competition anyway? These three wisdoms are in accord for they have substantial Wisdom – the divine *Logos* – as their common origin.

Now for Thomas – inspired here by the Wisdom books of the Old Testament quite as much as by the Greeks – it is the proper task of wisdom to judge and to order. Taken in its subject, then (that is, ourselves), wisdom is an habitual disposition of the mind, a mind-set which, when perfect of its kind, enables us to carry out that judging and ordering activity proper to wise persons with exactitude and ease.

To achieve this task, Thomas pressed a variety of ancient philosophies into service, as well as the work of more modern commentators thereon, not only Christian but Jewish and Muslim as well.

> All of the writings of Aquinas are fugues in which dissonant technical vocabularies are brought into some truthful harmonious relation . . . [50]

Thomas explains his aim[51] as so to teach hearers that they may come to a real understanding of the truth. This means, then, the pursuit of reasons, a searching into *veritatis radix*, the 'root of truth': a making hearers know in what way what is said is true. Without that, so Thomas feared, the hearer may have the certainty that things are as the 'teacher of Catholic truth' says they are, but she will acquire no real 'science', no thorough understanding, and so depart empty.[52] Part of St Thomas's seriousness as a Dominican, a member of the *ordo praedicatorum, ordo doctorum*, was that he was not willing to let this happen.

11.
Thomas and the Idea of Theology

In looking at Thomas's picture of theology, it is worth noting at the outset how comparatively little Thomas has to say about this subject. He did not get lost in methodology, or entangled by an over-sophisticated and ultimately obfuscating hermeneutics. He took his Bible, a decent metaphysics, the antecedent theological tradition, and got on with the job.

Nowhere does he offer a full account of the activity he calls in one place *praecipuum vitae meae officium*, the 'central occupation of my life'.[1] Nor is it easy simply to infer his idea of theology from his practice, because that practice was bound up with a variety of very different purposes. We saw as much when considering 'Thomas in his Time'. These purposes range from initiating beginners in the study of the faith in the *Summa theologiae* through – on, at least, one widely held view of the matter – arming missionaries with a handbook of arguments in the *Summa contra Gentiles*, to dealing with highly particularised requests, as in the *De regimine principum*, written for the Latin king of Cyprus, or his *Contra errores Graecorum*, written for pope Urban IV as a contribution to his reunion negotiations with the Byzantine Church. So a study of Thomas's 'method' would have to place special reliance on a small number of brief but interesting passages as well as cautious but assiduous reference to Thomas's actual practice.[2]

The prologue to the 'Writing on the Sentences': The 'modes' of theological discourse

The two places where Thomas's theology is chiefly outlined are his comments on the prologue of Peter Lombard's *Liber sententiarum* and the opening question of the *Summa theologiae*. These passages deal with the teaching of the Christian religion in its fullest sense, and especially with its biblical basis – neither excluding, therefore, what we today would call 'theology' nor restricting Aquinas thereto. So much is plain by considering the earlier of these two texts, the commentary on the prologue of *First Sentences*, dealing as this does with the nature of *sacra doctrina*. The culminating issue Thomas raises here deals with the different modes (*modi*) of discourse used in what he terms 'this knowledge', *scientia*, 'of which we are speaking'. Six such 'modes' are mentioned, and it rapidly becomes plain that five of them are not what we should immediately think of as *theological*, strictly, though they are certainly *biblical*.

Thus Thomas speaks of the *modus revelativus*, in 'revelatory' discourse, such as the accounts of visions of divine things in the prophetic books of the Canon; the *modus orativus*, in 'praying' discourse, like in the Psalms; and the *modus narrativus* or 'narrative' discourse – a term that for him covers, first, the recital of miracles confirming revelation and secondly, telling the story of exemplary actions that draw out the moral implications of revelation. Next, Thomas mentions the *modus metaphoricus* (also called *symbolicus* or *parabolicus*): such metaphorical language assists in representing revealed reality. By contrast, 'exhortatory' discourse in the *modus praeceptivus*, which he divides into submodes either 'threatening', *comminatorius*, or 'promissory', *promissivus*, has essentially the same purpose as in narratives of exemplary actions. The largely scriptural bent of the categories mentioned so far is confirmed by Thomas's commentary on the Psalter, which describes three of them as characteristic forms of biblical discourse.

The sixth and last of the modes of discourse in the comments on Peter Lombard's prologue identifies a form of expression conventionally taken as central to, at any fate, fundamental or philosophical and dogmatic or systematic theology, and this is what Thomas calls the *modus argumentatiuus*. Although the commentary on the Psalms finds such argumentative discourse in the Book of Job and the Pauline Letters – and therefore in the Bible itself – it is at this point of Aquinas's 'Writing on the *Sentences*' that we find for the first time illustrative reference to extra-biblical texts, both the works of the Fathers and the post-patristic doctrinal construction of the author of the *Book of the Sentences* himself. In *First Sentences*, Thomas treats 'argumentative' discourse as both defending the faith against errors that deform it and also 'discovering' or 'contemplating' truth in those *quaestiones* – questions or difficulties – which Scripture suggests to the mind. But if we *do* regard this 'mode' as central to the theological enterprise, we must also pay due attention to the wider context in which Thomas places argumentation: namely, the entire ensemble of divine revelation as passed on in the Church.

In *First Sentences*, the characteristics Aquinas ascribes to Christian theology are shared with all revelation-based teaching activity. Like revelation itself, such theology is founded on God's own knowledge of himself and all things. It is both speculative and practical – that is, concerned with objective truth for its own sake (speculative) and immediately directive of human action (practical). It stands higher than every other kind of human knowledge not only because of its object but also because of the light in which it sees that object. For Thomas, all these features belong to the expression of revelation as a whole – and therefore to sacred theology which is one mode of possessing or transmitting revealed truth. This theology – the term as used here must not be confused with that 'divine science or theology' which is one of Thomas's three names for metaphysics – is homogeneous with the word of God, a word it expresses in a new medium. At the start of his 'exposition' of Denys's *The Divine Names*, accordingly, Thomas declares that, although the affirmations of theology may not, as such, be contained in Scripture, they are nonetheless not 'alien from' or 'other than' its teaching: *non aliena ab hac doctrina*.[3] Nonetheless, it is clear from this early discussion as a whole that Thomas's primary desideratum for theology is that it be soaked in

Scripture: not for nothing was a high medieval master in theology first of all a lecturer on the 'sacred page'. It is, we can say, vital for the health of Catholic theology, in the twenty-first century as in the thirteenth, that it seek to give to the faithful, at all levels of sophistication, the entire revelation found in Scripture, using all the tools – from humble philology to mystical interpretation – which sane exegesis and the Church's tradition admits.

The Great *Summa*'s first question: (1) Holy teaching or sacred science?

If we turn now to the opening question of the *Summa theologiae*, we find a cognate but rather more speculatively developed account. The Great *Summa* belongs, of course, to the period of Thomas's maturity, the 'Writing on the *Sentences*' to his comparative youth. In this question, theology is described as a 'holy teaching' communicative of divine truth. By 'teaching', Thomas means not only a doctrine taught, but also – and primarily – the action of teaching it. (In his commentary on the first book of Aristotle's logical work *The Posterior Analytics* he explains that *doctrina est actio eius qui aliquid cognoscere facit*, 'teaching is the action of the one who makes something known'.[4]) Later on in the *Prima Pars*, Thomas will offer a lengthy reflection on the nature of teaching activity.[5] To the astonishment, doubtless, of present-day pedagogical theorists, he sees teaching as one fundamental way in which human beings share in the divine governance of the world.[6] God moves the creation towards the end he has elected for man. Human beings share in, and forward, this process by teaching others about their supernatural destiny.[7]

In Thomas's use of the phrase *sacra doctrina*, it would be a great mistake to think that the word *sacra* is just some loosely used pious adjective. It bears its proper meaning of 'divine'. Only God is the Teacher or Doctor in this *sacra doctrina*, just as only he is the Taught or Doctrine. The rest of us 'are its *doctores* only as the instruments for the imparting of a *veritas* which he alone strictly knows'.[8]

Apart from the importance of this thought in teaching theologians humility (not their most salient characteristic in modern

Catholicism!), it is also pertinent to the much discussed *second* article of the question, *utrum sacra doctrina sit scientia*, 'whether this holy teaching is knowledge'. In his little book *Is Theology a Science?* Père Chenu claims that *sacra doctrina* includes the functions of a science in the broadest sense of that word.[9] Theology can work 'deductively', deriving some predicate contained in a subject, or it can operate 'resolutively', working back to presuppositions that render some assertion intelligible. It can also proceed 'axiomatically', establishing the meaning of a term by reference to other terms. It will certainly make use of propositions, entailing, then, acts of judgement – either by way of putting forward an hypothesis, or more categorically saying how things are.[10] For St Thomas, *scire* is to know something in, with and through its ground, and therefore to know why it is so. Inasmuch as we merely *believe* the *sacra doctrina*, we do not (in this sense) *know* it. And yet *the divine Teacher* knows what he is teaching, and in *sacra doctrina* it is his knowledge that is impressed on human minds by faith.[11] According to Chenu, the fact that theological knowledge, building itself up in these procedures into scientific form, remains a *participated* knowledge, a share in the divine knowledge, does not subvert its (truly) scientific status. After all, a (natural) scientist's knowledge (and the man or woman in the white coat is surely the contemporary paradigm for someone with 'hard' knowledge to offer) is not absolute either. Evidence is always evidence *within a field*, and one 'system' (e.g. physics) can be subsumed under another more architectonic one (e.g. cosmology).

It needs to be said, however, that not all Thomas's 'procedures' are of this type. His theological presentation of the contents of revelation by ways of ideas of *convenientia* – fittingness, harmony – seems much closer to aesthetics (there are parallels to be drawn here with the work of that great modern theologian of beauty, Hans Urs von Balthasar).[12]

What strikes the present-day theological student as curious – if stimulatingly so – about Thomas's notion of *sacra doctrina* is the way it runs together the ideas of revelation, Scripture, Tradition and theology. True, all of these express some aspect of a cognitive relationship between man and God. But to say this is hardly to claim they are conceptually indistinguishable! St Thomas's statements, such as – at one point – his seeming identification of *sacra doctrina* and Scripture,[13] do not imply this. They imply only that for certain purposes and in certain respects *sacra doctrina* may be defined by reference to one of these disparate concepts. The inter-relations are complex, and can be traced only by going beyond the first question. Some of the material surveyed in this 'miniature' helps us to do that tracing.

The Great *Summa*'s first question: (2) The use of philosophy

The pedagogic, evangelical and even, we might go so far as to say, pastoral character of St Thomas's account of theology is well brought out in the question's fifth article, 'Is Christian theology more valuable (*dignior*) than all the other sciences?' Returning the answer 'Yes!', Thomas has to meet the objection that, in point of fact, theology is parasitic on philosophy – and thus to deal with the issue of the place within *doctrina* of the 'philosophical disciplines'. Thomas writes:

> This knowledge [i.e. the holy teaching] can draw upon philo-sophical disciplines, not because it has absolute need of them, but for the greater clarification of what is conveyed in this knowledge. For it does not draw its premises from other sciences, but directly from God through revelation. Thus it does not draw upon other sciences as though they were superior to it, but it makes use of them as its subordinates and handmaids, just as master-building employs subsidiary crafts and the civil authority makes use of military arts and sciences.

To drive the point home, Thomas adds for good measure:

> And the fact that it [the holy teaching] thus makes use of them is not on account of any deficiency or inadequacy in itself, but is on account of the deficiency of our understanding, which is more easily led to those matters that transcend reason and are set forth in this science by means of such matters as are known by natural reason and from which other sciences arise.

The *ancillary* role, then, of philosophy in the holy teaching is that of meeting the subjective requirements of the learner. For Thomas, theology is controlled by the needs of preaching and teaching the faith and of the cure of souls – and yet in given cases (the *Summa theologiae* is one) those very needs may be best satisfied by offering an architectonic vision of truth as an integrated whole. Hence the later Thomistic goal of constructing a systematic, scientific discipline of theology-with-philosophy as an end in itself (albeit, of course, in revelation's service) is not without its 'Thomasian' foundation, a rooting in the historical Thomas Aquinas.

Evidently, Thomas has not abandoned, in the *Summa theologiae*, his earlier idea of how theology has, importantly, an 'argumentative mode' in the *Scriptum super Sententiis*. As he will stress in the eighth article of the *Summa*'s opening question ('Is this teaching probative?'), the holy teaching does indeed make use of rational arguments. Thomas expatiates on how such rational argumentation needs to be variously employed if it is to serve the diverse kinds of human being with whom the teacher will deal. Called as he is to work with all sorts and conditions of men, the *doctor veritatis catholicae* will surely encounter those who already accept some but not all of the items of the *doctrina* as well as those who, being without faith, accept none at all. The person who concedes some but denies others can be shown how the items she denies follow upon or tie in with the items she accepts. With regard to the outright unbeliever, the teacher cannot prove the faith to her but he can, on the basis of natural reason and without explicit reference to revelation, help her to dissolve false reasonings which are an obstacle to faith.

The need to show, positively, the coherence of the contents of the Creed and, negatively, to rebut arguments against the articles of faith, is one important (bipartite) rationale for the large amount of natural theology the *Summa theologiae* contains. It is not that Thomas gives priority to rational argumentation *vis-à-vis* the witness of Scripture and Fathers, the texts that testify to revelation. Rather is it that such arguments are an indispensable constituent of *sacra doctrina* inasmuch as they constitute irreplaceable equipment for a teacher of the Catholic faith.

There is also another rationale Thomas offers for the presence of a good deal of philosophical-sounding material within a theological work. Revelation does not consist exclusively of truths that go beyond the range of human reason, even though theological science, in his words, 'bears principally on what, by its elevation, transcends reason'.[14] In addition, God has revealed truths that are actually accessible to reason but, alas, not readily so.[15] The chief precepts of the natural law, formulated in the Ten Commandments, are a good instance of this.

And in fact it follows from Thomas's insertion of *sacra doctrina* into a very human context of teaching and learning that we might expect it to respect the intrinsic nature of human *ratio*, of natural reason. At the same time, thanks to the supernatural nature of the holy teaching's content, it is also predictable that Thomas will insist that we allow such *ratio* to be suitably illumined from above by the light of faith.

Reason and faith, philosophy and holy teaching, are not the same but neither do they live in two hermetically sealed compartments. They are distinct, but not unrelated.

To deal with the distinctness first.[16] Faith and reason are distinct in terms of their sources, in terms of their procedures and in terms of their subject matter. Thus, as to *sources*: faith draws its principles from divine revelation, the foundational truths expressed in the Creed, whereas philosophy acquires its basic principles from intellectual research aimed at gaining a knowledge of the structure of reality. As to *procedures*: reason proceeds by synthesising the experiential knowledge it gains, analysing this and drawing appropriate conclusions, whereas the holy teaching rests on the divine authorisation of the Creed, while using concepts, principles and observation as well as solid philosophy to penetrate more deeply the meaning of what has been revealed. This (enormous) difference between the sources and procedures of the two is justified by the difference of their *subject matter*, which in the case of holy teaching is God, inasmuch as he has revealed himself and his saving design for man, and in the case of philosophy is man, nature and – key phrase for metaphysics – being *qua* being. Here we rejoin that distinction between the anabatic and the katabatic explored in Chapter 3 of this study, on 'God and Creation'.

Thomas was keenly interested in philosophy for its own sake

as well as for its possible services to the faith. Despite the limitations of the texts at his disposal, he can be called a critical historian of the philosophical tradition, who grappled successfully with the diverse tendencies of the Platonist and Aristotelian schools. He took philosophical truth with great seriousness, not least because this foundational knowledge also prompts what I have called the 'anabatic' approach from creatures to God.

The distinction, then, between philosophy and the holy teaching is only too apparent. But not less so, according to Aquinas, is the harmony. Both natural reason and the doctrine of faith have their origin in God who has given man the principles of each to work with. Contradiction between them is out of the question.[17] The supernatural order presupposes the natural order and brings it to fulfilment – so happy collaboration between them is the order of the day. Of course, the philosophy in question must be a *true* philosophy (otherwise it is worse than useless), and one symptom of the putative truth of any philosophical affirmation will be its congruence with what we know from revelation to be the case. The issue of using the right philosophical tool in Catholic theology is an extremely pertinent one today both in dogmatic theology (one thinks of the attempt to deploy Marxian categories in 'Liberation Theology') and in moral theology (compare the employment of Utilitarian ethics in their 'Proportionalist' form in that moral theology known as 'moderated teleology', which found itself under papal fire in the encyclical *Veritatis splendor*).

The Great *Summa*'s first question: (3) Turning to the images

Thomas's penultimate article in this question returns to the topic of that 'metaphorical mode' of theological discourse which earlier figured in the 'Writing on the *Sentences*'. Should the holy teaching use metaphorical or symbolic expressions? At Leo XIII's insistence, the edition of Thomas's works which bears the pope's name began in somewhat unseemly haste with an imperfectly critical version of the *Summa theologiae*. That Leonine edition reads at this point, 'Is it fitting that "sacred *Scripture*" uses metaphor?'

But it would seem that 'sacred *doctrine*' is what Thomas really wrote. While, it is true, the article has chiefly to do with the symbolic, metaphorical and parabolic language of the Bible, its principles are meant to apply to any vehicle of the holy teaching. Here again, it is the requirements of the learner that are paramount. God, as Thomas says, provides for all as befits their nature. But the nature of human consciousness is such that it is led from sense images to intellectual understanding. As he will put it in a later question of the *Prima Pars*:

> By the revelation of grace, the natural light of the intellect finds itself reinforced by the infusion of the light of grace; and sometimes, equally, phantasms [images] are formed under the divine action in the imagination of man – phantasms that express divine things more than those we draw in natural fashion from sensuous realities.[18]

Thomas as mystical theologian

That Thomas must have something to say about Christianity's mystical dimension follows ineluctably from his theological epistemology and even, indeed, from his theological method. The higher knowledge given in revelation is wholly by grace – and therefore the work of God – and yet happens to us as the perfecting of our intellectual natures.[19] So likewise, theology respects and responds to the intrinsic nature of human reason while at the same time insisting that, thanks to revelation's supernatural content, reason here must be illumined from above by the light of faith.[20] This light is for Thomas light shining from the End, an anticipation of the light of glory. And this can be seen from the tendency of theological reason to abolish itself as a way of understanding and be resolved into *intellectus*, a simple, unitive, 'at-a-glance' kind of knowing.

But then there is also, in Thomas's corpus, a whole series of references to a way of perception that is closer to things – even divine things – if also more 'confused' than the knowledge acquired by theological study. In the opening question of the *Prima Pars* he speaks of judgement by bent, *per modum inclinationis*, in contrast to judgement by enquiry, *per modum cognitionis*. He refers to this flair for the reality that underlies and lies beyond, for conceptualisation, as a sure discernment by kinship, *propter connaturalitatem*.

Elsewhere in the Great *Summa*, he treats it as a recognition arising from natural attraction and setting up a relation of *affinitas*, as of marriage. He can describe it as a familiarity from habit or second nature; as sympathy, *compassio*, and 'undergoing', *patiens*, rather than learning about, *discens*; as acting with instinctive sureness rather than rational certitude; as a prompting – *instinctus* – and touching – *contactus* – as well as real union; as *assimilatio* or 'being made like', in an experience that is charged with love, a *cognitio affectiva sive experimentalis*.[21] This perception of an existential and mystical depth to theology is especially developed in Thomas's account of the Gifts of the Holy Spirit where Trinitarian theology and moral theology come together,[22] as well as in his accounts of the effects of love[23] and ecstatic rapture.[24] Such love, says Thomas, generates a reciprocal abiding – *mutua inhaesio*; a transport – *extasis* – out of self towards the other; a melting – *liquefactio* – so that the heart is open to be entered; a longing in absence – *languor*; fervour in pursuing – *fervor*; and enjoyment in presence – *fruitio*. God's self-communication by grace takes up the purely natural psychological phenomenon of *appetitus*, our movement towards some perceived good out of a desire for union with the real: takes it up and draws it into an apprehension of the Trinity, one of whom became incarnate for us.

Revelation – and this is a point likely to be lost to view in a naturalistic age – has a power to affect souls going way beyond what even the most cogent philosophising can manage. In his commentary on the Apostles' Creed, Thomas describes how revelation, as received by Christian faith, brings four good things in its train: union with God; the inchoate knowledge of God; direction for this present life; victory over temptations.[25] In this sense, the supernatural counterpart of the philosopher is not so much the theologian as the saint – and the truly decisive contrast is not between two intellectual methods but rather two *ways of life*.[26]

Conclusion on theology

In Chapter 2, we were able to see how, for Thomas, revelation does not consist so much of public events as of cognitive acts in which the intellect works on its materials according to a *lumen propheticum*, a way of conferring greater luminosity on beings that transcends the 'natural light of the intellect' (*lumen naturale intellectus*) and yet still enjoys an analogous relation with that lesser light. It is – so far as the New Covenant is concerned – a vision in the inspired mind of apostle and evangelist, a vision above all in the prophetic human mind of Jesus Christ. Thomas distinguishes 'prophetic light' *both* from the beatifying *lumen gloriae* which represents an 'intellectual light in the mode of a permanent, perfect form'[27] *and* from the 'light' that makes possible the act of faith – an act cognitively imperfect since the assent made to truth by the mind in believing is given to a knowledge possessed not by the believer himself but by some other.[28] However, for Thomas *any* genuine cognition of God, even in the inchoate form of the habit of faith, has an eschatological character, in that it bears explanation only in terms of a sharing in God's own knowledge of himself. It is a distant approximation (brought closer by the Gifts of the Holy Spirit at play in the lives of the mystics) to that *scientia beatorum* which the saints enjoy not in the order of grace, simply, but in the order of glory. As I ended my account of 'Thomas in his Time', his theology, 'no matter how speculative its flights, had never had an ultimate goal different from that of Benedict or Bernard in the heavenly city of God'.[29]

This gives formal epistemological expression to the soteriological value of revealed knowledge. And indeed, the unifying concept that holds together all the varied aspects of revelation is *salus*, 'salvation'.

> It was necessary for the salvation of man that he should have, beyond the philosophical disciplines investigated by human reason, a teaching that proceeds from divine revelation.[30]

What is revealed, in all its diversity, is, in each and every case, some instance of 'everything the knowledge of which can be useful for salvation'. St Thomas's concept of theology as *sacra doctrina* follows from St Dominic's idea of *sancta praedicatio,* the holy preaching. We know that the greater part of his *praedicatio* consisted in long and gruelling discussions with Albigensian leaders – and followers. When he dispersed his brethren into the great urban and University centres of Europe it was to teach and evangelise not least by acquainting themselves with how the people of the time were thinking, what were their needs and the ways in which those needs might be met. But this is not to be taken in some merely pragmatist sense! To Thomas's way of thinking, human salvation and the perfection of man as an intellectual being are one and the same. As the *Summa contra Gentiles* puts it, 'the ultimate salvation of man is that he may be perfected in his intellectual aspect by the contemplation of the First Truth'.[31]

Conclusion

It is his combination of breathtakingly simple intellectual confidence in revelation and the tireless industry with which mental acumen is set to explore it for the good of souls that makes Thomas so valuable an icon of the Christian mind in the Church today. Thanks to its clarity and comprehensiveness, the apostolic value of St Thomas's thought and writing is very great, and his achievement still needed in the Church.

Even at the catechetical level his work remains of enormous use. One could put together an excellent commentary on the new *Catechism of the Catholic Church* by reading for instance: for Book 1 (on the Creed), the *Expositio symboli apostolorum* and the *De articulis fidei*; for Book 2 (on the Liturgy), the treatise *De ecclesiae sacramentis*; for Book 3 (on morals), the *De decem praeceptis et lege amoris*; for Book 4 (on prayer), the *Expositio orationis dominicae*. There is a whole course of first-rate Christian initiation here just waiting to be given.

At the level of theology proper, however, the hermeneutical over-sophistication of much Catholic theology today, and the weak metaphysical sense of many of its practitioners, are major obstacles to the retrieval of classical Thomism in seminaries and University faculties. If one believes that in Thomas the tradition of the Fathers at last met a philosophical culture worthy of them, this can only be judged a regrettable circumstance.

Hermeneutics has become a bogey with which to frighten the children, and yet, when not envenomed by a relativistic and epistemologically agnostic attitude towards truth, its message is really rather simple. Appropriating ancient – including medieval – texts requires an effort of understanding and not just philological skills.

Of course, no one can deny that numerous features in my

cultural environment as well as my personal life-story *do* furnish me with certain schemata, a tendency to understand a text from the past according to preconceived notions. But a more satisfactory hermeneutic will treat such schemata as essentially corrigible, capable of correction by the text as understanding grows. For all human beings share a common potential to be other than they are. They are not obliged to see everything from one viewpoint. It is significant that, in the theological context, those who most insist that, hermeneutically, understanding is always situated and there-fore non-objective are, in matters of foundational theology, the most likely to propose a notion of the primacy of 'praxis' (practical action) over theory – even though in the non-theological context, hermeneutical theory and the Marxian concept of praxis have little or no original points of contact. The denial that we can transcend our situation sufficiently to attain that correct understanding of past texts which alone deserves the name 'knowledge' – in the theo-logical case, the knowledge of revelation found in Scripture and ecclesial tradition – necessarily creates a vacuum which the idea of the primacy of praxis alone is suited to fill. A concept of transforma-tive action so set up as to be defined at any rate dialectically, in part, over against theory of every possible sort, is, for the non-objective interpreter of the Christian's 'story', the answer to a maiden's prayer.

But Thomas would have us see that *veritas sequitur esse rerum*, 'Truth follows upon the being of things'. This key notion, and its fellow, namely, that truth is the real relation between *intellectus*, mind, and *res*, 'thing' – that is, reality – are desperately needed today. The enrichments the Catholic theological tradition has received from revivals in patristics, liturgics, and biblical exegesis, the broadening of human sense and sensibility it has undergone through encounters with philosophies like phenomenology, per-sonalism, existentialism, and from the (not always so scientific!) human sciences, depend for any enduring value on the perpetuation of a sane and adequate metaphysics in the Church. The hour is striking when a recall to the ontological theology of Thomas is urgent.

My task of helping readers to 'discover' Aquinas is done. This book has presented Aquinas in miniature. It has tried to recapture the lucidity and splendour of Thomas's thought, qualities already apparent in the image chosen for the cover. Reflecting on the confused and unattractive face contemporary Christianity often shows the world, the reader may be struck by the contrast of the beauty this 'miniature' displays.

Bibliography

Texts of St Thomas's writings

A critical text of all Thomas's authentic works is being prepared by the Leonine Commission, so called from its foundation by Pope Leo XIII in 1880. When complete, the edition will fill 50 folio volumes. Meanwhile, the most convenient form of the Latin text is generally that published by the house of Marietti (Turin and Rome).

The *Summa contra Gentiles* is available in English as *On the Truth of the Catholic Faith* (New York, 1955–7), in five volumes.

For the *Summa theologiae*, the Anglophone reader may choose between two translations brought out under the aegis of the English Dominican Province, one more literal (London, 1912–36) in 22 volumes, reprinted in a 3–volume edition at New York in 1947–8, and one more fluent if also paraphrastic, in 60 volumes (London and New York, 1964–77).

For the *Compendium theologiae*, a useful précis by Thomas, there is *Compendium of Theology* (St Louis, 1947), reprinted as *Light of Faith. The Compendium of Theology* (Manchester, NH, 1993).

English readers are poorly served where the biblical works of Thomas are concerned, but there exist translations of his commentaries on Galatians and Ephesians (Albany, NY, 1966), as well as First Thessalonians and Philippians (Albany, 1969). There is a part translation of the commentary on the Gospel according to John (Albany, 1980). One should not forget the Tractarian translation of the 'continuous gloss on the Gospels', the *Catena Aurea* (Oxford, 1841–5, reprinted Southampton, 1997).

A number of the sets of 'disputed questions' have been translated, notably: *On Truth* (Chicago, 1952–4), in 3 volumes; *On the Power of God* (London, 1932–4), in 3 volumes (reprinted at Westminster, MD, 1952); *On Spiritual Creatures* (Milwaukee, 1951); *The Soul* (St Louis, 1949); *On the Virtues in General* (Providence, RI, 1951); *On Charity* (Milwaukee, 1960).

Translations are extant of Thomas's commentaries on Aristotle's corpus: *Aristotle on Interpretation* (Milwaukee, 1962); *Commentary on the Posterior Analytics of Aristotle* (Albany, NY, 1970); *Commentary on Aristotle's Physics* (New Haven, 1963); *Aristotle's 'De Anima' with the Commentary of St Thomas Aquinas* (New Haven, 1951); *Commentary on the Metaphysics of Aristotle* (Chicago, 1964); *Commentary on the Nicomachean Ethics* (Chicago, 1964).

Another major commentary by Thomas which has found its way into English is that on the *De Trinitate* of Boethius: *The Trinity and the Unicity of the Intellect* (St Louis, 1946), with further part translations: *On Searching into God* (Oxford, 1947); *Divisions and Methods of the Sciences* (Toronto, 1953).

A particularly painless way to enter Thomas's spiritual and intellectual world is via his sermons on the Apostles' Creed, Our Father, and Hail Mary, published in English as *The Three Greatest Prayers* (London, 1937).

For further details of translations of the minor works, see the full (at time of publication) listing in J. A. Weisheipl, *Friar Thomas d'Aquino. His Life, Thought and Works* (Washington, 1983, 3rd edition).

Bibliographical sources

V. J. Bourke, *Thomistic Bibliography, 1920–1940* (St Louis, Missouri, 1945).

R. Busa (ed.), *Index Thomisticus* (Stuttgart-Bad Canstatt, 1974–80).

C. Giacon, 'Sussidi lessicali e bibliografici per lo studio di S. Tommaso', *Seminarium* 29 (1977), pp. 918–93.

R. Ingarden, *Thomas Aquinas. International Bibliography, 1977–1990* (Bowling Green, Ohio, n.d. but c. 1993).

F. P. Mandonnet and J. Destrez, *Bibliographie thomiste* (Kain, 1921).

T. L. Miethe and V. J. Bourke, *Thomistic Bibliography, 1940–1978* (Westport, CT and London, 1980).

P. Wyser, *Thomas von Aquin* (= *Bibliographische Einführungen in das Studium der Philosophie 13–14*) (Berne, 1950).

P. Wyser, *Der Thomismus* (= *Bibliographische Einführungen in das Studium der Philosophie, 15–16*) (Berne, 1951).

See also for an ongoing survey, *Rassegna di letteratura tomista* (Naples, 1969–), which continues the former *Bulletin thomiste* (Le Saulchoir, 1923–68).

Chapter 1: Thomas in his Time

D. A. Callus, 'Les sources de Saint Thomas: état de la question', in L. de Raeymaker (ed.), *Aristote et saint Thomas* (Louvain-Paris, 1957).

M.-D. Chenu, *Introduction à l'étude de saint Thomas d'Aquin* (Montreal-Paris, 1954, 2nd edition); Eng. translation, *Toward Understanding Saint Thomas* (Chicago, 1964).

B. Davies, *The Thought of Thomas Aquinas* (Oxford, 1992).

R. Garrigou-Lagrange, *La Synthèse thomiste* (Paris, 1946).

N. Kretzmann and E. Stump (eds), *The Cambridge Companion to Aquinas* (Cambridge, 1993).

J. Pieper, *Hinführung zu Thomas von Aquin: Zwölf Vorlesungen* (Munich, 1958).

F. Selman, *Thomas Aquinas, Teacher of Truth* (Edinburgh, 1994).

J.-P. Torrell, *Initiation à saint Thomas d'Aquin* (Fribourg-Paris, 1993); Eng. translation, *Saint Thomas Aquinas, I. The Person and his Work* (Washington DC, 1996).

J.-P. Torrell, *Saint Thomas d'Aquin: maître spirituel* (Paris, 1996).

D. Tracy (ed.), *Celebrating the Mediaeval Heritage: a Colloquy on the Thought of Aquinas and Bonaventure* (= *Journal of Religion Supplement*, 1978).

S. Tugwell, *Albert and Thomas. Selected Writings* (New York and Mahwah, NJ, 1988).

J. A. Weisheipl, *Friar Thomas d'Aquino. His Life, Thought and Works* (Washington DC, 1983, 3rd edition).

Chapter 2: Revelation

Revelation at large

L. Elders (ed.), *La doctrine de la révélation divine de saint Thomas d'Aquin* (= *Studi tomistici* 37) (Vatican City, 1990).

V. White, 'St Thomas's Conception of Revelation', *Dominican Studies* I. 1 (1948), pp. 3–34.

P. E. Persson, *Reason and Revelation in Aquinas* (Eng. translation, Oxford, 1970).

The Bible

M. Aillet, *Lire la Bible avec s. Thomas. Le passage de la 'littera' à la 'res' dans la 'Somme théologique'* (Fribourg, 1993).

M. Arias Reyero, *Thomas von Aquin als Exeget* (Einsiedeln, 1971).

M.-D. Mailhot, 'La pensée de saint Thomas sur le sens spirituel', *Revue Thomiste* 59 (1959), pp. 613–63.

C. Spicq, 'Saint Thomas d'Aquin exégète', *Dictionnaire de théologie catholique* 15. 1 (Paris, 1946), cols. 94–738.

P. Synave, 'La doctrine de saint Thomas d'Aquin sur le sens littéral des Ecritures', *Revue biblique* (1926), pp. 40–65.

B. E. Smalley, *The Study of the Bible in the Middle Ages* (2nd edition, Oxford, 1952).

B. E. Smalley, *The Study of the Gospels in the Schools, c. 1100–c. 1280* (London and Ronceverte, 1985), pp. 257–79.

Tradition

L.-J. Bataillon, 'Saint Thomas et les Pères: de la *Catena aurea* à la *Tertia pars*', in C.-J. Pinto da Oliveira (ed.), *Ordo sapientiae et amoris. Image et message de saint Thomas d'Aquin à travers les récentes études histo-riques, herméneutiques et doctrinales* (Fribourg, 1993), pp. 13–36.

Y. Congar, 'Tradition et *sacra doctrina* chez saint Thomas d'Aquin', in J. Betz and H. Fries (eds), *Eglise et Tradition* (Le Puy, 1963), pp. 157–94.

E. Ménard, *La Tradition. Révélation, Ecriture, Eglise selon saint Thomas d'Aquin* (Bruges-Paris, 1964).

Faith

B. Duroux, *La psychologie de la foi chez saint Thomas d'Aquin* (Tournai, 1963).

E. Schillebeeckx, 'L'instinct de la foi selon saint Thomas d'Aquin', *Revue des Sciences philosophiques et théologiques* 48 (1964), pp. 377–408.

Chapter 3: God and Creation

J. A. Aertsen, *Nature and Creature. Thomas Aquinas's Way of Thought* (Leiden, 1988).

E. Bailleux, 'La création, oeuvre de la Trinité, selon saint Thomas', *Revue thomiste* 62 (1962), pp. 27–50.

D. Burrell, *Aquinas. God and Action* (Notre Dame, Ind., 1975).

H.-F. Dondaine, 'Cognoscere de Deo *quid est*', *Recherches de théologie ancienne et mediévale* 22 (1955), pp. 72–8.

R. Garrigou-Lagrange, *Dieu, son existence et sa nature* (Paris, 1915).

R. Garrigou-Lagrange, *De Deo uno* (Rome, 1937).

R. Garrigou-Lagrange, *De Deo trino et creatore* (Rome, 1945).

W. Hankey, *Aquinas's Doctrine of God as expounded in the 'Summa theo-logiae'* (London, 1987).

N. Kretzmann, *The Metaphysics of Theism. Aquinas's Natural Theology in 'Summa contra gentiles' I* (Oxford, 1997).

J. Maritain, *St Thomas and the Problem of Evil* (Milwaukee, 1942).

J. Owens, *St Thomas Aquinas on the Existence of God. Collected Papers of Joseph Owens* (Albany, NY, 1980).

V. White, 'The Prolegomena to the Five Ways', *Dominican Studies* V (1952), pp. 134–58.

Chapter 4: The Trinity

E. Bailleux, 'Le personnalisme de saint Thomas en théologie trinitaire', *Revue thomiste* 61 (1961), pp. 25–42.

E. Bailleux, 'La création, oeuvre de la Trinité selon saint Thomas', *Revue thomiste* 62 (1962), pp. 27–50.

E. Bailleux, 'Le cycle des missions trinitaires d'après saint Thomas', *Revue thomiste* 63 (1963), pp. 166–92.

F. L. B. Cunningham, *St Thomas' Doctrine on the Divine Indwelling in the Light of Scholastic Tradition* (Dubuque, Iowa, 1955).

J. F. Dedek, *Experimental Knowledge of the Indwelling Trinity: an Historical Study of the Doctrine of S. Thomas* (Mundelein, Ill., 1958).

G. Emery, *La Trinité créatrice. Trinité et création dans les commentaires aux Sentences de Thomas d'Aquin et de ses précurseurs Albert le Grand et Bonaventure* (Paris, 1995).

A. Krempel, *La doctrine de la relation chez saint Thomas. Exposé historique et critique* (Paris, 1952).

B. J. F. Lonergan, *Verbum: Word and Idea in Aquinas* (Notre Dame, Ind., 1967).

A. Malet, *Personne et amour dans la théologie trinitaire de saint Thomas d'Aquin* (Paris, 1956).

Chapter 5: The Trinity in Man

E. Bailleux, 'A l'image du Fils premier-né', *Revue thomiste* 76 (1976), pp. 181–207.

L.-M. de Blignières, 'La dignité de l'homme image de Dieu selon saint Thomas d'Aquin', *Studi tomistici* 42 (Vatican City, 1991), pp. 199–220.

I. Hislop, OP, 'Man the Image of the Trinity according to Saint Thomas', *Dominican Studies* III. 1 (1950), pp. 1–9.

M.-J. S. de Laugier de Beaureceuil, 'L'homme image de Dieu selon saint Thomas d'Aquin', *Etudes et recherches* 8 (1952), pp. 45–82; 9 (1953), pp. 37–97.

D. J. Merriell, *To the Image of the Trinity, A Study in the development of Aquinas's teaching* (Toronto, 1990).

Chapter 6: Angelology

J. D. Collins, *The Thomistic Philosophy of the Angels* (Washington, 1947).

M. L. Guérard des Lauriers, 'Le péché et la causalité', *Bulletin thomiste* XI (1962), pp 553–637.

C. V. Héris, OP, *Les Anges*, (= *Revue des Jeunes* edition and translation of *Summa theologiae*, Ia., qq. 50–64) (Paris, 1952).

D. Keck, *Angels and Angelology in the Middle Ages* (New York and Oxford, 1998).

D. P. Lang, 'Aquinas's Proof for the Existence and Nature of the Angels', *Faith and Reason* 21, 1–2 (1995), pp. 3–16.

J. Maritain, *The Sin of the Angel* (Westminster, MD, Eng. translation 1959).

Chapter 7: Grace and the Virtues

Grace

H. Bouillard, *Conversion et grâce chez saint Thomas d'Aquin. Etude historique* (Paris, 1944).

C. Ernst, *The Theology of Grace* (Dublin and Cork, 1974).

B. J. F. Lonergan, *Grace and Freedom: Operative Grace in the Thought of St Thomas Aquinas* (London, 1971).

A. Williams, 'Deification in the *Summa Theologiae*: a Structural Interpretation of the *Prima Pars*', *The Thomist* 61 (1977), pp. 219–55.

A. Williams, *The Ground of Union. Deification in Aquinas and Palamas* (New York and Oxford, 1999), pp. 34–101.

The Virtues

Ch.-A. Bernard, *La théologie de l'espérance selon saint Thomas d'Aquin* (Paris, 1961).

R. Cessario, *The Moral Virtues and Theological Ethics* (Notre Dame, Ind., 1991).

P. Geach, *The Virtues* (Cambridge, 1977).

L.-B. Geiger, *Le problème de l'amour chez saint Thomas d'Aquin* (Montreal-Paris, 1952).

R. McInerny, 'Ethics', in N. Kretzmann and E. Stump (eds), *The Cambridge Companion to Aquinas* (Cambridge, 1993), pp. 196–216.

S. Pinckaers, *Les sources de la morale chrétienne* (Paris, 1987).

J. Porter, *Recovery of Virtue. The Relevance of Aquinas for Christian Ethics* (Louisville, Kentucky, 1990).

E. Schockenhoff, *Bonum Hominis. Die anthropologischen und theologischen Grundlagen der Tugendethik des Thomas von Aquinas* (Mainz, 1987).

The Gifts of the Holy Spirit

A. Gardeil, *The Gifts of the Holy Ghost in the Dominican Saints* (Eng. translation, Milwaukee, 1952).

M. M. Labourdette, 'Dons du Saint-Esprit: doctrine thomiste', *Dictionnaire de spiritualité* 3 (Paris, 1956), cols. 1610–35.

M. M. Philipon, 'Les dons du Saint-Esprit chez saint Thomas d'Aquin', *Revue thomiste* 59 (1959), pp. 451–83.

Chapter 8: Christ, Church, Sacraments
Christology

A.-M. Carré, *Le Christ de saint Thomas d'Aquin* (Paris, 1944).

G. Lohaus, *Die Geheimnissse des Lebens Jesu in der 'Summa theologiae' des heiligen Thomas von Aquin* (Freiburg im Breisgau, 1985).

F. Ruello, *La Christologie de Thomas d'Aquin* (Paris, 1987).

L. Scheffczyk, 'Die Stellung des Thomas von Aquin in der Entwicklung der Lehre von den *Mysteria Vitae Christi*', in M. Gerwing and G. Ruppert (eds), *Renovatio et reformatio. Festschrift für Ludwig Höll* (Münster, 1986), pp. 44–70.

M. Seckler, *Das Heil in der Geschichte. Geschichtstheologisches Denken bei Thomas von Aquin* (Munich, 1964).

J.-P. Torrell, OP, *Le Christ en ses mystères. La vie de Jésus dans l'oeuvre de Thomas d'Aquin* (Paris, 1999).

Ecclesiology

Y. Congar, 'L'Idée de l'Eglise chez S. Thomas d'Aquin', *Esquisses du mystère de l'Eglise* (Paris, 1953), pp. 59–91.

Y. Congar, '"Ecclesia" et "populus (fidelis)" dans l'ecclésiologie de saint Thomas', in A. Maurer (ed.), *St Thomas Aquinas, 1274–1974. Commemorative Studies* (Toronto, 1974), I, pp. 159–74.

Y. Congar, 'Vision de l'Eglise chez Thomas d'Aquin', *Revue des sciences philosophiques et théologiques* 62 (1978), pp. 523–42.

A. Dulles, SJ, 'The Church according to Thomas Aquinas', in *A Church to Believe In. Discipleship and the Dynamics of Freedom* (New York, 1983), pp. 149–69.

M. Grabmann, *Die Lehre des heiligen Thomas von Aquin von der Kirche als Gotteswerk. Ihre Stellung im thomistischen System und in der Geschichte der mittelalterlichen Theologie* (Regensburg, 1903).

A. Osuna, 'La doctrina de los estadios de la Iglesia en Santo Tomàs', *Ciencia tomista* 88 (1961), pp. 77–135, 215–66.

G. Sabra, *Thomas Aquinas's Vision of the Church: Fundamentals of an Ecumenical Ecclesiology* (Mainz, 1987).

E. Vauthier, 'Le Saint-Esprit, principe d'unité de l'Eglise d'après saint Thomas d'Aquin. Corps mystique et inhabitation du Saint-Esprit', *Mélanges de science religieuse* 5 (1948), pp. 175–96; 6 (1949), pp. 57–80.

Sacramentology

J.-H. Nicolas, 'Réactualisation des mystères rédempteurs dans et par les sacrements', *Revue thomiste* 58 (1958), pp. 20–54.

C. O'Neill, *Meeting Christ in the Sacraments* (New York, 1964; revised edition by R. Cessario, New York, 1991).

C. O'Neill, *Sacramental Realism: a General Theory of the Sacraments* (Wilmington, Del., 1983).

Chapter 9: Thomas in History

S.-T. Bonino (ed.), *Saint Thomas au XXe siècle. Actes du Colloque du centenaire de la 'Revue thomiste', 25–28 mars 1993, Toulouse* (Paris, 1994).

C. Fabro, 'San Tommaso d'Aquino', *Enciclopedia cattolica* XII (1959), pp. 252–98.

C. Fabro, *Introduzione a San Tommaso. La metafisica tomista e il pensiero moderno* (Milan, 1983).

A. Gardeil, OP, 'La réforme de la théologie catholique', *Revue thomiste* 11 (1903), pp. 197–215; 428–57.

R. Garrigou-Lagrange, 'Thomisme', *Dictionnaire de théologie catholique* XV (Paris, 1950), cols. 823–1023.

C. Giacon, *La seconda scolastica. I grandi commentatori di s. Tommaso* (Milan, 1943–6).

E. Gilson, *History of Christian Philosophy in the Middle Ages* (New York, 1955).

D. W. Hudson and D. W. Moran (eds), *The Future of Thomism* (Notre Dame, Ind., 1992).

P. Mandonnet, 'Frères Prêcheurs (théologie dans l'Ordre de)', *Dictionnaire de théologie catholique*, VI (Paris, 1950), cols. 864–924.

G. A. McCool, *Catholic Theology in the Nineteenth Century: the Quest for a Unitary Method* (New York, 1977).

G. A. McCool, *From Unity to Pluralism. The Internal Evolution of Thomism* (New York, 1989).

G. Prouvost, *Thomas d'Aquin et les thomismes. Essai sur l'histoire des thomismes* (Paris, 1996).

F. van Steenberghen, 'L'avenir du thomisme', in van Steenberghen, *Introduction à l'étude de la philosophie médiévale* (Louvain-Paris, 1966), pp. 240–56.

K. Werner, *Der heilige Thomas von Aquin III. Geschichte des Thomismus* (Regensburg, 1859; New York, 1963).

Chapter 10: Thomas and the Practice of Philosophy
Overviews

E. Gilson, *The Philosophy of St Thomas Aquinas* (2nd edition of Eng. translation, Cambridge and St Louis, 1929).

E. Gilson, *The Christian Philosophy of St Thomas* (New York, 1956).

M. de Wulf, *An Introduction to Scholastic Philosophy, Mediaeval and Modern* (Eng. translation, Dover, Mass., 1956).

Metaphysics

J. A. Aertsen, 'Die Transzendentalienlehre bei Thomas von Aquin in ihren historischen Hintergründen und philosophischen Motiven', *Miscellanea mediaevalia* 19 (1988), pp. 82–102.

F. D'Agostini, 'Analitici, Continentali, Tomisti: la filosofia e il sense dell' "essere" ', *Divus Thomas* 24 (1999), pp. 53–79.

J. C. Doig, *Aquinas on Metaphysics: a Historical-Doctrinal Study of the Commentary on the Metaphysics* (The Hague, 1972).

L. Elders, *The Metaphysics of Being in St Thomas Aquinas* (Leiden, 1993).

C. Fabro, *Participation et causalité selon saint Thomas d'Aquin* (Louvain-Paris, 1961).

J. de Finance, sj, *Etre et agir dans la philosophie de saint Thomas* (Paris, 1943).

A. Forest, *La structure métaphysique du concret selon saint Thomas d'Aquin* (Paris, 1931).

L. B. Geiger, *La participation dans la philosophie de saint Thomas d'Aquin* (Paris 1953, 2nd edition).

M. D. Jordan, 'The Evidence of the Transcendentals and the Place of Beauty in Thomas Aquinas', *International Philosophical Quarterly* 29 (1989), pp. 394–407.

H. Lyttkens, *The Analogy between God and the World in St Thomas. An Investigation of its Background and Interpretation of its Use* (Uppsala, 1953).

R. McInerny, *The Logic of Analogy. An Introduction to St Thomas* (The Hague, 1961).

J. F. Wippel, *Metaphysical Themes in Thomas Aquinas* (Washington DC, 1984).

J. F. Wippel, 'Metaphysics', in N. Kretzmann and E. Stump (eds), *The Cambridge Companion to Aquinas* (Cambridge, 1993), pp. 85–127.

Man

M. Brasa Diez, 'La historicided del hombre según Santo Tomàs', *Atti del VII Congresso Tomistico Internazionale* (Rome-Naples, 1981), pp. 219–27.

O. J. Brown, *Natural Rectitude and Divine Law in Aquinas: An Approach to an Integral Interpretation of the Thomistic Doctrine of Law* (Toronto, 1981).

M.-D. Chenu, 'Création et histoire', in A. Maurer (ed.), *St Thomas Aquinas, 1274–1974. Commemorative Studies* (Toronto, 1974), pp. 391–400.

L. Hayen, 'Le thomisme et l'histoire', *Revue thomiste* 62 (1962), pp. 51 – 82.

P. Hoenen, *La théorie du Jugement d'après saint Thomas d'Aquin* (Rome, 1946).

J. Isaac, 'La notion de la dialectique chez saint Thomas', *Revue des Sciences philosophiques et théologiques* 34 (1950), pp. 481–506.

N. Kretzmann, 'Philosophy of Mind', in N. Kretzmann and E. Stump (eds), *The Cambridge Companion to Aquinas* (Cambridge, 1993), pp. 128–59.

F. Manthey, *Die Sprachphilosophie des heiligen Thomas von Aquins und ihre Anwendung auf Probleme der Theologie* (Paderborn, 1937).

A. A. Maurer, *St Thomas and Historicity* (Marquette, 1979).

J. P. Ruane, 'Self-knowledge and the Spirituality of the Soul in St Thomas', *The New Scholasticism* 32 (1958), pp. 425–42.

A.-D. Sertillanges, 'L'Etre et la connaissance dans la philosophie de saint Thomas d'Aquin', in *Mélanges thomistes* (Paris, 1934), pp. 175–97.

W. A. Wallace, *Causality and Scientific Explanation* (Ann Arbor, MI, 1972–4).

Philosophical sources

R. I. Henle, *Saint Thomas and Platonism. A Study of of 'Plato' and 'Platonici' Texts in the Writings of St Thomas* (The Hague, 1956).

M. D. Jordan, *The Alleged Aristoteleanism of Thomas Aquinas* (Toronto, 1992).

K. Kremer, *Die neuplatonische Seinsphilosophie und ihre Wirkung auf Thomas von Aquin* (Leiden, 1971).
J. Owens, 'Aquinas as Aristotelean Commentator', in A. Maurer (ed.), *Saint Thomas Aquinas, 1274–1974. Commemorative Studies I* (Toronto, 1974), pp. 218–38.
P. Quinn, *Aquinas, Platonism and the Kingdom of God* (Aldershot, 1996).

Chapter 11: Thomas and the Idea of Theology

G. van Ackeren, *Sacra doctrina. The Subject of the First Question of the 'Summa Theologica' of St Thomas Aquinas* (Rome, 1952).
J. F. Bonnefoy, *La nature de la théologie selon saint Thomas d'Aquin* (Paris, 1939).
M.-D. Chenu, *Is Theology a Science?* (Eng. translation, London, 1959).
M. Corbin, *Le chemin de la théologie chez Thomas d'Aquin* (Paris, 1974).
L. Elders, *Faith and science: an Introduction to St Thomas' 'Expositio in Boethii de Trinitate'* (Rome, 1974).
M.-M. Labourdette, 'La théologie, intelligence de la foi', *Revue thomiste* XLVI (1946), pp. 5–44.
M.-M. Labourdette and M.-J. Nicolas, 'L'analogie de la vérité et l'unité de la science théologique', *Revue thomiste* XLVII (1947), pp. 417–66.
G. Lafont, *Structures et méthodes dans la Somme théologique de saint Thomas d'Aquin* (Bruges, 1961).
G. Narcisse, 'Les enjeux épistémologiques de l'argument de la convenance selon saint Thomas d'Aquin', in C.-J. Pinto de Oliveira (ed.), *Ordo sapientiae et amoris. Image and message de saint Thomas d'Aquin à travers les récentes études historiques, herméneutiques et doctrinales* (Fribourg, 1993), pp. 143–67.
P. E. Persson, *Sacra doctrina. Reason and Revelation in Aquinas* (Eng. translation, Oxford, 1970).
J.-P. Torrell, OP, 'Le savoir théologique chez saint Thomas', *Revue thomiste* 96 (1996), pp. 355–96.
V. White, OP, *Holy Teaching. The idea of Theology according to St Thomas Aquinas* (London, 1958).

Thomas as mystical theologian

C. N. Still, 'Gifted Knowledge: an Exception to Thomist Epistemology', *The Thomist* 63, 2 (1999), pp. 173–90.
J. Maritain, *Distinguer pour unir, ou les degrés du Savoir* (Paris, 1932; 1934); Eng. translation, *The Degrees of Knowledge* (London, 1937), pp. 305–57.

Notes

Preface

1. Cited in B. Sewell, *In the Dorian Mode. A Life of John Gray, 1866–1934* (Padstow, 1983), p. 174.
2. *Quaestiones disputatae De veritate*, q. 9, a. 4.
3. *Expositio Libri Posteriorum*, I., lect. 8, 1; J. Wébert, 'L'image dans l'oeuvre de saint Thomas et spécialement dans l'exposé doctrinale sur l'intelligence humaine', *Revue thomiste* 31 (1926), pp. 427–45.
4. A. Nichols, OP, *Dominican Gallery. Portrait of a Culture* (Leominster, 1997), pp. 402–3.
5. *Super librum Dionysii De divinis nominibus*, c. 7, lect. 4.
6. On whom see my *Dominican Gallery* (Leominster, 1997), pp. 184–222; for a fair example of his lyrical yet philosophically alert expositions of Aquinas, try Appendix 10, 'The Dialectic of Love in the Summa', in T. Gilby, OP, *St Thomas Aquinas, Summa theologiae. Volume I, Christian Theology [1a. 1]* (London, 1964), pp. 124–32.
7. See, for example, H. McCabe, *St Thomas Aquinas, Summa Theologiae. Volume 3, Knowing and Naming God [1a. 12–13]* (London, 1964); B. Davies, *The Thought of Thomas Aquinas* (Oxford, 1992).
8. Not that this excludes, *pace* the older English writers, all elements of a poetic presentation of Aquinas: far from it, as such a study as Dominique Millet-Gérard's *Claudel thomiste?* (Paris, 1999) suggests. What we find in Claudel is a poet not only instructed by Thomas in the treatises on God as One and Three, creation, the angels, beatitude, but also endeavouring to apply Thomas's metaphysical realism to poetic language with its vocation to order all things to the God who is the plenitude of being, to see language in the light of the divine Word himself.
9. M. Grabmann, *The Interior Life of St Thomas Aquinas* (Eng. translation, Milwaukee, 1951), pp. 1–2. Cf. R. Gibbs, *Tommaso da Modena. Painting in Emilia and the March of Treviso, 1340–80* (Cambridge, 1989), pp. 50–87. The figure of Thomas is, unfortunately, badly damaged and therefore could not be used, as I would have liked, as the cover image of this book.
10. The phrase occurs in two important programmatic statements by

Aquinas of what theology is, as found in his commentaries on Boethius' *De Trinitate* (q. 2, a. 2), and Peter Lombard's *Book of the Sentences* (I., prologue, a. 3, sol. 1).

11. See on this A. Gardeil, OP, *The Gifts of the Holy Ghost in the Dominican Saints* (Eng. translation, Milwaukee, 1942).

12. *Lectura super Joannem*, sub. loc. 5, 16.

13. *Expositio et lectura super Epistolas Pauli Apostoli, II. ad Corinthos*, 2, lect. 3, with a citation of Gen. 27:27.

Chapter 1: Thomas in his Time

1. T. Leccisotti, 'Il dottore angelico a Montecassino', *Rivista di filosofia neoscolastica* 32 (1940), pp. 511–47.

2. J.-P. Torrell, OP, *Initiation à saint Thomas d'Aquin, Sa personne et son oeuvre* (Fribourg, 1993), pp. 7–8.

3. Ibid., p. 21.

4. M.-D. Chenu, OP, *St Thomas d'Aquin et la théologie* (Paris, 1959), p. 11.

5. *Contra doctrinam retrahentium a religione*, 15. I owe these points to Père Torrell's magisterial study.

6. M. L. Corish, 'Teaching and Learning Theology in Mediaeval Paris', in P. Henry (ed.), *Schools of Thought in the Christian Tradition* (Philadelphia, 1984), pp. 106–24.

7. F. Marinelli, *Personalismo trinitario nella storia della salvezza: Rapporti tra la ss.ma Trinità e le opere ad extra nello 'Scriptum super Sententiis' di San Tommaso* (Rome, 1969), and, more widely, G. Marengo, *Trinità e creazione: Indagine sulla teologia di Tommaso d'Aquino* (Rome, 1990).

8. J.-P. Torrell, OP, *Initiation à saint Thomas d'Aquin* (Fribourg, 1993), p. 72.

9. L. J. Bataillon, OP, 'Les sermons attribués à saint Thomas: Questions d'authenticité', *Miscellanea mediaevalia* 19 (1988), pp. 325–41.

10. The *Expositio super primam et secundam Decretalem* (the Fourth Lateran Council's confession of faith and its reprobation of the theology of history of Joachim of Flora); and the *De articulis fidei et Ecclesiae sacramentis* respectively.

11. L. Boyle, OP, *The Setting of the 'Summa Theologiae' of Saint Thomas* (Toronto, 1982).

12. *Compendium theologiae*, 201.

13. N. Lash, *The Beginning and End of Religion* (Cambridge, 1996), pp. 141–2.

14. J. Leclerq, OSB, *The Love of Learning and the Desire for God: A Study of Monastic Culture* (Eng. translation, New York, 1961, 1974).

15. J.-P. Torrell, OP, *Initiation à saint Thomas d'Aquin* (Fribourg, 1993), p. 365.

Chapter 2: Revelation

1. J.-P. Torrell, OP, 'Le traité de la prophétie de S. Thomas d'Aquin et la théologie de la révélation', in L. Elders (ed.), *La doctrine de la révélation divine de saint Thomas d'Aquin* (= *Studi tomistici* 37) (Vatican City, 1990), pp. 171–95.
2. V. White, OP, 'St Thomas's Conception of Revelation', *Dominican Studies* I. 1 (1948), pp. 10–11.
3. *Expositio et lectura super Epistolas Pauli Apostoli, ad Romanos*, 11., lect. 1.
4. *Summa theologiae*, Ia. IIae., q. 102, a. 4.
5. Acts 7:30, 35, 53; Gal. 3:19; Heb. 2:2.
6. *Quaestiones disputate De veritate*, 12, 3.
7. *Summa theologiae*, IIIa., q. 7, a. 7.
8. R. Schenk, '*Omnis Christi actio est nostra instructio*. The Deeds and Sayings of Jesus as Revelation in the View of Thomas Aquinas', in L. Elders (ed.), *La doctrine de la révélation divine de saint Thomas d'Aquin* (Vatican City, 1990), pp. 103–31.
9. *Expositio et lectura super Epistolas Pauli Apostoli, I ad Corinthios*, 1, lect. 1.
10. *Expositio et lectura super Epistolas Pauli Apostoli, ad Romanos*, 8, lect. 5.
11. A. Lemmonyer, OP, 'Les apôtres comme docteurs de la foi d'après saint Thomas', *Mélanges thomistes, publiés par les Dominicains de la Province de France à l'occasion du VIe centenaire de la canonisation de saint Thomas d'Aquin, 18 juillet 1323* (Kain, 1923), p. 171.
12. *Summa theologiae*, IIa. IIae., q. 1, a. 9, ad. i.
13. *Expositio et lectura super Epistolas Pauli Apostoli, II ad Thessalonicenses*, 2, lect. 3.
14. *Expositio super Job ad litteram*, 1, lect. 2.
15. J. van der Ploeg, OP, 'The Place of Holy Scripture in the Theology of St Thomas', *The Thomist* 10 (1947), pp. 398–422.
16. *Quaestiones quodlibetales*, 9, 16.
17. *Lectura super Joannem*, 1, lect. 13.
18. B. Smalley, 'Thomas Aquinas', in B. Smalley, *The Gospels in the Schools, c. 1110–c. 1280* (London and Ronceverte, 1985), pp. 266–70. Cf. the discussion in M. D. Jordan, *Ordering Wisdom. The Hierarchy of Philosophical Discourses in Aquinas* (Notre Dame, 1986), pp. 26–30. Over against most if not all previous writers on the topic, Jordan understands the authorial intention spoken of by Thomas in the opening question of the *Prima Pars* as referring to the authorship of the Holy Spirit. This enables Jordan to enclose the spiritual senses altogether within the literal. 'The Spirit foreknows all truthful readings of Scripture and *intends* them', ibid., p. 28.

19. B. Duroux, OP, *La psychologie de la foi chez saint Thomas d'Aquin* (Tournai, 1963), pp. 194–5.

Chapter 3: God and Creation

1. *Summa contra Gentiles*, IV. 1.
2. Cf. *Summa theologiae*, IIa. IIae., q. 175, a. 3, on which M. D. Jordan comments, 'Of course, rapture itself is a transient anticipation of beatitude and an explicit violation of the mortal condition – a foretaste of death. So the general principle stands: there is no present vision of the divine essence.' Thus *Ordering Wisdom* (Notre Dame, 1986), p. 201.
3. Cf. A. Nichols, OP, *Say it is Pentecost. A Guide through Balthasar's Logic* (Edinburgh, 2000), pp. 69–72, 95–100. Balthasar's neologisms – 'ana-logic', 'cata-logic' – are, however, used of God as, specifically, *triune.*
4. T. Gilby, 'Introduction', *St Thomas Aquinas. Theological Texts* (Durham, North Carolina, 1982), pp. xi–xiv.
5. Thomas himself would consider that his work combines two 'wisdoms'. 'Mundane' wisdom, won through philosophy, judges 'lower' causes – that is, *caused* causes – judging in their terms. 'Divine' wisdom considers higher – that is, divine – causes, and judges according to *them*. Thus *Quaestiones disputatae De potentia*, q. 1, a. 4, corpus.
6. N. Lash, *The Beginning and End of Religion* (Cambridge, 1996), p. 144, citing W. Hankey, *God in Himself. Aquinas's Doctrine of God as expounded in the 'Summa theologiae'* (Oxford, 1987), pp. 10, 37, 39, 131. We should note, however, that Hankey's study somewhat overestimates the use of Neoplatonic dialectic in the *Prima Pars*: Thomas did not at that date know the (pseudo-Proclean) *Liber de causis.*
7. L. Elders, *The Philosophical Theology of St Thomas Aquinas* (Leiden, 1990), p. viii.
8. *Super Boetium De Trinitate*, 4.
9. *Sententia super Metaphysicam*, prologue.
10. P. F. Strawson, *The Bounds of Sense* (London, 1966), p. 207.
11. For a classic modern account, see E. L. Mascall, *He Who Is. A Study in Traditional Theism* (London, 1943); E. L. Mascall, *Existence and Analogy. A Sequel to 'He Who Is'* (London, 1949).
12. *Summa theologiae*, Ia., q. 2, a. 1, ad. i. On the famed 'natural desire for God', Thomas holds that all human beings have a natural desire to know the cause, once they are aware of things around them as effects: thus *Summa theologiae*, Ia., q. 12, a. 1.
13. J. Maritain, *A Preface to Metaphysics* (Eng. translation, New York, 1961), pp. 15–16.
14. Cf. the comments of Professor Keith Ward on the attempt of Peter Atkins in his *Creation Revisited* (Harmondsworth, 1994) to 'get a uni-

verse out of nothing'. Ward writes: 'What he refers to as "nothing" . . . is actually a rich realm of possibilities from which an actual universe somehow arises. My response has been to say that the postulate of such a realm of possibilities is not absurd, but that it is best conceived as located in the mind of God . . . The mind of God is not "nothing", though one may well say that it is not a finite thing. It is a necessarily existing source of all actuality, which actualises a subset of possibilities by a contingent act of will', *God, Chance and Necessity* (Oxford, 1996), p. 38.

15. This is why the other Four Ways can be presented in its light, as in my *A Grammar of Consent. The Existence of God in Christian Tradition* (Notre Dame and London, 1991), pp. 88–91.

16. *Summa theologiae*, Ia., qq. 3–11.

17. *Summa theologiae*, Ia., qq. 14–26.

18. *Summa theologiae*, Ia., qq. 12–13.

19. M. D. Jordan, *Ordering Wisdom* (Notre Dame, 1986), pp. 164–5. And cf. the *Quaestiones quodlibetales*, 6, 1, a. 1.

20. Many things can be said to be 'complete' or 'achieved' and so in his commentary on the *De causis*, Thomas (with accompanying explanation) prefers to call God 'super-complete'. That which is complete in creation 'although it be not per se subsistent is in a way sufficient unto itself – in the sense that it does not need another in which to adhere as in a subject. However, because the form that is the principle of action is in it limited and participatory, it cannot act through the mode of creation or outpouring, as that which is totally form acts – that which, by participation in itself, is according to itself totally productive of other things. Since, therefore, that is so among us in those things that are diminished and complete, it follows that God is neither diminished nor simply complete but rather super-complete. For he does not lack action, like diminished things, and he acts in the mode of creating or pouring out – which those things that are complete among us cannot do', *Super librum De causis*, lect. 22, nn. 379–80.

21. *Summa theologiae*, Ia., q. 4, a. 1

22. V. White, OP, 'The Prolegomena to the Five Ways', *Dominican Studies* V (1952), pp. 134–58 and here at p. 148.

23. M. D. Jordan, *Ordering Wisdom* (Notre Dame, 1986), pp. 168–9.

24. Leaning on the theological work of (now Cardinal) Walter Kasper, I have made this point in connection with the Eastern Orthodox apophaticism of Vladimir Lossky in my *Light from the East. Authors and Themes in Orthodox Theology* (London, 1995), pp. 39–40.

25. Later Scholasticism will call such divine Names 'impure perfections' or 'closed names', because they express in the first instance particular substances with their accidents.

26. The 'open Names' of the Later Scholastics.

27. Given its importance, we are surprised to hear the following statement from Colin Dexter's 'Inspector Morse': 'These were good people, who rejoiced in the simple ties of family and Christian fellowship; who thought of God as a father, and who never in a month of Sabbaths could begin to understand the aberrations of the new theology which thought of him (if it thought of him at all) as the present participle of the verb "to be".' Thus C. Dexter, *Service of All the Dead* (London, 1979, 1980), p. 165. The error is compounded by being set in a notional 'St Frideswide's church hall' only half a mile from the studium of the Dominicans in Oxford!

28. G. Lafont, osb, *Structures et méthode dans la Somme théologique de saint Thomas d'Aquin* (Bruges, 1961), p. 473.

29. *Summa theologiae*, Ia., q. 14, a. 4.

30. D. Dubarle, *L'ontologie de Thomas d'Aquin* (Paris, 1996), p. 122.

31. *Summa theologiae*, Ia., q. 18, a. 3, corpus.

32. Dubarle points out that whereas modern philosophy (and sensibility) increasingly susbstitutes freedom for the ancient stress on intelligibility as the hallmark of the highest value, Thomas, in his concept of the divine – and human – mind and will holds freedom and intelligibility together. Thus *L'ontologie de Thomas d'Aquin* (Paris, 1996), p. 123.

33. *Summa theologiae*, Ia., q. 13, a. 2.

34. *Summa theologiae*, Ia., q. 32, a. 1.

35. *Quaestiones disputate De veritate*, 10, 13.

36. *Quaestiones disputatae De potentia*, 8, 1.

37. *Summa theologiae*, Ia., q. 27, a. 5.

38. *Scriptum super Sententiis*, I., dist. 10, q. 1, a. 1, sol.

39. D. J. Merriell, *To the Image of the Trinity. A Study in the Development of Aquinas's Teaching* (Toronto, 1990), p. 89.

40. c.f. *Summa theologiae*, Ia., q. 44, a. 1, with q. 45, a. 6, and q. 14, a. 8.

41. *Summa theologiae*, Ia., q. 45, a. 6 and a. 7, ad iii.

42. *Summa theologiae*, Ia., q. 45, a. 7, corpus.

43. *Summa theologiae*, Ia., q. 44, a. 1.

44. D. Dubarle, *L'ontologie de Thomas d'Aquin* (Paris, 1996), p. 215.

45. *Summa theologiae*, Ia., q. 47, a. l.

46. *Summa theologiae*, Ia., q. 5, a. 3.

47. *Summa theologiae*, Ia., q. 6, a. 4.

48. *Summa theologiae*, Ia., q. 48, a. 1.

49. *Summa theologiae*, Ia., q. 49, a. 2.

Chapter 4: The Trinity

1. T. de Régnon, sj, *Etudes de théologie positive sur la Sainte Trinité* (Paris, 1892–6).

2. J. Lebon, 'Le sort du consubstantiel nicéen', *Revue d'histoire ecclésiastique* 47 (1952), pp. 485–529.

3. 'Their theology of the hypostasis was not precise enough to enable them to see the impossibility of placing person and nature on the same level in the act of generation': thus A. Malet, *Personne et amour dans la théologie trinitaire de saint Thomas d'Aquin* (Paris, 1956), p. 14.

4. A. Malet, *Personne et amour dans la théologie trinitaire de saint Thomas d'Aquin* (Paris, 1956), p. 17.

5. For his 'sophiological' attempt to overcome the divide between Greek 'Monopatrism' and Latin 'Filioquism', see S. Bulgakov, *Le Paraclet* (Paris, 1946), pp. 171–82.

6. H. U. von Balthasar, *Liturgie cosmique* (Paris, 1947), p. 59.

7. I. Chevalier, *Saint Augustin et la pensée grecque: les relations trinitaires* (Fribourg, 1940), pp. 51–63.

8. Augustine, *De Trinitate*, VII. 6.

9. A. Malet, *Personne et amour dans la théologie trinitaire de saint Thomas d'Aquin* (Paris, 1956), p. 22: echoing Chevalier's study.

10. M. E. Williams, *The Teaching of Gilbert Porreta on the Trinity as found in his Commentaries on Boethius* (Rome, 1951).

11. M.-D. Chenu, OP, 'Le dernier avatar de la théologie orientale en Occident', *Mélanges Auguste Pelzer* (Louvain, 1947), pp. 159–81. Chenu makes a further (highly speculative) proposal. If, at the Fourth Lateran Council, the opponents of Gilbert's disciples were also hostile to the nascent Dominican and Franciscan movements, this may have been owing to a connection they divined between a Trinitarian theology stressing that the divine being is a communion of subjects whose ceaseless interflow simply is the divine life (a communion only to be explored by those who open themselves to it in the overflow of the Liturgy in personal prayer) and the new sense of fraternity, the lyrically expressed devotion to Christ, the concern for the poor, all of which led the friars to transgress the boundaries of the 'clerical social structures' of the time.

12. G. Dumeige, SJ, *Richard de Saint-Victor et l'idée chrétienne de l'amour* (Paris, 1952).

13. *Quaestiones disputatae De potentia*, 9, 2, ad xii. And indeed, even outside divine studies, in philosophical anthropology, as a later age would call it, the person is the *sub-positum*, the foundation on which there rests all else that is the case with a subject. Cf. *Summa contra Gentiles*, IV. 38.

14. Alexander of Hales, *Summa*, I. 407.

15. Thus Thomas is a target for V. Lossky in *La théologie mystique de l'Eglise d'Orient* (Paris, 1943), and in *Théologie de Dieu et connaissance négative chez Meister Eckhart* (Paris, 1960).

16. D. Dubarle, 'L'ontologie du mystère chrétien selon saint Thomas d'Aquin', *Angelicum* 52 (1975), pp. 227–301, 485–520; 53 (1976), pp. 227–68.

17. D. Dubarle, *L'ontologie de Thomas d'Aquin* (Paris, 1996), pp. 188–9.
18. W. Norris Clarke, *Person and Being* (Milwaukee, 1993).
19. *Scriptum super libros Sententiarum*, I., dist. 4, q. 1, a. 2.
20. *Summa theologiae*, Ia., q. 39, a. 4, ad v.
21. *Summa theologiae*, Ia., q. 29, a. 3.
22. A. Malet, *Personne et amour dans la théologie trinitaire de saint Thomas d'Aquin* (Paris, 1956), pp. 41–2.
23. cf. *Summa theologiae*, Ia., q. 45, n. 3; q. 41; and q. 43, a. 3.
24. *Summa theologiae*, Ia., q. 43, a. 5, ad ii. With reference to Augustine, *De Trinitate*, IX. 10 and IV. 20.
25. *Summa theologiae*, Ia., q. 43, a. 3.
26. cf. *Summa theologiae*, Ia., q. 38, a. 1; Ia., q. 43, a. 3; a. 4, ad i; a. 5; *Summa contra Gentiles*, IV, 18 and 21; *Quaestiones disputatae De veritate*, q. 27, a. 2, ad iii.

Chapter 5: The Trinity in Man

1. For this great theme of high medieval theology, see more widely G. Emery, *La Trinité créatrice. Trinité et création dans les commentaires aux Sentences de Thomas d'Aquin et de ses précurseurs Albert le Grand et Bonaventure* (Paris, 1995).
2. See J. E. Sullivan, OP, *The Image of God. The Doctrine of St Augustine and its Influence* (Dubuque, Iowa, 1963).
3. *Scriptum super Sententiis*, I., dist. 3, q. 3, a. 1, sol.
4. *Sententia Super Metaphysicam*, IV.
5. I. Hislop, OP, 'Man, the Image of the Trinity, according to St Thomas', *Dominican Studies* III. 1 (1950), p. 4.
6. Augustine, *De Trinitate*, XII. 10.
7. A. Squire, OP, 'The Doctrine of the Image in the De Veritate of St Thomas Aquinas', *Dominican Studies* IV (1951), p. 176. With reference to the *Quaestiones disputatae De veritate*, q. 10, a. 7.
8. As a recent student has written, 'Thomas understood that Augustine found the image of the Trinity at its best in man's acts of knowing and loving God because in these acts man reflects the eternal processions of the Son as the eternal Word from the Father and of the Holy Spirit as Love from the Father and the Son. Thus Aquinas conceived of the image of God as an ineradicable capacity for God in man, the foundation for man's participation in the life of the Trinity to which man is called by God's grace': D. J. Merriell, *To the Image of the Trinity. A Study in the Development of Aquinas' Teaching* (Toronto 1990), p. 4.
9. *Expositio et lectura super Epistolas Pauli Apostoli, ad Colossenses*, 1, lect. 4.
10. *Scriptum super Sententiis*, I., dist. 10, q. 1, a. 1.
11. *Summa theologiae*, IIIa., q. 23, a. 3.

12. See *Scriptum super Sententiis*, II., dist. 26, q. 1, a. 3; *Summa theologiae*, Ia IIae., q. 110, a. 2, ad ii.
13. *Summa theologiae*, IIIa., q. 7, a. 13.
14. *Summa theologiae*, Ia., q. 93, a. 4.
15. L.-M. de Blignières, 'La dignité de l'homme image de Dieu selon saint Thomas d'Aquin', *Studi tomistici* 42 (Vatican City, 1991), pp. 199–220, and here at p. 207. Italics added.

Chapter 6: Angelology

1. A. Pope, *An Essay on Man* (1733), Epistle ii, 1–2.
2. *Summa theologiae*, Ia., q. 50, q. 1.
3. G. Tillotson (ed.), *Newman. Prose and Poetry* (London, 1958), p. 822.
4. For a thorough study of Aquinas on cosmic order, see O. Blanchette, *The Perfection of the Universe according to Aquinas: a Teleological Cosmology* (University Park, PA, 1992).
5. P. Boyde, *Dante Philomythes and Philosopher: Man in the Cosmos* (Cambridge, 1981), pp. 132–71.
6. Dante Alighieri, *La Divina Commedia*, 'Paradiso', canto XXX, lines 61–2.
7. *Summa theologiae*, Ia., qq. 54–8.
8. K. Foster, OP, *St Thomas Aquinas, Summa Theologiae, volume 9, Angels [Ia. 50–64]* (London, 1968), pp. 72–3.
9. Ibid., p. 92.
10. Ibid., p. 81.
11. *Summa theologiae*, Ia., q. 58, a. 3.
12. *Summa theologiae*, Ia., q. 62, a. 5.
13. *Summa theologiae*, Ia., q. 63, a. 1, ad iii.
14. *Summa theologiae*, Ia., q. 63, a. 3.
15. K. Foster, OP, 'Appendix 2. Satan', in K. Foster, *St Thomas Aquinas, Summa theologiae. Volume 9. Angels [Ia. 50–64]* (London, 1968), p. 318; see also M. L. Guérard des Lauriers, 'Le péché et la Causalité', *Bulletin thomiste* XI (1962), pp. 553–637.

Chapter 7: Grace and the Virtues

1. C. O'Neill, *Meeting Christ in the Sacraments* (New York, 1964), p. 71.
2. R. Cessario, *The Moral Virtues and Theological Ethics* (Notre Dame, Ind., 1991).
3. F. Kerr, 'Resolution and Community', *New Blackfriars* 50. 589 (1969), p. 478.
4. Thus J. F. Danby, *Shakespeare's Doctrine of Nature* (London, 1949).
5. F. Kerr, 'Resolution and Community', *New Blackfriars* 50. 589 (1969), p. 477.
6. B. M. Ashley, 'What is the End of the Human Person? The Vision of God and Integral Human Fulfilment', in L. Gormally (ed.), *Moral Truth*

and *Moral Tradition. Essays in Honour of Peter Geach and Elizabeth Anscombe* (Dublin, 1994), p. 79.

7. Ibid., pp. 80–81.

8. *Summa theologiae*, Ia., q. 12, a. 5.

9. *Revue thomiste* CII. 1 (2001), (= *Surnaturel. Une controverse au coeur du thomisme au XXe siècle. Actes du colloque organisé par l'Institut Catholique de Toulouse, les 26–27 mai 2000 à Toulouse.*)

10. For a fuller critique of the view that there is no hierarchised and ultimately single 'telic' completion to the good life for man, see R. Hittinger, *Critique of the New Natural Law Theories* (Notre Dame, Ind., 1987).

11. *Summa contra Gentiles*, III. 37.

12. R. A. Armstrong, *Primary and Secondary Precepts in Thomistic Natural Law Teaching* (The Hague, 1966); W. A. Wallace, *The Role of Demonstration in Moral Theology. A Study of Methodology in St Thomas Aquinas* (Washington DC, 1963).

13. Cf. *Scriptum super Sententiis*, III., q. 1, a. 2, ad ii.

14. S. Tugwell, OP, 'The Old Wine is Good', *New Blackfriars* 53. 631 (1972), pp. 558–63.

15. See P. Hall, *Narrative and the Natural Law. An Interpretation of Thomistic Ethics* (Notre Dame, Ind., 1994); the 'fields and spacious palaces' formula is a reference to Augustine's *Confessions* at X. 8.

16. P. Lefébure, 'Anarchy and Grace: St Thomas', *New Blackfriars* 50. 589 (1969), pp. 465–6.

17. The difficulty of this balance is seen in the divergence between the two 'continuators' who completed Thomas's unfinished political works. Ptolemy of Lucca (d. 1326), who finished the *De regimine principum*, was a clericalist republican who would have tightened the organisation of Christendom under the supreme jurisdiction of the Pope. Peter of Auvergne (d. 1304), who completed Aquinas's commentary on Aristotle's *Politics*, pictured a regional State smaller than Christendom and unaffected by the Church.

18. Cf. *Summa theologiae*, Ia. IIae., q. 95, a. 2, and more widely, T. Gilby, OP, *Between Community and Society* (London, 1953); T. Gilby, *Principality and Polity* (London, 1958).

19. *Summa theologiae*, IIIa., q. 61, a. 2.

20. Beautifully expressed in the essays of Josef Pieper on the cardinal virtues: thus J. Pieper, *The Four Cardinal Virtues*, (Eng. translation Notre Dame, IN, 1967).

21. M. Seckler, *Instinkt und Glaubenswille nach Thomas von Aquin* (Mainz, 1961).

22. Grace as 'physical premotion' – anti-Pelagianism in its most metaphysical mood – has sometimes been regarded as the most formative of the distinctive theses of the Thomist school.

23. *Summa theologiae*, Ia. IIae., q. 110, a. 1.

24. *Summa theologiae*, Ia. IIae., q. 110, a. 4.
25. *Summa theologiae*, Ia., q. 20, a. 2.
26. *Summa theologiae*, IIa. IIae, q. 23, a. 1, ad ii.
27. *Summa theologiae*, IIa. IIae, q., 27, a. 6.
28. T. McDermott, *St Thomas Aquinas, Summa Theologiae: a Concise Translation* (London, 1989), p. 327.

Chapter 8: Christ, Church, Sacraments

1. See the laudatory comments of C. Spicq, *Esquisse d'une histoire de l'exégèse latine au moyen âge* (Paris, 1944), p. 315.
2. D. Bourke, 'Introduction', in D. Bourke and A. Littledale, *St Thomas Aquinas, Summa Theologiae. Volume 29, The Old Law [1a.2ae. 98–105]* (London, 1969), pp. xx–xxvii.
3. M. Seckler, *Das Heil in der Geschichte. Geschichtstheologisches Denken bei Thomas von Aquin* (Munich, 1964).
4. See for instance, A. E. Lewis, *Between Cross and Resurrection. A Theology of Holy Saturday* (Grand Rapids, Mich., and Cambridge, 2001), p. 150.
5. c.f. *Summa theologiae*, IIIa., q. 2, a. 1.
6. D. Dubarle, *L'ontologie de Thomas d'Aquin* (Paris, 1996), p. 357.
7. *Summa theologiae*, IIIa., q. 2, a. 2.
8. *Summa theologiae*, IIIa., q. 2, a. 2.
9. *Summa theologiae*, IIIa., q. 2, a. 2, ad ii.
10. *Summa theologiae*, IIIa., q. 2, a. 6.
11. *Summa theologiae*, IIIa., q. 6, a. 6.
12. *Summa theologiae*, IIIa., q. 17, a. 2.
13. E. P. Persson, *Sacra Doctrina. Reason and Revelation in Aquinas* (Eng. translation, Oxford, 1970), pp. 195–6.
14. Ibid., p. 198.
15. *Summa theologiae*, IIIa., q. 3, a. 8.
16. *Summa theologiae*, IIIa, q. 18.
17. I. Backes, *Die Christologie des heiligen Thomas von Aquins und die griechischen Kirchenväter* (Paderborn, 1931).
18. A. Williams, *The Ground of Union. Deification in Aquinas and Palamas* (New York and Oxford, 1999), pp. 34–101.
19. A principal basis for the comparison sometimes made between Thomas and Maximus the Confessor.
20. J.-P. Torrell, *Saint Thomas d'Aquin. Maître spirituel* (Fribourg, 1996), pp. 182–5.
21. Y. M.-J. Congar, 'Le sens de l'Economie salutaire dans la "théologie" de saint Thomas d'Aquin [Somme Théologique]', *Festgabe J. Lortz. II. Glaube und Geschichte* (Baden-Baden, 1958), pp. 73–122 and here at p. 83. Cf. J. Lécuyer, 'La causalité efficiente des mystères du Christ selon s. Thomas', *Doctor communis* (Rome, 1953), pp. 91–120.

22. G. Lohaus, *Die Geheimnisse des Lebens Jesu in der 'Summa Theologiae' des heiligen Thomas von Aquin* (Freiburg, 1985), pp. 17, 19.

23. Ibid., p. 66.

24. E. Vauthier, 'Le Saint-Esprit, principe d'unité dans l'Eglise d'après saint Thomas d'Aquin. Corps mystique et inhabitation du Saint-Esprit', *Mélanges de science religieuse* 5 (1948), pp. 175–96; 6 (1949), pp. 57–80.

25. *Scriptum super Sententiis*, III., d. 13, q. 2, a. 2. cf. *Expositio et lectura super Epistolas Pauli Apostoli, ad Ephesios*, c. 1, lect. 8.

26. Y. Congar, 'The Idea of the Church in St Thomas Aquinas', in *The Mystery of the Church* (London, 1960), pp. 97–117; Y. Congar, 'La vision de l'Eglise chez Thomas d'Aquin', *Revue des Sciences philosophiques et théologiques* 62 (1978), pp. 523–41.

27. *Scriptum super Sententiis*, IV, d. 15, q. 3, a. 1, sol. 4, ad i.

28. *Summa theologiae*, IIIa., q. 65, a. 3; IIIa, q. 73, a. 3.

29. Ibid., and *Lectura super Joannem*, 6, lect 8.

30. *Scriptum super Sententiis*, IV, d. 1, q. 1, a. 2, sol. 5, ad i.

31. P. M. Gy, 'Avancées du traité de l'Eucharistie de saint Thomas dans la *Somme* par rapport aux *Sentences*', *Revue des Sciences philosophiques et théologiques* 77 (1993), pp. 219–28. Père Gy shows how Thomas does not, in his later work, opt for a theory of signification over against one of causality, but holds that the sacrament, before being the sign of a sacramental effect, is the sign of its cause, Christ the high priest acting in the sacrament.

32. Cf. the words of Dom Anscar Vonier, 'The Thomistic view of the sacrament is clear; it unites indissolubly cult and sanctification', *A Key to the Doctrine of the Holy Eucharist* (London, 1925), p. 48.

33. A. Patfoort, OP, 'Morale et pneumatologie. Une observation de la Ia. IIae.', in A. Patfoort, OP, *Thomas d'Aquin. Les clés d'une théologie* (Paris, 1983), pp. 71–102.

Chapter 9: Thomas in History

1. For the late-thirteenth-century debates about Thomas's teaching, see F. J. Roensch, *The Early Thomistic School* (Dubuque, Iowa, 1964).

2. In the long-windedly entitled *Novarum defensionum doctrinae angelici doctoris beati Thomae de Aquino super quattuor libris Sententiarum quaestiones profundissmiae et utilissimae* (1517).

3. P. Mandonnet, OP, 'Frères Prêcheurs (la théologie dans l'Ordre de)', *Dictionnaire de théologie catholique* VI (Paris, 1950), col. 894.

4. *Collationes in 'Ave Maria'*, a. 2; see also T. R. Heath, 'Appendix I. Historical Survey of the Writings of St Thomas on our Lady', in T. R. Heath, *St Thomas Aquinas, Summa theologiae. Volume 51, Our Lady [3a. 27–30]* (London, 1969).

5. P. O. Kristeller, *Le Thomisme et la pensée italienne de la renaissance* (Montreal-Paris, 1967), pp. 80, 89.

6. Ibid., p. 125.
7. Ibid., pp. 17–18.
8. G. Prouvost, *Thomas d'Aquin et les thomismes. Essai sur l'histoire des thomismes* (Paris, 1996).
9. A. Nichols, OP, 'Introduction' to the republished edition, *Catena Aurea. Commentary on the Four Gospels out of the Works of Church Fathers by Saint Thomas Aquinas* (Southampton, 1997), pp. v–xxi.
10. In the words of J. Augustine Di Noia, OP the key new reading of St Thomas 'depends on an account of the properly theological use to which Aquinas put philosophical analogy and construction as he sought to exhibit the intelligibility of the Christian faith': thus 'Thomas after Thomism. Aquinas and the Future of Theology', in D. W. Hudson and D. W. Moran (eds), *The Future of Thomism* (Notre Dame, Ind., 1992), p. 231.
11. 'They': representative names might be, in the English-speaking world, P. Geach, A. MacIntyre, R. McInerny, E. Stump, W. J. Wippell; in German-speaking Europe, M. Rhonheimer, E. Schockenhoff; in Francophone Europe, S.-T. Bonino, J.-L. Bruguès, B.-D. de La Soujeole, G. Narcisse, S. Pinckaers, J.-P. Torrell; in Italy, G. Cottier, D. Mongillo.
12. Pierre Mandonnet remarks how, on the one hand, Thomas would never have written a *Summa philosophiae* and, on the other, how 'metaphysics . . . commands the entire economy of his work'. 'Metaphysics is the unifying principle of all the sciences as of the real order, and it is because Thomas Aquinas surpassed the mass of thinkers of his time as metaphysician that it was reserved for him to produce a unique work'. Thus 'Frères Prêcheurs (la théologie dans l'Ordre de)', *Dictionnaire de théologie catholique* VI (Paris, 1950), cols 883, 879–80.

Chapter 10: Thomas and the Practice of Philosophy

1. G. Lafont, OSB, 'Mystique de la croix et question de l'Etre. A propos d'un livre récent de Jean–Luc Marion', *Revue thomiste* LXXIX (1979), pp. 259–304. Lafont points out, relevantly, that Scripture affirms not only God's otherness but also his propinquity. On the whole debate, see also *Saint Thomas et l'ontothéologie*, (= *Revue thomiste* XCV. 1) (1995).
2. A. Dulles, SJ, 'Vatican II and Scholasticism', *Commonweal* (May 1990), p. 8.
3. *Humani generis*, 48.
4. A. Dulles, SJ, 'Vatican II and Scholasticism', *Commonweal* (May 1990), p. 9.
5. Ibid., p. 10.
6. Thomas's methodologically vital notion of 'modes of consideration', by which different disciplines can treat the same subject matter from different, hierarchically related standpoints, is laid out in his commen-

tary on the *De Trinitate* of the sixth-century Latin Christian philosopher Boethius, sometimes described as the last of the Romans and the first of the Scholastics. The *modi considerandi* idea lies behind the typically Thomistic notion of 'distinguishing in order to unite': see, for example, J. Maritain, *Les degrés du savoir. Distinguer pour unir* (Paris, 1932).

7. In physical science, intellect abstracts from matter insofar as the latter is the principle of individuating things ('signate' matter) but not from matter considered as the basis of sensuous qualities (*materia sensibilis vel communis*); in mathematics intellect abstracts from the latter but not from material substance considered as quantified ('material intelligibility').

8. G. B. Phelan, *Selected Papers* (Toronto 1967), p. 77.

9. *Quaestiones disputatae De potentia*, q. 7, a. 7; cf. *Summa theologiae*, Ia., q. 3, aa. 5–6.

10. T.-D. Humbrecht, 'Dieu, a-t-il une essence?', *Revue thomiste* CXV (1991), p. 17.

11. *Quaestiones disputatae De veritate*, q. 1, a. 1. Italics are, of course, added.

12. *Pulchrum*, 'the beautiful', is sometimes described by modern Scholastics as a 'derivative transcendental' because apprehended by the conjoined power of knowledge and appetite. For *verum*, 'the true', and *bonum*, 'the good', designate being insofar as it has reference to, respectively, the cognitive and appetitive powers: what *verum* and *bonum* signify is the reality of being as grounding the orders of knowledge and appetition.

13. *Summa theologiae*, Ia., q. 5, a. 1.

14. *Summa theologiae*, Ia., q. 13, a. 4, ad ii.

15. *Quaestiones disputatae De potentia*, 7, 2, ad iv.

16. J. L. Marion, *God without Being* (Eng. translation, Chicago, 1991).

17. T.-D. Humbrecht, OP, 'Dieu, a-t-il une essence?', *Revue thomiste* CXV (1991), p. 17.

18. M. D. Jordan, *Ordering Wisdom*, (Notre Dame, 1986), p. 108.

19. Ibid., p. 110.

20. J. de Finance, SJ, *Etre et agir dans la philosophie de saint Thomas* (Paris, 1943).

21. Cf. *Super librum Dionysii De divinis Nominibus*, c. 4, lect. 9: 'The very orientation or aptitude of appetite to something as to its good is called love. Everything that is ordered to something as to its good somehow has that present to itself and united according to some similitude, at least one of proportion, as the form is somehow in matter insofar as matter has an aptitude and an order to it.'

22. *De ente et essentia*, 4.

23. In the title of a famous book by P. Rousselot, SJ, *L'intellectualisme de saint Thomas* (Paris, 1924, 2nd edition).

24. M. Pollan, *The Botany of Desire. A Plant's Eye View of the World* (New York, 2001), p. 65.
25. *Quaestiones disputatae De veritate*, 1, 9.
26. *Quaestiones disputatae De veritate*, 8, 6.
27. T. Gilby, *St Thomas Aquinas. Philosophical Texts* (Durham, North Carolina, 1982), p. 215.
28. See *Quaestiones disputatae De veritate*, 1, 9.
29. J. de Finance, SJ, *Etre et agir* (Paris, 1943), p. 32.
30. R. O'Connor, *The Theology of Work. Analogies between the Principal Mysteries of the Faith and the Operation of the Practical Intellect using Thomistic Principles* (Castleisland, Kerry, 1995), pp. 49–50.
31. *Summa theologiae*, Ia., q. 79, a. 8.
32. *Summa theologiae*, Ia., q. 75, a. 1.
33. *Summa theologiae*, Ia., q. 75, a. 2.
34. M. D. Jordan, *Ordering Wisdom* (Notre Dame, 1986), p. 133.
35. *Summa theologiae*, Ia., q. 87, a. 1, ad i.
36. cf. *Summa theologiae*, Ia., q. 76, a. 1. Here de Finance's term 'anti-nomic' seems justified – or at least Fr Edward Booth's milder 'aporetic': see E. Booth, *Aristotelean Aporetic Ontology in Islamic and Christian Thinkers* (Cambridge, 1983).
37. *Summa theologiae*, Ia, q. 12, a. 5.
38. F. Kerr, OP, 'Aquinas after Marion', *New Blackfriars* 76. 895 (1995), p. 357. Note, however, that, for many scholars, Thomas's tardily renewed interest in Aristotle was caused by external factors: the revival at Paris of an Averroist interpretation of Aristotle's corpus. See Chapter 1 above, at p. 13.
39. M. D. Jordan, *Ordering Wisdom* (Notre Dame, 1986), p. 16.
40. Ibid., pp. 30–31.
41. Cf. *Summa theologiae*, Ia. IIae., q. 91, a. 1, ad iii.
42. *Summa theologiae*, Ia., q. 62, a. 3.
43. L. Menand, *The Metaphysical Club. A Story of Ideas in America* (New York, 2001), p. 279.
44. K. Ward, *God, Chance and Necessity* (Oxford, 1996), pp. 92–3.
45. *Summa theologiae*, supplement to the *Tertia Pars*, q. 41, a. 1, ad iii.
46. *Summa theologiae*, IIae. IIae, q. 174, a. 6.
47. E.g. *Summa theologiae*, Ia. IIae., q. 97, a. 1.
48. *De substantiis separatis*, c. 9; cf. *Summa contra Gentiles*, III. 48.
49. *Summa theologiae*,, Ia., q. 62, a. 1.
50. M. D. Jordan, *Ordering Wisdom* (Notre Dame, 1986), pp. 4–5.
51. *Summa theologiae*, Ia., q. 1, a. 8, ad ii.
52. *Quaestiones quodlibetales*, IV. a. 18.

Chapter 11: Thomas and the Idea of Theology

1. *Summa contra Gentiles*, I. 2, citing Hilary of Poitiers' *De Trinitate*, I. 37.
2. The virtue of Dom Ghislain Lafont's *Structures et méthode dans la Somme théologique de saint Thomas d'Aquin* (Bruges, 1961).
3. *Super librum Dionysii De divinis nominibus*, I. 1. xi.
4. *Expositio Libri Posteriorum*, I. 1. 1.
5. *Summa theologiae*, Ia., q. 117, a. 1.
6. *Expositio et lectura super Epistolas Pauli Apostoli, ad Galatas*, c. 1, lect. 5.
7. L. Elders, 'L'éducation des hommes dans l'histoire du salut', *Sedes Sapientiae* 75 (2001), pp. 15–37. Elders notes how the divine pedagogy in Thomas also embraces such factors as just chastisement of human sin and the testing that is adversity, as well as the role of the ceremonial or ritual (and not just moral and judicial) precepts of the Torah in arousing in Israel dispositions which would permit her to receive Christ.
8. V. White, OP, *Holy Teaching* (London, 1958), p. 8.
9. M.-D. Chenu, *Is Theology a Science?* (Eng. translation, London, 1959).
10. For a fuller account of Thomas's procedures, see M.-D. Chenu, *Understanding Saint Thomas* (Eng. translation, Chicago, 1964).
11. In his commentary on Boethius' *De Trinitate*, Thomas explains that there is a hierarchy of *scientiae* whereby one 'science' (e.g. music) may draw on another (e.g. mathematics) so as to access truths fully available only to the second, superordinate *scientia* in each such pair: *Super Boetium De Trinitate*, q. 5, a. 1, ad v. This model of the 'subalternated science' is, evidently, how he understands theology's scientific status *vis-à-vis* God's own knowledge.
12. G. Narcisse, 'Les enjeux épistémologiques de l'argument de convenance selon saint Thomas d'Aquin', in C.-J. Pinto de Oliveira (ed.), *Ordo sapientiae et amoris. Image et message de saint Thomas d'Aquin à travers des récentes études, historiques, herméneutiques et doctrinales* (Fribourg, 1993), pp. 143–67.
13. *Summa theologiae*, Ia., q. 1, a. 2, ad ii.
14. *Summa theologiae*, Ia., q. 1, a. 5. Cf. *Summa contra Gentiles* IV. 1.
15. *Summa theologiae*, Ia., q. 12, a. 12; Ia., q. 32, a. 1; *Summa contra Gentiles* III. 47.
16. I rely here on L. Elders, 'Foi et raison, la synthèse de saint Thomas', *Sedes Sapientiae* (2001), pp. 1–20.
17. *Super Boetium De Trinitate*, q. 2, a. 3, 2: perhaps the fullest programmatic statement in Thomas of the contribution of philosophy to theology.
18. *Summa theologiae*, Ia., q. 12, a. 13, c.
19. Cf. *Summa contra Gentiles*, IV. 42.
20. *Super librum Boetii De Trinitate*, 8, 1.
21. T. Gilby OP, 'The Dialectic of Love in the '*Summa*' has numerous

references to Thomas' corpus along these lines. My summary reflects Gilby's account.

22. *Summa theologiae*, Ia. IIae., q. 68.
23. *Summa theologiae*, Ia. IIae., q. 28.
24. *Summa theologiae*, IIa. IIae., q. 175.
25. *Collationes in Symbolum Apostolorum*, prologue, 1–4.
26. M.-D. Chenu, 'Les *philosophi* dans la philosophie chrétienne médié-vale', *Revue des Sciences philosophiques et théologiques* 26 (1937), pp. 27–40.
27. *Summa theologiae*, IIa. IIae., q. 171, a. 2 corpus: '*Lumen intellectuale . . . per modum formae permanentis et perfectae*'.
28. Thus *Quaestiones disputatae De veritate*, 14, 9: '*propter testimonium alienum*'.
29. See here on p. 18.
30. *Summa theologiae*, Ia., q. 1, a. 1.
31. *Summa contra Gentiles*, IV. 42.

Index of Names

Abelard 65, 67
Abraham 52
Albert 5, 129
Alexander IV 7
Alexander of Hales 66, 67
Ambrose 27
Andrew of Rhodes 132
Anselm 14
Aristotle 3, 4, 5, 10, 13, 14, 16,
    22, 45, 46, 54, 57, 75, 87, 95,
    96, 97, 135, 149, 150, 156,
    161, 164, 169
Ashley, B. 93, 94, 96
Athanasius 61, 140
Augustine 62, 63, 64, 70, 71, 72,
    74, 77, 101, 104, 160, 163
Austen, J. 98
Averroes 13
Avicenna 45
Ayglier, B. 4

Bañez, D. 133
Baptista of Mantua 133
Barth, K. 41, 43
Benedict 4, 18, 98
Benedict XV 137, 138
Bernard 18, 98
Blignières, L.-M. de 80
Boethius 41
Bonaventure 66, 67
Bourret, E. 130
Boyle, L. 9

Bulgakov, S. B. 63
Burckhardt, J. 99
Butler, C. 140

Cano, M. 133
Casel, O. 118
Cassian 98
Chenu, M.-D. 4, 65, 171
Chesterton, G. K. viii
Chevalier, I. 64
Chrysostom 138
Clarke, W. N. 68
Columbus, C. 131
Comte, A. 137
Congar, Y. M.-J. 21, 121
Corvinus, M. 131
Cyril of Alexandria 113

Daniélou, J. 21
Dante 86
Darwin, C. 137, 163, 174
David 52
Davies, B. ix
Dawkins, R. 163
de Lubac, H. 94
Demetrios of Thessalonica 3
Denys viii, 5, 30, 51, 123, 169
Descartes, R. 161
Dewey, J. 43, 135
Diego de Deza 131
Dominic 179
Dubarle, D. 54

Dulles, A. 148
Dumeige, G. 66
Duns Scotus 131, 137
Durand de Saint-Pourçain 130
Duroux, B. 35

Eckhart 130
Elders, L. 40

Ficino, M. 134
Finance, J. de 157, 159
Foster, K. 87
Francis of Assisi 4
Frederick II 3, 5

Gauguin, P. 143
Gauthier of Saint Victor 65
Gilbert de la Porrée 65, 66
Gilby, T. viii, ix, 71, 159
Giles of Rome 131
Godefroid de Fontaines 130
Gray, J. vii, ix, x
Gregory the Great 4
Gregory X 18
Gregory of Nyssa 61
Gregory Palamas 62
Grisez, G. 92, 95
Grosseteste, R. 5
Guidi, U. 130
Günther, A. 27

Hawking, S. 90
Hegel, G. F. W. 141
Heidegger, M. 141
Henry of Ghent 131
Henry of Würzburg 130
Hesiod 83
Hislop, I. 76
Hooker, R. 92
Hopkins, G. M. viii, 124

John, evangelist x, 24, 33, 56,
   66, 73, 84, 85
John XXII 129
John XXIII 148
John Capreolus 131
John of Damascus 54, 113, 116
John of Montenero 132
John Paul II 142
John the Teuton 4, 6
John of Turrecremata 132
John of Wildeshausen *see* John
   the Teuton
Jordan of Saxony 4
Jordan, M. 51, 157, 162
Journet, C. 119

Kalteisen, H. 132
Kant, I. vii, 41, 59, 135, 159
Kerr, F. 92, 161
Kierkegaard, S. 42
Kilwardby, R. 129, 130, 131
Kristeller, P. O. 134, 135

Lafont, G. 54
Lash, N. 12
Leclerq, J. 14
Leo XIII 136, 137, 175
Leonardo 77
Lohaus, G. 119
Louis IX 7

McCabe, H. ix
Maimonides 6, 52
Malet, A. 63, 64, 71
Mandonnet, P. 129, 131
Mantuanus *see* Baptista of
   Mantua
Marion, J.-L. 147
Maritain, J. 44
Mary 28, 86, 132
Mascall, E. L. viii
Maximus 63, 115

Medina, B. de 133, 135
Michael the Irishman 3
Milton, J. 89
Moses 26, 43, 52, 85

Newman, J. H. 7, 8, 85
Nicholas ix, 17

O'Neill, C. 91
Origen 27

Parmenides 150
Pascal, B. 135
Patfoort, A. 125
Paul 8, 27, 29, 30, 32, 78, 101, 107
Peckham, J. 15
Persson, P. E. 113
Peter Lombard 6, 66, 67, 124, 168
Peter Niger 131
Phelan, G. B. 151
Pico della Mirandola 134
Pilgram, F. 121
Pius V 134, 136, 139
Pius IX 136
Pius X 134, 136, 139
Pius XII 93, 140, 148
Plato vii, 135, 150, 151
Plotinus 84
Pollan, M. 159
Pope, A. 82
Proclus 157
Prouvost, G. 136

Rahner, K. 141
Reginald of Piperno 101

Régnon, T. de 60, 61, 65
Richard of Saint Victor 65, 66, 69, 71

Sayers, D. L. viii
Scotus *see* Duns Scotus
Shakespeare, W. 92, 142
Silvestri, F. 133
Soto, D. de 133
Stephen 25
Strabo, W. 86
Strawson, P. F. 41, 43
Suarez, F. de 136

Tempier, E. 129, 130
Theodore of Mopsuestia 33
Thierry of Freiburg 130
Thomas de Lentini 4
Thomas of Naples 130
Tommaso da Modena ix
Torrell, J.-P. 4, 17
Turner, J. M. W. 77, 156, 157

Ulrich of Strassburg 130
Urban IV 9, 124, 130, 167

Vitoria, F. de 133
von Balthasar, H. U. 21, 38, 63, 171
von Hügel, F. 139

Ward, K. 164
Werner, K. 134
White, V. 23, 51
William de la Mare 131
William of Saint Thierry 65
Wittgenstein, L. 135